Who Turned Up The Silence

Andy Turner

Colorful Crow Publishing

Published by

Colorful Crow Publishing

96 Craig Street Suite 112-304 East Ellijay, Georgia 30540

http://www.colorfulcrowpublishing.com

First Edition

Library of Congress Control Number: 2023943202

ISBN 979-8-9881845-5-3 (Hb)

ISBN 979-8-9881845-6-0 (Pb)

ISBN 979-8-9881845-7-7 (eB)

http://www.whoturnedupthesilence.com

Cover photo by Ronnie Wolf/Ronnie Wolf Studios

Contributions by Austin Turner, Kaedon Turner, Bronson Turner, Lexi Turner, and Kelly Turner

ANDY TURNER

Dear Reader,

I can think of a few reasons why you have picked up this book today. Maybe you found the cover enticing or the back matter interesting. Maybe you are familiar with the individuals involved; possibly a friend showing support and love. Or maybe you have heard this story as it has been unfolded through news outlets, social media, or the myriad of low-budgeted YouTubers.

Whatever that reason is, I am glad this book found its way into your hands. I hope its story finds its way into your heart.

Sincerely,
Andy Turner

Preface

"There are 3 sides to every story..."

I have always been an avid reader with a fondness for history and a desire to know what the facts were. Having traveled to Israel many times, I have always found it amazing to stand and read the Bible at the very place where the story actually happened. It brings an amazing insight and emotional appeal to what is being told. Many tour guides begin with, "This is the exact spot," and they are dogmatic in the statement. Other times you'll hear that this is "tradition" and a likely or potential place where the events could have occurred.

I must admit that each time, in all the many travels I have been blessed to embark upon, hearing this diluted the experience and lessened the emotional connection that I felt. I wanted to connect to a true geographical location and hear facts.

The need for the facts is always present.

I have endured living a story that is unique; one of heartbreak, loss, sadness, and with people who have sought to devour and destroy. I have listened as others told the story that I lived firsthand with my children, and none have told the story accurately. I had to embrace and learn to avoid conflict for safety's sake.

With mounting death threats now topping the 1000s, constant security has become a necessity for my children's protection, and that security has been utilized many times. Our homes and cars have been vandalized while we were mocked and ridiculed in public, asked not to attend churches, schools, restaurants, events, and kids' sports.

WHY?

Because people simply decided to tell a story without the facts. Today people embrace social media and the advances in communication. There is great opportunity to utilize technology for good, to bring about change, to illicit connection with loved ones. But there is also open opportunity for those same tools to be used for bullying, gossip, spying, and creating fear and harm. People abuse the justice system, social media, and government entities. We have experienced this firsthand. And when these efforts did not produce the effects they desired, they took to podcasts, more social media platforms, TV, movies, and the entertainment industry. In this book, our family is breaking our silence for the first time, to tell the facts and the story of what we have had to endure.

"Shit doesn't stink as bad if you don't stomp it!"

We have had many lawyers tell us to stay quiet—to not engage. When seeking legal advice against the claims that were slanderous, claims that over time have caused me to lose eight jobs, claims that defamed my family, we were repeatedly told to stay silent. We were told that, "shit doesn't stink as bad if you don't stomp it!" We were told to continue to endure until the time was right. The right time to file lawsuits, the right time to speak up, the right time to tell our story. And while it has been very difficult to learn to bite my jaw in the face of complete and utter ridicule and maltreatment, it has been even more difficult to sit idle while my children are hurt, crying, and being torn apart by people who are only looking to gain attention or their 15 minutes of fame at the expense of others' pain and torment.

Now is the time for us to set the stories straight and tell, without remorse, not only what all has transpired but the people, organizations, agencies, and bandwagoners who have willfully and wrongfully tried to destroy us. From the many brash phone calls pushing for interviews, to the countless damaging encounters we have had to endure, our family has looked forward to this moment.

We are finally able to set the record straight and it is our hope that it will ultimately allow us the ability to move on, heal, mourn, and in some instances give the opportunity to tell the right people where they can stick it! As you embark on this journey and learn why all resemblance of peace was stripped and robbed and how it happened you will understand not only the meaning but **_WHO TURNED UP THE SILENCE_**.

Chapter One

Going Through the Fire

"...this book will be a breath of fresh air."
-John Schneider

November 18, 1980. I remember the date well because it was my kid brother's second birthday. I'd spent the early part of the day riding around in the yard pretending that my bike was Evil Knievel's famed motorcycle. I looked for things to jump, reasons to slide the back end around, making the sounds of the engine with my mouth as I peddled past people. Exhausted and in need of a break, I ran up on the porch. As I did, my foot caught the lip of the concrete causing me to trip, throwing my hand through the glass fixed in the door, causing it to shatter. My dad and grandfather were not very pleased with me. If there was ever a good time for such an accident, this was the furthest away from it.

With birthday preparations halted, everyone's focus shifted to me and the urgency to go get some glass to put in the door of our house.

I'll never forget the long ride down to Super D and the look on my grandfather's face when the lady told him how much the glass was going to be. Yeah, it was an accident, and I had a lot of those because I was a rambunctious kid. I was always into something, because I liked to play, and I had quite an imagination. In my day Xbox, Nintendo and PlayStation did not exist. We had our imaginations, *Kick the Can*, and the woods. I was always outside! This was the norm at the time. When you got thirsty you went to a spigot on the side of someone's house and got a drink, then went back to battle or playing the ball game. On this day, I was riding a little too recklessly and much like Evil's famous jumps, mine ended in the same manner.

I dropped my head and knew that punishment would be coming when we got back to the house. While my dad and grandfather were installing the glass, I heard a noise in the back part of the house. I started walking toward the sound, then my granddad called out to me, "You best be going up to the house, so your grandmother can get your pajamas on and get you started on your homework." I was in first grade, Sandy Steele's class, and was in a group reading a dinosaur book. I had to read a chapter every night and I hadn't read mine yet. Every day there was a quiz on what we had read. Obeying Paw-Paw, I ran up to his house. Ma-T, my grandmother, helped dress me in my Yoda footed pajamas and I got up on the couch with my reading book. I watched my brother as he was getting ready for his party. Mama dressed him in the most awful sailor suit with the little round hat. He was running around and wrestling with our family members that came by. He looked like he was going to be on a gay pride float. I was sitting on the couch when Granddad came in and sat down beside me. I continued reading my book. Cody played on the floor as they passed around slices of cake. They gave him this little train that you pull on a rope causing every one of the cars to turn, each one making a different noise.

I remember thinking, *what an awful gift*! I knew I'd have to listen to that thing crack, pop, and whistle. I could only imagine trying to sit down and play with my Star Wars men, having great battles over the Empire, all while having to listen to the cracking, popping, and whistling as my two-year-old brother ran by with this train on a rope. It seemed I wasn't the only one wondering who in the world would buy a present like that as I looked up at my granddad, who was looking down at the train with a long face ending in a deep frown. You could tell he wasn't happy because he had stopped chewing his chewing tobacco. My granddad really chewed his Redman chewing tobacco. I mean like it was a whole pack of Hubba Bubba Bubble Gum. Sometimes it got loud and irritating and my grandmother would say, "Robert, stop chewing that." He would reply, "Hun, it's not holding tobacco, it's chewing tobacco and I'm on the porch enjoying it!"

Granddad wasn't saying anything, just staring at this noise factory in the living room when all of a sudden, a man kicked the front door open and started yelling. I watched my granddad, who was a military man, jump to his feet. My granddad was an Army Veteran, who served in Normandy on D-Day, and he had that look in his eyes, like a man about to be in a fight. He looked stunned when the man yelled, "The house next door is on fire." I stopped and looked up from my book because the house next door was my house. I peered through the crack around the man, and I could see the flames coming through the roof of my home. We all ran out, stood in the front yard, and watched my grandfather bust out the glass of the same front door which he had just installed. He was trying to get the door open to run into the house and put the fire out. My grandmother was in the front yard screaming, "Robert, don't go in, it's too big!"

Standing in the yard I looked down at my pajamas and my feet were beginning to get cold. I watched as snowflakes started to stick to my pajama pants. My mom was on the front porch holding my brother's hand, he was still looking ridiculous in that little sailor outfit. My dad and grandfather had entered the front door of the house and immediately came out, because the fire was all-consuming and wildly raging. Something caught my eye in the window, the window right over my bed, and I realized what was lying on that bed. It was my Snoopy. You see, Snoopy was probably the greatest toy ever at the time and if you'd ever been to Lionel Playworld in 1980, you would have seen this bowling Snoopy. You pull his arm back, you put a ball in it, set up the pens, and you wait. After some time, Snoopy releases the ball all on his own and knocks the pins down. To me that was a state-of-the-art toy. I loved playing with it, but I see fire now on my bed and it's right in front of that window and my toy is gone.

Firemen were all over the place and they said there were eight to ten fire trucks everywhere. I remember them pulling up, I remember people running around and I remember the police standing in front of me. They were telling everyone to back up, because my dad's bullets had been engulfed in the fire and were being set off. As bullets are exploding and sending shrapnel in every direction, no one is taking account of me, seven years old, everything I own on my back. I have no toys anymore, no clothes, and everything that we own is ascending to the Heavens as smoke and returning to the Earth as ashes. The world around me was void of sound. I never heard one fire truck. I never heard the sirens, I never heard one police officer, I never heard one fireman. This is the first time that I recall in my life that noise was happening without doubt because I could see it but for some reason my ears were turned off. The only thing that was there was silence. I can't explain it, but it happened.

But then I heard her. The only voice I remember hearing, that broke the silence, the chaos, was a lady that had shown up from the American Red Cross. Her name was Ms. King. Martha King had seen a little boy standing in the snow, in the middle of everything going on and she picked me up and she said, "What's your name?"

"My name is Andy."

"Are you okay?"

"Yes."

"Were you in the fire?"

"No ma'am."

I looked at Ms. King. She was dressed very nicely. I had never seen a woman have what looked like a big colorful handkerchief tied around her neck and tucked into her blouse before. It looked fancy. What caught my eye the most was the Red Cross symbol on the shoulder of her jacket.

"Is that your house?" she asked. I replied, "It was."

I began to cry. Ms. King looked me in the eyes and told me with assertion, "I give you my word that everything will be okay."

I remember laying my head on this lady's shoulder, a complete stranger, someone I'd never met, and I felt comfort. Her words were bold, and I felt like she meant them. I felt like they would be true and as I laid there for a moment; the silence went away. Then suddenly, my mind filled again with my toy, the one toy that I did not want to lose. You see, I grew up very poor and didn't have many toys. Many Christmases, it was not uncommon for me not to get something or if I did, it would not be in abundance. So, what I did have, I appreciated and took care of.

"Ms. King, my toy is laying there on the other side of that window," my voice desperate. "It's a Snoopy from Lionel's Playworld and its melting. He's my best friend."

"Andy, I'll make sure that you get another Snoopy." Then, she hugged me real tight, and she said, "Let's get you warmed up, you're freezing out here."

She carried me up towards my grandparents' house, not even knowing that was my family. As a matter of fact, I didn't even know where my family had been during this time or how long the time had been. It's like I was in a bubble, just kind of standing there on my own. I knew that a good bit of time had lapsed, because now the top of the house was gone—no roof and burnt down to the top of the windows. Some of the fire trucks were rolling up their hoses and my feet were freezing. Ms. King carried me into my grandparents' home. My grandmother was sitting at the table crying and my granddad was doctoring his hand, which he cut when he busted the door's glass. My parents were holding my brother. He's crying for some reason. I felt like I just got overlooked, but Ms. King, that Ms. King, she sure was a sweet lady.

I remember the next morning; she showed up really early and I was at the breakfast table with my grandmother. Ma-T made me some biscuits and gravy, homemade. Now, my grandmother, she didn't measure a thing. She did everything by feel. She couldn't tell you how to make biscuits and gravy with measurements. She would just go in there and start doing it and it's always the same, because she knew what it felt like to make the perfect batch. I was sitting there eating a fresh slice of cantaloupe and a biscuit with gravy, along with a glass of milk. I thought that's what kings and rich folks ate. I had no idea that we were poor people.

There was a knock on the door. Ms. King comes walking in the door with Snoopy. It wasn't a bowling Snoopy; it was a stuffed Snoopy and she went to Lionel Playworld to get it. She made that special trip just for me and she sat down beside me.

"Hey! Look what I found! I found your Snoopy."

I didn't have the heart to tell her this wasn't a bowling Snoopy, because I knew that she was trying so hard to be my friend. Then honestly as I looked at it, it wasn't a bad looking toy. He was one I could drag around the yard, take on motorcycle rides, I decided he'd be all right. I still wanted the other one, because he was able to bowl but I was very thankful and appreciative, and I offered her half of my biscuit, which she politely declined.

"Hey, you're wearing those same clothes," she noticed. "I'm going to take you and get you some clothes to wear for school and some for church and some shoes."

I remember thinking that this lady right here must be rich, because I only went shopping for back-to-school and Easter. She put me in the car, and we went to town. I got a pair of shoes, some jeans, some khakis and two shirts. That was the first time that anybody had ever taken me and bought me something like that, other than my mom, one of my grandparents, or my Aunt Jan. Aunt Jan is my mom's sister and most of the time, her and my grandmother would take me to do my back-to-school shopping or to go get my Sunday Easter outfit. If not for Aunt Jan, I think most of the time, I wouldn't have had any clothes. Ms. King, she took me, and she made sure that everything fit. She checked the shoes and made sure that my toes were at the end. I didn't have to go over to the cheap section. She let me go get a good pair of shoes and it's the first time that I ever had a pair of Nikes. I remember when we went up to pay, I watched her real close and she smiled. She was happy to be able to do something for me. I got in the car, and I just held the bags.

I looked at her and said, "Ms. King, thank you." She stopped and looked back at me.

"You're most welcome." She leaned over and gave me a hug.

"Why do you do this?" I asked her.

"Well honey, it's my job, but I love doing this. There's no greater joy in my life than to help people, when they need it the most." I remember thinking about that many times in my life, when I needed somebody, and I wondered where Ms. King was, hoping she would wheel in and save the day again.

Ms. King was a tall, slim lady. She had very dark eyes, a big smile and when she smiled, she had really big teeth. Her smile just kind of took up her whole face. She always wore a scarf tied around her neck and it went down in her blouse every time I saw her. She was different. She was unique, she wasn't like anybody in my family or anybody I'd ever been around. She always wore perfume that was different and smelled good. She was the first black lady that I ever spent time with like this. She was loving, she was kind, and she made an impact on my life by doing nothing but being kind. Later in my life, I heard a quote from Maya Angelou, that stated, "It is so true that people will forget what you said, they will forget what you did, but they will never forget how you made them feel." I remember Ms. King and how she made me feel, even now as I am going on fifty years old. She made me feel happy. With her, my life was very comforting, but more importantly, she broke that silence. That moment when I was locked in, staring, everything was going wrong. Flames through the roof of the house and people running everywhere. She was the one that broke it, she was the one that made it better and all it took was the effort. How many other people could have simply given that effort? My own family walked by me and neighbors that knew me walked by me. Our house was attached to our little family store and yet no one there stopped to acknowledge me. Cars went up and down the road, how many other people could have stopped and done the same thing? People that knew my name? Why did it take a stranger, someone that was different, someone that I never saw to make this impact? Where were the people that I grew up with? Where were the people that told me they loved me every day? Where were the people that told me they were my friends? At seven years old, I learned a lesson and then I learned it over and over and over again. It put something in me.

Andy, be the Ms. King in the world, be the difference, invest in people, listen to people, help people, care for people, and break the damn silence!

That silence will drive people crazy, the silence that's deafening to people. The silence that makes people want to give up, the silence that makes people feel lonely, the silence that makes people want to die. You see, when you sit there long enough, eventually you'll start to believe what's on your mind. I've seen it happen to others and I appreciate the Ms. Kings in my life, but what I've seen over and over again, is it's never the people that it's supposed to be. It isn't always the ones that surround you, that say they'll be there for you. Often, it's the ones that come from outside. They are the ones that you least expect.

I read a quote a few years ago that stated if you do not have expectations of people then you will not be disappointed when they fail to act properly. I have pondered this for some time and asked myself, *does expectation cover common decency, kindness, helpfulness, compassion, or simply the golden rule to do unto others as you'd have them do unto you?*

I will say that Ms. King was the first King that entered my life and made a lasting impact but was not the last King.

Chapter Two

KAL-EL

"Many boys and girls dream about flying and wanting to be like Superman. I was lucky enough to learn to fly and built my career as an international airline pilot. I'm certain Andy would have enjoyed it too and thrived in the profession—given his talents and personality."
-Sam Mason

The early years were pretty typical for me. I got up in the morning, I went outside, and I was supposed to be back in when the streetlights came on. However, it wasn't out of the ordinary for me to be in the house about twenty minutes after the streetlights came on, because I was busy playing. In my mind, I was always some kind of superhero, or I was riding a motorcycle, which was actually my bicycle with a makeshift gas tank on the front. Wherever my mind was at the time, it's what I became.

One particular day, I had a beach towel with Superman on the back of it. I tied it around my neck and used my brother's diaper pen, the one with a duck on the front, to hold my cape together. I was running around the front yard, but in my mind, I was flying down the street saving dames, beating up bad guys, and stopping crime. Being poor,

I didn't own a swing set. We had a rope tied in a tree, and I'd swing back and forth so the wind would go through my hair, making the cape come up to emulate flying. A reporter happened to be driving by, and when he saw me, he stopped and took my photo. He asked me some questions and my grandparents came out to see why a strange man was in the front yard taking my picture. My photo appeared in the local newspaper and in the Atlanta Journal-Constitution and it read "Superman comes to Dallas."

This took my love for Superman to another level because now everybody at school saw me in the paper. They started calling me Superman. My very first tattoo was of Superman's Shield. I bear it on my left arm to this day. I have a framed picture of the photo that the man took of me. I was about 5 years old with that cape around my neck, in that rope swing. I even kept the towel and still have it. You can see the dirt stains at the bottom of the towel and the holes from the many fights with bad guys — the bullets that it deflected. I keep it to remind me of a simpler time, of a better time.

There's a certain day that Superman went to church. I recall my family taking me to church on this specific day. The pastor preached a sermon, "that if you believe and you trust in God and you ask in his name, that whatever you believe and ask, it'll be granted." I've not missed a day of Sunday school since I was born. I know what faith is, I know what prayer is because I went to church and was dragged to church, even when I didn't want to go. We didn't miss Sunday morning, Sunday night, Wednesday, Vacation Bible School, we attended every Revival, we even went to church when there wasn't church. We had to go cut grass or clean the church or sometimes just to go sit in the parking lot. I don't know what in the world my parents were doing, but I'd be sitting there. On this day, I was listening because I felt like the preacher was tapping into something important to me.

In my mind as a little kid, I was Superman when I put that towel on. I don't know if you ever believed in such a thing so much when you were a kid. Maybe you didn't, maybe it's ludicrous, but when that towel went around my neck, I was the Man of Steel. Now the preacher had just confirmed that if I had faith and I believed, I could fly. Now because he said if I had the faith just of a mustard seed, that I can move mountains, well I got more than enough faith. I will be able to fly! When I got home, I put the cape on. I went over to the side of the house, and I looked up to the top of it. We had a TV antenna that my grandfather had nailed to the fascia board and wrapped an old belt around, nailing it on the other side to hold it up. I climbed the TV antenna and went to the top of the house. I got up to the very pitch of the roof and I stood there. I looked all the way down Benson Street, and I said, "I believe and I'm about to put this in faith, and the preacher said it and it's in the Bible, it's got to be true." I took off running and I dove right off the top of the house and I was actually flying — for about three seconds. Suddenly, gravity took control and I fell, breaking both my arms as I crashed like the greatest American hero. I was in the yard crying when my grandmother came outside.

"What have you done?"

"Ma-T, the preacher lied. I can't fly!"

As I was sitting in the emergency room getting casts put on both of my arms, it dawned on me that I needed to have a chat with the preacher. My parents came in and wanted to know what the heck could make me jump from that high. I told them that the preacher was a liar. I got a whipping in the hospital, while getting casts put on my arms, for disrespecting the pastor. It didn't go any better when I saw him the following Sunday. I walked in there and told him to his face that he lied to me and he was the reason that both my arms were in casts. Nobody appreciated it, but still today I find it humorous. I don't think anybody can argue that was faith put into action. If anybody believed, I sure did at that time, or maybe I was an idiot. I guess you could look at that in different ways outside of these events. I was a pretty normal kid; times were just different.

I loved growing up in those times, we never had to lock our doors. Everybody knew each other, in fact, everyone that came to our store, I pretty much knew. I liked having the Little Country Store, my entire family worked there, my mom, my dad, my grandparents, and my uncles. Heck, I don't even know how everybody was getting paid for working there. It was our income, and I knew that every Saturday the candy man rolled up and unloaded boxes of candy. I always wanted to help my granddad put it on the shelf for some reason. I never got paid for doing it. So, I always felt like sticking candy in my pocket was my pay for helping him work. Until one day, they called me in the store.

"Hey, we noticed that we're not able to make any profit on all this candy. Seems to be a lot of it's coming up missing."

"Oh yeah," I said. "I wonder who's coming in and stealing all the candy."

"Well, we seem to think maybe it's you, when you're helping us put it out."

I just looked around like I was flabbergasted to be accused of such a thing. Until suddenly, they revealed that they had found my wrappers where I'd been hiding them. I was no longer allowed to help put up the candy or even be near it.

When I was somewhere around six or seven, my time working in that little store came to an end. I remember it all too well. At the end of a workday, I sat outside and watched as everyone finished their tasks and left. It was hot out and I decided I would get myself an ice cream out of the freezer. Those old freezers were the ones that had big push-slide doors and felt like you were pushing them up Mount

Everest. So, I pushed it, so hard that my feet were no longer touching the ground. I'm all the way up on my rib cage pushing these things in an effort to reach the one type of ice cream that I wanted, the Mickey Mouse ice cream. The ears were chocolate, his face was vanilla and somehow, they made his eyes, nose, and mouth chocolate. Not sure how Disney did that magic, but it sure was delicious. I was pushing where I could get within reach of that Mickey Mouse bar and even though I got the door open, I couldn't reach. So, I just climbed into the cooler. The Georgia sun was very hot, and it was cool sitting right there in the freezer. I opened up that Mickey Mouse ice cream and I bit that chocolate ear off. It was so good, and it felt so cool, I didn't even notice when the lid right above my head slid shut. I was just enjoying my ice cream and quickly discovered a box of Star Wars popsicles. I decided I would have one of those, too. So, there I sat, holding a popsicle in one hand and a Mickey Mouse ice cream in the other. As I'm eating my frozen treats, I realize this is the first time I've ever eaten ice cream without it melting down my hand. It was staying cool, keeping everything on the stick. I finished those and decided I might as well get another one. So, I ate another Mickey Mouse ice cream. I didn't want another Star Wars popsicle, but I did want one of the Bomb Pops. It was at the other end of the freezer and as I was crawling down there, I realized the lid had slid shut. I reached up to the glass to push it open, but the condensation on the inside would not allow me any grip. Suddenly, I forgot about the Bomb Pop, my heart started to beat fast as I began trying to figure out how in the world I was going to get out of there. I remember thinking that must have been what Jonah felt like when he was in the belly of the whale. So, I thought, maybe I should pray.

"Please let me get out of this thing alive. I don't want to freeze to death."

But then, I got distracted by the Mickey Mouse ice cream again and thought if I was going to die, I might as well die with a belly full of Mickey Mouse ice cream bars. I went ahead and ate my third Mickey Mouse bar, a Bomb Pop, and two more Star Wars popsicles. I took all the wrappers, and I rolled them up, sticking them down in my little overall pants. I'd been in there probably close to 45 minutes and was beginning to get cold. My parents and my granddad already locked up the store. I wasn't supposed to be in there. See, I found out that there was a bar put over the door in the back. That was supposed to be the lock. You could stick any piece of metal through the crack and go up and knock the bar off. That was a way to break in the back door and that's what I did. So, I sat there, trapped, everyone else gone with no reason to suspect I'm in the store. But then I heard my granddad, he always called me Boo.

"Boo, you in here?"

For a minute I thought it would be stupid to respond, to let him know that I was in the freezer, eating up all the ice cream. I knew I would get a whipping after he got me out, but my only other alternative was to sit there and freeze to death. I actually contemplated which was going to be the best option. I grabbed a Popeye's popsicle while I weighed my options. Granddad came over and stood over the freezer.

"What are you doing?"

"Well, I'm freezing," I replied. "Can you push the lid up, reach down, and pull me out?"

"Why are you in there?"

"So, you're not going to believe it, but I came to get me an ice cream because you told me I couldn't get any more candy bars, but you didn't say anything about the ice creams. So, I came to get one and when I climbed in, the lid slid shut. You can see where I was trying to open it, by all those handprints. I was praying that God was going to send somebody to come get me and here you are. You're an angel, Paw-Paw."

He did not look amused.

"Well, I'm an angel about to beat your tail, because you know you ain't supposed to be breaking into the store and getting stuff. You can't come in the store anymore. We can't make money with you eating everything and it's already tight enough as it is."

"Well Paw-Paw, since I can't come get the good stuff, I'm just going to run away. I have no other choice. I need to pack a hobo stick and I'm getting down the road."

He started laughing as he handed me a handkerchief. I filled it up with candy, tied it to a stick, and put it over my shoulder like I'd seen in the Droopy cartoons. I took off down the road. I could hear him sitting on the porch, still laughing at me. I got past the courthouse of Dallas, Georgia, and was headed up Highway 61 towards Cartersville. It wasn't long before the sheriff, who always got gas at our store, pulled over on the side of the road because I was hitchhiking.

"Andy, what are you doing?"

"I'm hitchhiking," I said matter-of-factly. "I'm running away. They told me I couldn't get any more ice creams and candy out of our store, so I packed this up and I'm going down the road."

"Where are you going?"

"I don't know."

"How far are you going to go?"

"I don't know."

"What are you going to do when you get there?"

"I don't know."

"Let me see your bag of goodies," he said as he began untying the handkerchief. "Oh man, you got some good-looking stuff in here."

I watched as he opened one of my goodies and began eating it. I wasn't planning on sharing, that's what I was going to live off of for the next twenty years until I was grown and able to get my own stuff. Next thing I know, he's opened up another pack. He must have been hungry, too. After he helped himself to all my candy, he shifted his focus back to me.

"Well, I don't reckon you got enough to survive on, I need to take you back. Hop in the police car. Let me drive you back down to the store. I'm buying," he tempted.

"I can't go back in the store," I replied.

We pulled up in the front yard and my family was standing there. They were confused as to why I'm in the front seat of a police car. The sheriff got out and told them he picked me up, along with my hobo stick. He said I was running away but didn't know where I was going and that I thought I had enough food to make it for twenty years. He said he ate it all in about ten minutes. I was trying to explain the story of how fast he was eating my food. After being chastised about the dangers of hitchhiking and how bad it was to get into the car with a stranger, I remember thinking, well, he wasn't a stranger. But now as I am writing this, we all know you aren't supposed to hitchhike or talk to strangers, but every day I pull up my Uber App and every day I go get in a stranger's car and talk to them. Man, how times have changed.

Being banned from the goodies, I now had to be creative on how I was going to get candy. So, I took to the Big Wheel and start writing tickets. When people came to our store for gas, I would pull up behind them, like I was a police officer. I'd write them a ticket and to pay the ticket, they had to go in and get a certain type of candy bar. Most people laughed, but about two out of three came out and paid the fine, which I was quite appreciative of, and gathered quite the collection of candy bars, eating them out back without my parent's knowledge.

They were quite happy to see the sales of certain candy bars going up and I was in control of that without them knowing. At quite a young age, I controlled the P&L of their store.

The very same Big Wheel was also my transportation to school. You see, I didn't ride the bus and of course, no one in my family was going to drive me, as we lived right next door to Dallas Elementary School on Hardy Street. It was less than one hundred yards away. Instead of walking to school, I decided I had a perfectly good Big Wheel to get me there. I think I was the only kid that was driving to elementary school. But it fit my persona as I truly was an early bloomer. I think everything in my life I achieved kind of early. I was shaving at ten, having sex at twelve, driving at thirteen. Born destined to be an early bloomer, what was wrong with driving to school in first grade? It was more fun for me! I do, however, recall the stares from the other students as I drove through the hallway and into Ms. Steele's room, parking beside my desk. Principal Jim Henson would enter the room and give the same speech he gave every other day.

"Andy, you can't be driving to school."

That was something I never understood. If he'd have told me I couldn't drive up a tree, that I would have believed. But to tell me I couldn't drive to school didn't make sense. I had driven to school, on my Big Wheel. I had driven it there and parked it right in that classroom. I never seemed to be able to follow what grown-ups were saying. He was telling me I couldn't do something that I was doing every day. And each day, I'd walk the same walk into the principal's office where he would call my folks.

"Hey, Andy drove to school again."

They would have to come get my Big Wheel, take it back to the house and the process would repeat the next day all over again, and the next day and the next. Before too long, they gave up and I was given a designated parking spot right by my desk. With the rules, I couldn't touch it until school was over to drive it home. I remember it took me exactly two months to break them, and yeah, I'm grinning as I'm writing this because I remember the feeling of victory. I also remember accepting their new rules about it and deciding to never break them because all I wanted to do was just be able to drive to school, even with the flat, crushed front tire from where I'd been spinning out and locking the brakes down, throwing it sideways. The bike would make a clap when it went around and hit that one flat spot, but to me it was a perfect Big Wheel. It was my car and those days were simpler days, fun days. The biggest problems I had was what I was going to have for lunch or what I was going to wear, especially after the house fire as I had to wear the same outfits over and over that Ms. King had bought for me.

I did have one other problem though — Ms. Steele. For some reason, she just didn't like me very much. Every day she found a reason to take me out in the hallway and paddle my butt. Now I must admit, most of the time she didn't have to look too hard for a reason, it just kind of showed up in front of her. However, some days she did create them. I remember one incident in particular. It was the Halloween prior to the fire, I did not have a whole lot of anything. Being the poor kid, the kind that stands out, makes you a target. I remember going to my grandmother asking for candy to take to school for the Halloween party.

"The teacher said if you don't bring candy, then you can't participate in the party," I pleaded.

I sure did want to participate because they were giving out all kinds of different candy. Since I wasn't allowed to go in the store, I was depending on my grandmother to have some candy for me to take. All she had was a box of old-people peppermint sticks. These were my grandmother's second favorite candy, the first being Circus Peanuts, and still to this day, every time I see them, I think of Ma-T.

"Honey you can take these, this is all I've got."

So, I took them. I got on my Big Wheel and I went to class, excited for the party. I had candy which was my invitation in. As I sat at my desk, I noticed the other students coming in. I was always the first kid at school every day. I've always been that person. I was first at school, first at class, first at work, everywhere I go I always show up early. My granddad taught me that. It was the military in him.

"Son, if you're on time, you're late and if you're ever late for somewhere, you're showing disrespect to people," he would tell me. "It means you don't care about their time, and you disrespect them. Don't ever be that person."

So, if I'm running on time, I have that anxiety about disrespecting people and being late. I'll show up an hour early and just sit and wait — but I'm never, ever late.

As I sat there watching, the first kid that came in was wearing a costume. He was dressed as Fred Flintstone, and I thought it was really cool. Then a girl came in, she was Betty Boop. They kept filing in one after another. All these fantastic costumes. One kid came in his Darth Vader costume, and I thought it was the greatest costume I'd ever seen in my life. He had a lightsaber, which was no more than a flashlight with a long plastic tube that fit down over the other end. When you turned the flashlight on, it lit up down the tube. I thought to myself if I were to have that, I'd be making people disintegrate like he did Obi-Wan Kenobi.

I looked down at the same clothes that I had worn on Monday. It was Thursday but I had worn the same clothes because I didn't have a lot to choose from. I had school clothes and I had church clothes. For my school clothes, I had one pair of pants and about three shirts.

I wore the same stuff, and I got picked on a lot. I certainly didn't have a Halloween costume. Ms. Steele was going around the class making nametags for the other kids based on what they were dressed up as. She was putting the tags on their costumes. I remember when she came to Tina and said,

"Tina, what are you dressed up as?"

"I'm Strawberry Shortcake," Tina said excitedly.

Ms. Steele wrote it on the tag, and she put the sticker on Tina. Then she moved on to the next student. She went all the way down the row until she got to me. She saw that I didn't have on a costume, and she asked, "Well, Andy, what are you dressed up as?"

I looked at her, trying not to show how embarrassed I was feeling. But I was embarrassed, enough that tears were sitting on the edges of my eyes, threatening to spill. I tried to suck them back in, feeling angry, but trying to control my emotions. I just looked up and said, "Well, I've got this box of candy that my grandmother gave me. I'm just going to be the Candy Man. Yeah, I'm the Candy Man, that's who I am."

In my mind, I'm thinking I came up with a good story. At least I'm somebody, I'm something instead of a nobody. I'm here, I'm participating, and then I hear her laughing. It was a snicker, a smart-ass snicker. I stared at her and her yellowing teeth, thinking about how unkind she was. The rest of the class started laughing. She wrote Candyman on a sticker with a laughing face and I was left fighting tears. A few moments later the bell rang, and it was time to go to recess. Instead of going to recess, I got on my Big Wheel, and I pedaled my ass home, deciding I would not be returning to school — that party could kiss my ass. There was no way I was going to be a part of it and be made fun of by Ms. Steele.

When I rode up in front of the house, my granddad was sitting on the porch and he asked, "Boy what's wrong with you?"

As soon as he spoke, the dam that had been holding back that flood of tears cracked and I could not hold it back any longer. I started crying and saying everything that I was thinking, both were obviously a mistake. You see, being raised in the preacher's house, you're not allowed to talk ugly. You can think it all you want, but you weren't allowed to say it. Well, I said what I was thinking about Ms. Steele, and to my poor legs demise, my grandmother heard me, and she came out with a hickory. She spanked my legs, which may have been the start of the MC Hammer Dance. My granddad just sat there looking at me. I could tell something was bothering him. Once I got my whipping for saying the ugly things — that I meant every word of — I went over and sat down beside him.

"You know that lady should not have done you that way."

"Yes, sir," I replied.

"You shouldn't have said what you said."

"Yes, sir, you're right. I apologize."

He told me to get in the car and I knew for sure I was in bigger trouble. I just knew he was about to drive me to wherever my parents were, and I was in for another whipping. My granddad went in the house to talk to Ma-T, then he got in the car, and I could tell he was visibly upset. He had tears in his eyes, and he wasn't talking. I didn't realize a couple of cuss words were so serious to my granddad, who had been in the military. He spent time fighting overseas, surely, he had said a couple of bad words. We made a stop that I stayed in the car for and at the next stop, we were in front of Super D.

Super D was the place that had everything. They had a wall of Matchbox cars that looked like I had died and gone to Heaven. There was a section on one side for Hot Wheels and on the other side a section for Matchbox, the cheaper ones. In the middle were the ones for a nickel, the ones that had the plastic bottoms that came apart.

They rolled fine, and they were good to play with, but they were not the name-brand ones. Those plastic bottoms were the ones I bought most of the time.

They also sold shovels, hoes, garden hoses, clothes — they had a little bit of everything. On this day, my granddad took me over to the aisle where they had Halloween costumes. What I didn't know is that during the stop we had made on the way to Super D, he sold his watch. He did that to have a little bit of cash so he could buy me a Halloween outfit.

"You pick out any one of them that you want," he pointed to the ones in boxes.

They were plastic and had a face with the rubber band that went around the back of your head. Once you put it on a couple of times the rubber band would break and if you stuck your tongue out the hole of the mask, it was going to cut your tongue — quite possibly requiring stitches.

I looked at my Granddad. He was still sucking back those tears. I saw the Superman costume, but I already had a Superman towel. I was the real Superman, so I asked the man working there, "Sir, do you have a Darth Vader one?"

"Son, I don't think so. We have this Superman."

"I'm already Superman and I got a towel. I want the Darth Vader if you have one."

He said he would go in the back to check for one. We heard some fumbling while he foraged around in the back storage area. I went back to searching the shelf, but a Darth Vader costume was nowhere to be found. Granddad began pointing out some others. There was the Six Million Dollar Man, Starsky and Hutch, Green Lantern, and Flash. I assured him that I liked them all but I had seen a Darth Vader and that was what I wanted most. A few minutes later, the clerk returned and asked, "Son, what size are you?"

"Sir, I'm little."

"I know you're a little guy. What size are you?"

"I don't know, I'm little."

"Come here," he said and from around his back, he pulled out a Darth Vader costume — size small. He pulled it out of the box, and I tried it on. It was made just for me. It fit perfectly! He said I could take it off and he would put it back in the box.

"I'll just keep it on." I was beaming.

He started laughing and said, "Mr. Turner, now this has an accessory. I don't know if you're interested in it, but it comes with a lightsaber."

"The one that lights up?"

"Yeah."

"It's the long plastic thing that lights up? Does it turn red?"

"No, it's just a light-up."

"That's good enough! Paw-Paw, do you have enough money?"

The clerk turned to my granddad and said, "Well, Halloween's over. You just give me an extra nickel and you can take it."

I promised to help Granddad in the garden, to cut okra, or whatever else I had to do for that nickel. I kept on that Darth Vader outfit, mask and all, and I got in the car. On the ride back, I lit up the car fighting the Jedi. Back home, I got out of the car and walked in the house telling Ma-T to get her hickory. We were about to battle. Funny enough, she did, she pulled out her hickory and we went across the living room floor, just like Luke and Darth. This went on for probably twenty minutes. I heard my granddad chuckling and laughing, and when they told me it was bedtime, I slept in my costume. I took the mask off and slept holding the lightsaber.

The next morning was Friday, and I wore that costume to school even though it wasn't costume day, and it definitely wasn't dress up for Halloween day, but I didn't give a shit. I walked in there and sat down at my desk with Darth Vader on.

"Ms. Steele, I'm Darth Vader today."

"Andy, today is not dress-up day."

"I'm aware, but yesterday I couldn't afford a costume and you laughed at me. Today, I got a costume, and I wore it."

"Well, you're going to have to take it off."

"I'm not." My responses grew more adamant.

"Today is not dress-up day."

Before I had time to process my thoughts, my next words slipped out, "Well you dressed up as ugly."

I will never forget when she sent me out to Jim Henson's office. He said to me, "I know what she said you said, but tell me again, what you said."

"I told her she dressed up as ugly."

Then he called in another teacher. "Tell her what you said."

"I told her she dressed up as ugly."

"Hold on a minute," he said and called in another teacher. He told me to tell her what I said and after that, he called in another teacher and went through the same spiel. After I had told about half the school faculty, his attention shifted back to me.

"I will have to call your daddy."

"No, call my granddad."

He let me call Paw-Paw, who came down immediately, and for the first time ever, I heard Jim Henson take my side.

"Listen, don't be hard on the boy," he told my granddad. "After all, he was just telling the truth."

I left that day, and I stopped being put down. "Thank you, Mr. Henson," I said.

"Oh no, you are still in trouble, but I appreciate what you said. It's good for somebody to be honest every now and then."

I got in the car and Paw-Paw asked why I was in so much trouble. I told him the whole story from start to finish. We went and got ice cream. Paw-Paw was a good man. I kind of took his philosophy in life. Sometimes there's a time to punish the kids and sometimes there's a time to let them vent. I needed to get it out. He realized that.

Those early years were fine, simpler times. They sure have changed, and they changed fast. You see, when you're not worried about costumes or candy, you must worry about real problems.

I remember right after the fire we moved into a little apartment, but we weren't there long before moving into a mobile home. I didn't know how poor we were until other kids told me. One particular Christmas was going to be a hard Christmas.

I spent time around many different types of kids, but I wasn't a bad kid. I was a straight-talking kid. I always told the truth. Sometimes I told it to be solid. I will never forget one day my kid brother and I were out playing. Cody and I grew up best friends; he was younger than me. My dad, being a Southern Baptist pastor, moved around frequently. In fact, on my twenty-first birthday, they moved into their twenty-first home. Sometimes we moved two or three times a year. Every time a U-Haul went by our house, the furniture aligned itself at the door. Something I always thought was strange, Dad would say God was leading him to a new church. He'd be at the church for a little while but when somebody would disagree with something that he said while preaching, God would tell him to leave and go somewhere else. He liked preaching, but he didn't really have people management skills. So, we moved, and we moved a lot. Because of this, Cody and I became really close. When you go to new schools, nobody knows you, and being the new kid in school is not easy. You get picked on, you are made fun of, and it takes you a while to earn your place. It's not like the kids that all grew up together. So typically, if you saw Cody, you saw me.

Now back to that one particularly hard Christmas. Cody and I were sitting on a stool together, my dad was sitting in front of us telling us how Santa Claus was not going to come that year. I remember thinking about all those Santa Claus movies I had watched. Even the orphan kids that didn't have parents got stuff for Christmas. I had just watched Santa Claus is Coming to Town, the animated one. He was taking toys to the poor and everybody got them. So why wouldn't I get gifts? It just didn't seem right. I remember that night when I went to bed, I laid down and just cried. It was just a couple days from Christmas and my spirit was shattered. A couple of days go by and it's Christmas Eve. I really don't have any reason to be excited; Santa Claus wasn't coming. Typically, Cody and I would watch Christmas shows, the cartoon ones, before bed. We always slept together on Christmas Eve night. We got up really early, so excited to see what Santa brought us. We would go running into the family room and dive into the presents, but on that night, we just went to bed early. We went to our own beds.

We had a leak in the roof of our trailer, and it dripped right in the dead center of my bed. On that night, it was raining and dripping, and I thought how fitting that was. Now I would have to move to the foot of the bed and lay the long way to avoid getting wet. I'm lying there upset and in the midst of it came that awful sound again. The same sound that I heard before, that high-pitched realness of silence. It would only be broken by the periodic drip of the water, as it would hit my blanket. It was terrible, laying there hearing it over and over, listening to the fight of the deafening shrill of silence and the drip of the water invading my private space. I couldn't tell which was worse at that specific time. That was a night that Santa Claus was in his sleigh flying around and he was just going to keep flying right on over us. He would not be stopping at my house.

Unbeknownst to me, there was a conversation that had taken place and my granddad found out about what was told to Cody and me a couple of days prior. He was not going to allow us to not get anything for Christmas. He went down to a junkyard and found a couple of bikes. The one for me was an old bicycle that had a flag on it. I'll never forget the flag. It seemed to me at the time that it was about twelve feet high, and it was attached to the seat. The bike had a big banana seat on it and that flag just stuck straight up. A big orange flag on it really served no purpose except to let everybody know, Hey I'm right here, you can't miss me. Maybe they didn't want me to get run over in the street. The back tire did not match the front tire. The rims consisted of real long spokes that held the front tire. I believe the tire came from a different bike or maybe it was custom-made. The big banana seat probably came from a girl's bike. For whatever reason, this was the bike that my granddad got for me. He took a can of gray spray paint and painted the entire bike, the tires, the wheels, the chain, the seat, everything but the flag. He brought it inside the trailer and they placed it under the tree just like Santa. Paw-Paw got my brother a little tricycle and he spray-painted it silver. Christmas morning, Cody and I got up and made our way down the hallway, not with our normal run down at 5:00 a.m. excitement, but more of a dreadful turn around the corner. However, there sat my granddad and when I looked up, I saw that bike. I was so excited! I ran and jumped on it.

"SANTA CAME!"

"You didn't think he would leave you out, did you?"

"Well, Dad told me that he wasn't coming. We couldn't afford to pay him."

"Well, he was wrong, Santa would never leave you out. You are too good of a boy."

I began riding the bike in the house, running over stuff and Granddad sent me outside.

"Hey, can I go down to the road? I want to show my friend."

I headed down the road towards the trussell on the back side of Mount Olivet Road. I got down to where Brian VicNair lived, and I remember a bunch of kids coming up to me. Everybody had brand new bicycles. One boy's bicycle looked like a motorcycle and for a minute I thought it was. It had a gas tank that was made of metal and had a number plate with the number sixty-eight on it. Except for the chain and the pedal, it looked like a real motorcycle. They saw my bike and they stared at me. Scott Bone came up and my cousin, Tommy Turner came over to my bike. Everybody was looking at the bikes and they all kept laughing. I remember thinking to myself, what are they laughing about? I quickly realized what they were laughing at was my bike.

"What happened to your bike?"

"What do you mean, what happened to it?"

"It's all gray."

"Well, that's the way it came."

They started verbally picking it apart and making fun of it. What was once joyful and made me happy; now suddenly was robbed from me. I stood there sad, while everybody began to point and laugh at me. I took my bike and started walking down a dirt road back toward my house. I got to the front yard and threw it down. I walked in the house and went back to bed. Paw-Paw came back and asked what was going on. I told him what happened.

"Don't worry about those kids."

"Paw-Paw, I'm not worried about those kids and what they say. I'm just tired of always being at the end of it."

"Son, what do you mean? What do you mean by always being at the end of it?"

"That's it, Paw-Paw. Have you ever been just always at the end of the line? Everybody always picks on you? Always got something smart to say?"

"No."

"You wouldn't understand if I tried to explain it to you."

He patted me on the head, got up, and walked out. I heard the door shut and I heard my dad go out. It sounded like there was an argument in the front yard. I was not sure what was being said, but it sounded like Granddad was winning because he was the loudest. Then my dad came in and I didn't see him the rest of Christmas Day. Granddad left and I stayed in my room, until we had to go to church. I wasn't really excited about going to church, but I went. It was a pretty good service that talked about the birth of Jesus and what Christmas is really about. It gave me a good perspective that it wasn't about Santa Claus and the presents. It was about celebrating Him. It helped get my mind back on a good plan, but I'm telling you, it sure sucked always being at the end of it. Kal-El was never at the end, he always came out on top and saved the day! That night I covered up with my Superman towel thinking about what it would really be like to have those powers.

Chapter Three

An Overachiever is Born

"One day I'm going to have these cars."
"Every one of them?"
"Yeah."

It didn't take me long to realize I didn't like being at the end of it. I wanted to do better. I wanted to be the best at everything that there was. At school, I wanted to have the best grades. When I played sports, I wanted to be the best. I wanted to win. I wanted to be like the guys in the movies. The ones that always got the hot girl. I didn't want to be the one at the end of it. Being that guy sucks. The guy at the end of it was the unlucky one and I damn sure didn't want to be that guy anymore. He had to sit back and listen to the silence. I wanted to be the one in the front. He listens to the cheerleaders and the praise. Everyone pats him on the back. He's got everything going great for him, that's the guy I wanted to be. So, I got a magazine, and I tore out my favorite cars. I said to myself, "One day, I'm going to have these cars." I got out another magazine and I found a house. I said to myself, "One day I'm going to have a house just like this." I hung those pictures on the wall. After a while, I had a lot of cars on the wall and a couple of different nice houses. I remember my dad came in and asked, "Why do you have all these cars on the wall?"

"One day I'm going to have these cars."

"Every one of them?"

"Yeah."

"There's no way you'll have every one of these cars. That's too many."

"You watch me. I'm going to be rich one day. I'm going to have every one of these cars."

He explained to me that people only have one or two cars. I remember him telling me how it would be impossible to own more than that. I listened but knew that what was impossible for him was not impossible for me. I had listened to people say I could do anything. I had gone to church and listened to pastors say I could do anything. I'd watched TV people say I could do anything; that nothing could stop me. And that was what I believed. That was what I wanted. I didn't want to be the one that got held back. I wanted to be the person that couldn't be held back, that couldn't be stopped.

I remember reading the story in the Bible about Peter. Peter walked on the water. It sounded doggone impossible. He figured it out. How did he do it? He looked at Jesus. Jesus asked him to come. He believed it and stepped out onto the water. He walked on the water until he looked away from Jesus. Now, if he would have been a little boy and he just told somebody he was going to walk on water one day, how many people would have told him he couldn't do it because it was impossible? How many people have shot down your dreams? I don't care how big your dream is, if anyone tells you it can't be done, tell them to kiss your ass. And then surround yourself with people who will stand by you. The ones that will help you buy floaties and hire a lifeguard and cheer you on while you walk on that water. Surround yourself with people like that.

When I was in high school, I met a man that taught me that I could do anything I set my mind to. He taught me business. He taught me loyalty. He taught me love. He told me he would help me to be more of a man. I'm thankful God sent him my way. At nineteen years old, I started my first business. At twenty-one years old, that business was worth over three million dollars. Every car that I had hanging on that wall, I've owned at one time in my life. I've owned more than eighty-three properties at one time. How did I accomplish that growing up with nothing? Because I had one person, that said I will teach you to walk on water. If you believe, you can do anything. I had a dream as a young kid to just be better than what I was. A dream to turn things around, to have something and I did. I remember standing one day and thinking, I made it. I can write a check for seven figures. I've made it. It didn't come by luck, it didn't come by inheritance, it came by hard work and by someone believing in me. Someone saying, "Hey kid I'll teach you." Just like when I was seven years old standing in front of a house burning to the ground, watching everything that I owned burn up and one lady saying, "Hey you're okay, you're going to be okay." It took one man saying to me, "You can be better. You can do better. You can rise above. You can have anything, and I'll show you the way. Follow me." I followed him and he kept his word. I refer to this guy often in my life. He is deceased now, but without him, I would not have learned the principles of business and the understanding of property. I would not have learned about investments and I'm thankful that I'm able to do and know and able to navigate and take care of my family, all thanks to him. I also learned something else, no matter what I've gone through, how bad it was, how big it was, or how small it was, he was there. First one in, last one out. Loyal, supportive, loving, and caring. Everybody needs someone like that. If I had not found him or he hadn't found me, I dare to think how my life would have turned out. It was through him that I was able to obtain the jobs that I did, the ability to run billion-dollar companies, to have VP-level positions, to run my own companies, all because of the knowledge that he gave me.

Can we go back to that little kid hanging up car posters and dreaming amongst a bunch of naysayers? This experience might have created in me a drive to do better for my own children. On more than one occasion I've been accused of being one of those over-the-top dads. You know what? I am. My kids' Christmases have been more than they needed, and I am aware that I was overcompensating for my Christmases growing up. I will tell you though, I loved every single minute of it. My kids have caught Santa Claus multiple times bringing in presents. He'd have the sleigh out front with reindeer hooked to it. Santa would sit down in a chair and tell them the stories of Christmas and how he really works for Jesus. We would read the Christmas story out of the Bible surrounded by a room stuffed full of presents.

I remember a couple of Christmases ago, my son, Kaedon asked, "Dad, can we take a break from opening these presents? Let's go get something to eat and take a break."

My kid was tired of opening present after present. I say that with joy in my heart, not out of pride, not out of bragging, but because I was able to watch my kids smile. I was able to see something in their eyes that lit up. They never had to feel what I felt because they never had to hear the silence. So yeah, I was an over-the-top dad. I still am. Because I love my kids. I love my family. I've always been a family person. I'm unapologetic for that, more men need to be. More men need to be dedicated men that love their wives and love their children. Don't spend your time chasing corporate dreams or anything else that fades, but stay focused on what's important. Unfortunately, not many men are focused on the right things. I've been able to feel the loss and have the gain. Being able to sit on this side and know what it feels like on that side. There's an education to it, there's an education in knowing what it feels like. There's a drive and wanting to prevent it and wanting to help others who go through it. Being able to spot it brings an appreciation for what you have and reminds you to not take it for granted. I soak up every moment of feeling the love that I have for my family, because we're not promised it tomorrow. How many times have you heard that? If you grew up in the South, you heard it probably every Sunday, if not every day. We're not promised tomorrow, so let's appreciate every moment today, growing on what we have, because when it's gone, you'll appreciate it a whole lot more. In the future, if you come to one of our parties they will be too much, and we will have the most fun laughing and enjoying the moments and loving the time!

Chapter Four

What Did I Just Do?

"Doc, you can quit now," I heard Paw-Paw say. "You can quit, because I SEE JESUS."

One year I drove home from college to meet dad for lunch. He was pastoring a church previously pastored by Garner Ballew. This stop in his journey of pastorates was, in my opinion, his best work. Garner had passed away from medical issues and had left the church with a great foundation. Due to the work completed, my dad was able to take this strong foundation and grow it into a decent size church. The church name was New Testament Baptist Church. At the moment of my arrival, they had just recently finished a new church auditorium and it looked beautiful. All our family put in money for the main chandelier with a plaque that was to honor my grandfather, Robert A. Turner. I recall walking into the church and pausing to look at the lights and remember all of the time Paw-Paw had spent with me. And like a flood the memory of the day he passed away came rushing back like a tidal wave.

I was still young, and dad was pastoring Oothcalooga Baptist Church in Adairsville, Georgia. I spent every moment I could at the home of Delmar and Elaine Height. They had become family to me. They lived in an old rock house that dated back to Civil War times. They had grown kids, Tonna and Greg, that I looked up to and enjoyed being around. I was at their house and fell asleep and dreamt that my granddad had passed away. It was a very vivid dream and one that bothered me greatly. I awoke and immediately started telling everyone. I had heard that if you have a bad dream and you tell someone that it wouldn't come true. Well, that tidbit of information was false. That night Elaine had cooked dinner, much like every night, and my parents showed up to eat. I was sitting by Delmar asking him to play "horse race" which was a card game similar to Rummy but with different hands and rules. We played it often and had so much fun. Amid my plight, their phone rang. This was way before cell phones. The Height's had a phone attached to the wall, now referred to as a "house phone," with a cord that had been stretched to reach about 25 feet; I think it may have been a six-foot cord when it was new. When I heard the first ring, I said out loud "it's about Paw-Paw." Tonna answered the phone, and it was one of my great aunts on the other end and sure enough, my granddad had been sitting in his chair that I always sat on the arm of and had a heart attack. They had rushed him to Paulding Medical Center. As Dad ran to the car, I followed and dove in. We rushed to the hospital. I do not recall the drive as I sat in that silence again. No car sounds. If Dad spoke to me, I never heard it. I was just fixed looking out the window in a daze as if I had been hypnotized. In moments, we were at the hospital, and I followed Dad through the labyrinth of people and doors until we came to the room where my granddad was lying. I remember a hand going on my shoulder and it put me against a wall between two metal beams that was just wide enough for me to fit. I watched doctors working on Paw-Paw.

I remember the monitors and the noise and one of the doctors, Dr. Sacs, saying, "Mr. Turner, you're going to be okay; we will get you fixed you up."

"Doc, you can quit now," I heard Paw-Paw say. "You can quit, because I SEE JESUS."

He raised his arms as if to hug and they fell across his chest. It was at that moment that the monitors went flat, and he breathed his last breath here and his first breath at Home. I remember the stillness and a calmness watching this. Through the years many people asked me what I thought he saw. Without any doubt in my mind or heart, I believe he saw what he had read about, prayed about, believed in faith that ended in sight as he saw his Savior in that moment. This event as a child sealed any doubt for me in what happens when we die. Oddly, there was no silent moment. Just a stillness and a peace. I wept until my dad lead me out into the hallway. My Uncle Johnny and Ma-T were coming down the hall. When they saw us, my precious 90-pound grandmother began to scream,

"NOOOOOO! Not Robert! No God, please don't take my husband. NOOOO!"

The echo of her scream can still be vividly heard in the memory banks of my mind to this day. Uncle Johnny picked her up, and he and Dad sat her on a gurney, and they began to pray at her feet. I stayed against the wall observing and trying to not add to her pain. I listened to her as they prayed, her screams began to change. Ma-T went from God, NO to thank you Lord, for the time we had, thank you for the love we shared. This went on for about thirty minutes as family began to flood into the hospital.

As I came back from this memory, I observed people walking out of the church with its new auditorium. They had ironically just finished a funeral. I had not known of this prior. I was just coming in from a very long drive to have lunch with Dad and enjoy a break from college with some fishing and boating at the lake. I entered the main auditorium and was walking down the aisle. I heard sniffling and whimpering. I looked up from my gate to locate the sound and on the front row was a young lady sitting and crying. I walked over and sat beside her, not speaking at first, giving her time to get it out and notice that I sat down, so she wouldn't be startled. When she looked up, I simply asked if she was ok.

"I don't know, we just finished my grandfather's funeral."

After my stroll down memory lane, I could relate to this. I said loss is hard, my grandfather passed away and I was closer to him than anyone. She put her head on my shoulder and cried and we sat there for a long time, neither of us saying anything. After what was likely an hour, my dad walked out of his office with a woman who looked very straggly and rough, to put it kindly. The woman walked over to the young lady and said let's go. The lady was the young girl's mother and Dad had just finished preaching her father's funeral. He had forgotten our lunch plans with the funeral arrangements and wasn't expecting to see me on the front pew. I decided to tag along for the graveside service and hopefully get some Chinese food afterward!

At the graveside, I stayed in the car as I wasn't dressed for the occasion. I didn't want to seem disrespectful. I sat and looked on and recalled the moment that I walked across the road holding Ma-T's hand at Mt. Olivet Baptist Church, watching as Paw-Paw was committed to the ground. Somewhere there's a photo of her and me sitting on the flowers atop his grave holding hands and crying. It's a picture I can't look at today and not immediately feel the same emotion.

Following the service, my stomach was growling Amazing Grace as I was past hungry. I was ready for Dad to stop running for mayor and just come on! If you were a preacher's kid growing up, you can relate to this statement for sure! Finally, he gets in the car. As my mouth began to water for Chinese food, I heard a tap on the window. It was the young girl. I rolled the window down and she handed me a rolled-up piece of paper. I put it in my pocket so I wouldn't have to listen to the years of whatever joke Dad would make out of this, one that he would repeat for years to come whenever he felt he had an opportunity to get one on you. We went and ate, and I think I licked the plate clean.

When I got to the house it was time to grab a shower and crash. I had driven for eight hours and had no idea I'd be attending a funeral, all for some Chinese food. As I entered, I saw my brother and it was time for some 8 Ball and Tecmo Bowl! Cody couldn't handle the Tecmo Bowl I brought having Marcus Allen and Bo Jackson on the same team! We played tournaments and he chased me across the field and back, diving to no avail. Touchdown Bo Jackson kept appearing on the screen followed by my laughter. Later, as I was getting ready for bed, that forgotten piece of paper fell out of my pocket.

The girl had written, Thanks for your kind words and just being there, signed Mende and a phone number. I put the paper in the drawer of my nightstand and was almost asleep on my much loved, and much missed, full-motion waterbed when the phone rang. I heard my mom yell up the stairs that the call was for me. Who could be calling me this late and would even know I'm home? I rolled over to grab the Sports Illustrated football phone that I thought was the coolest gift ever. As I got the receiver up to my half-asleep head, I heard a female voice say hey. I returned the hey and was hesitant to guess any names, knowing if I said the wrong one it would be like a Fat Boy going off in Japan. Then I heard a sniffle followed by, "It's Mende. I got the number to your house from mom." I heard my mother hang up the other phone now that she had nosily found out who was calling.

"I hope I didn't wake you," I heard Mende say. "I need to talk, and since you have been through it, I thought you wouldn't mind."

I told her I didn't, and she began to share how important her grand-dad was to her. He had been good to her. She shared stories about him and even talked about seeing him where he laid in the floor next to his chair for the last time. She would talk and then cry, regain her composure, and continue to share stories. She talked about her father who had divorced her mom and wasn't around much afterwards. Her stories were deeply heart breaking and sad. She talked about the times she spent sitting out by the mailbox waiting for her dad to come get her and he would never show. She talked about her mom's boyfriends and paramours that would sexually abuse her. I had never heard stories like these, and it made my heart hurt for her. Before I realized it, the sun was coming up and she was still telling stories. This was the first person I had known to have gone through these types of events. As we got off the phone, I pondered these for the rest of the day. The next evening the phone rang again, and it was the same event, but no stories were repeated. This went on for a few days, so one night we decided to go have breakfast the next morning.

At breakfast she pulled up in a VW Rabbit Cabriolet. It sounded rough and began leaking as soon as she shut it off. It reminded me of some of the cars my parents had growing up. Many times, I'd requested to be dropped off a block away from school so I could walk in without kids seeing our vehicle and bringing me more ridicule. Her car brought back a familiar childhood feeling. Looking at her car and clothes, I knew where she was and remembered all too well the struggles life brings upon us.

We ate and it was a good meal. I noticed that she wasn't timid like other girls — afraid to eat in front of a boy. She was hungry and ate quickly. She was also quiet unless telling her stories, often having awkward silence filling time until she remembered another story. She talked about her younger brother, Jason, who I grew to really like. He was a smart kid and had a personality that I connected with.

Mende's stories were always heart grabbing, but with one story in particular I felt a special connection. It was one of the few times she got to spend a holiday with her father. His current wife had told her and Jason to look under the Christmas tree at all the presents. Being kids they plopped down on the floor and stared at the colorful paper, wondering what might be inside the packages.

"None of those are for you," they heard her say.

Being a lover of Christmas and feeling I missed out a lot, her stories, this one especially, caused me to feel compassion and empathy. No one should have to endure being abused and mistreated.

When we left, her car would not start. I arranged to have it hauled to a local mechanic to get it looked at but every time I saw her, that little car was giving her more and more trouble.

Eventually she and I were talking every single day. I realized I wasn't talking to anyone else anymore and all my time was spent talking to Mende. I finished my college stint and came home and decided to build some houses. I had 10 started and in contract at drywall phase. This opened an opportunity for me to get into the concrete industry. With this I had multiple streams of income and life was going well. I was healthy, blessed, and it seemed the future was bright.

During my time with Mende, we decided to get married. I'm not sure at this point how we reached this decision. I believe for her it was an escape from where she was, where she lived, not having much, and looking to be more. I don't know what I was thinking, I was not in love at all. I guess what I was dealing with was the fact that I had met someone that I didn't want to see suffer. I wanted to give her a better life, to show her what it's like to be Cinderella. This is the best way I can describe it as a grown mature adult. As a young man just flowing through life it seemed like the thing to do, after all you can grow to love someone, right? The more I was around her mother, the more I felt sorry for Mende. Every story I heard made me feel more empathy.

One day, I went out and bought her a brand-new Dodge Neon. It was fire-engine red with keyhole rims, like the Gallardo. It was a five-speed manual that she picked up on quickly and mastered driving in a few days. It was her first new car ever. It was time to let the VW rest.

We set a wedding date and like lightning it rushed upon us. I called my friends from all over to be in the ceremony and asked my dad to officiate. It was quite beautiful, and we had over 750 guests attend. On the day of the ceremony, I stood in a side room with my groomsmen, waiting to walk out. My dad looked at me and said quite possibly the best advice he ever gave me — advice that I wish I would have listened to.

"Andy it's not too late, you can walk out that side door and get in the car and go. I'll tell everyone you had a migraine or changed your mind. Right now, is not too late."

I looked at every one of the guys there, they were silent. I peered out the door at the host of people in attendance, many I had not seen in years. While I knew in my heart that I was about to make a mistake, I felt I was too far in and couldn't turn back. So, we headed out.

Have you ever noticed that the first few chords of Here Comes the Bride start with DUM DUM DUM DUM? Or at least that's what I felt like the piano was saying to me right before everything went silent.

Andy, what are you doing man? Hello... I could hear my inner voice as I stood there. I was listening to that silence when I felt a tap on my shoulder. I turned and there she was, already on the stage in front of me. I repeated everything that Dad said like a parrot while thinking the acid in my stomach was about to go everywhere. Suddenly everything went loud and people were standing and clapping. I walked down the aisle to the back of the church and into the opening. I looked up at the chandelier honoring my grandfather and thought to myself, this is where all of this started.

We were to spend our honeymoon in a cabin I owned in Pigeon Forge. I had little to say as I ate a Checkers Big Buford and fries on the way. The reception was bursting with many wonderful, kind people. All the guests spoke such kind words to us, hugging my neck, giving advice and encouragement. It had kept me so busy; I hadn't had time to eat.

When we arrived at the cabin, Mende went straight to bed. As she slept, I called my dad.

"I've made a mistake."

His words to me were firm, "It's too late now, we don't believe in divorce. Make the best of it and do what you can."

That was not the advice I wanted to hear. I went to sleep, deciding I'd make a go of it, and do my best. The next morning felt like an episode of the Twilight Zone. My hand did not look right or feel right. What is this thing on my hand? I learned through all the years of playing football that nothing comes easy. It takes hard work, blood, sweat, and tears! I guess this was the first day of the two-a-days training camp to being married.

Boy, did I hate those two-a-days.

Chapter Five

Some Things Never Change

"A crack of lightning lit the sky and thunder so loud it made me jump.
I sat motionless until the silence crept in and took over."

I sold my home and we moved into a house on Burton Drive. I owned several houses there that I had built using the same floorplan and I felt this would be a good start for Mende and me. We wouldn't have to worry about a mortgage payment and there was an opportunity to turn it later for a decent profit.

One thing about Mende during these days, she was a kind person. She was kindhearted but had been through a lot and this left her defeated and cold. I felt like my efforts now of turning her whole world around would be met with enthusiasm and a demeanor like Tigger from Winnie the Pooh. But no matter what I did, nothing seemed to change the Eeyore face, mentality, or mood. Every day she was unhappy.

I wanted to show her the world and how big and beautiful it was, so I booked a 31-day tour of the entire country of Italy. I was absolutely mesmerized by the architecture, especially the breathtaking churches. We spent our days in vineyards on walking tours and spent nights in castles. We stomped grapes, which at first was very unappealing, but quickly turned into an opportunity to laugh at my inability to dance. We saw the statue of David, Sistine Chapel, even the Pope. We saw St. Peter's grave, took the gondola ride in Venice, had dinner at the spot where the very first pizza was created and learned why and how the creation of our most popular food came to be. The food, the culture, and the people were something that makes you want to stay forever. In fact, if I ever go back to Sorento, I'm not leaving.

On a visit to the ancient city of Pompeii, I was introduced to a 90-year-old lady, Ms. D., who was on the trip with her daughter and grandkids. We were at the castle and Ms. D. wanted to dance, so I obliged. During this time everyone was filming and laughing, even the staff. Mende left and went back to the room we were staying in.

"You two don't match," Ms. D. piped up, willing to speak her mind freely. "You are always talking and happy, she frowns and complains about every meal or the temperature or where she's sitting."

I had not noticed all of this until she pointed it out, but she was correct.

"We're nearing the end of the song, watch out I may go for the dip," I joked, my go-to method of deflection.

She and I made our way back to our seats where we were enjoying the evening with her family, our tour guide, Ornella, and an empty seat where Mende had been.

Ornella was an attractive lady who grew up in Florence. She was young and well put together, very well spoken and carried herself like she was a celebrity. I watched as everyone retired, leaving her and me at the table alone. Ornella moved to the chair beside me.

"Are you happy," she asked.

I was already thinking about why Mende was not happy and why my efforts of a home, cars, clothes, and trips had seemed to do absolutely nothing. But I had been laughing and dancing and having a great evening, why would she ask me this?

"I see you living life and making the most of the day, but I also see in your eyes that you're not happy," she went on to say.

I smiled and said it must be the wine. More deflection. But her words shook me. I knew I had made a mistake and was trying my darndest to make the most of it; however, I was not happy. I was focused on a task to make someone else happy at the expense of myself. Why? Was it youthful ignorance or had I just gone too far to the edge and couldn't back out because I felt pity for someone? Regardless, I found myself sitting in one of the most beautiful countries in the world, unhappy.

Ornella stood. "If you were my man, you would always be happy," she smiled big and took two steps before looking back and adding, "You know I'm in the great room on the top of the grand staircase to the right, if you decide you want to smile, just come in."

I sat in that chair another two hours until the fire turned to what looked like orange and black sticks with no flame. I'd be lying if I told you I didn't ponder walking up those steps in that castle. Ornella reminded me of the Raquel Welch poster that was on Andy Dufrene's wall in Shawshank. Same hair, same body type. The temptation was very high, especially with the inner tug-of-war I was dealing with. But I read the Bible every day and believed in it. It was almost sunup when I made my way to my room. I started getting ready for the day's tour. I was just out of the shower when Mende woke up and I asked her if she would join me on the terrace overlooking the valley and vineyards. She declined.

For the remainder of the trip, instead of seeing the sites, she opted to spend time alone, mostly shopping. She wasn't interested in the old buildings and was tired of the food from the tours. We went home with only a handful of photos of us together and many of the sites and locations. Following this we went on many cruises, to Israel, Puerto Rica, Panama, Belize and countless other places. Each place and every trip were all the same.

After a while I didn't want to even bother. The conversations went to necessity. Others began to notice and would ask questions. I felt like the other aspects of my life had been successful but no matter how hard I tried; I was failing in this area. I leaned hard on my love language of gift-giving. We sold our home. Mende, our first son, Austin, and I all moved into what is now referred to by my kids simply as the "green" house. It was a beautiful three-story craftsman-style home. Within its six-thousand-square-feet, we had a theatre room, five bedrooms, 30-foot ceilings in the grand room, hardwood and marble, all sitting on the top of a mountain. On the top porch you had an amazing view of the sunrise over the peaks every morning. I felt that, surely, this would make her happy. I never was more wrong. What I had created was now an expectation and entitlement for things. In my attempt to simply make her happy, to make her feel like Cinderella, I created someone who came from nothing and now felt that everyone owed her something for what she had been through.

She began trying to create happiness for herself by buying things. She became unhappy with what she had and knew happiness would be found in her next purchase. Desperate, I obliged.

Over a span of 10 years, I started to notice that my attitude was changing. At this junction, there have been so many attempts and nothing I did worked. I was pouring out trying to keep her filled and she absorbed like a cactus and never blossomed. By now, we had two sons, Austin and Kaeden. The boys had become my life. They were my joy, my happiness, my reason for working, my everything.

The boys and I stayed busy! We created games, one of our favorites we called, "Monster Truck Knockdown." We would line up all the standup toys from the toy box; army men, GI JOE, Star Wars, and Disney figures, anything that would stand. You could stagger them all over the floor, any way you wanted. Then the other players would use monster trucks that we bought at Monster Jam, pushing them on the ground several times to wind up the wheels, and then ziiiipppp, they would be released and make their way across the floor to knock down the toys. The last person with a figurine standing was the winner. Countless hours were spent on the floor, revving trucks and letting them fly!

We camped out in the backyard. We had all-night movie marathons. Austin and I built model cars, Kaedon and I built model planes. We constantly played ball, football, baseball, basketball, soccer. We played trash can basketball, which eventually evolved to toilet basketball. Yes, raising boys is a treat! And yes, we broke things and had to clean up messes. I never even cared.

I noticed that I stopped trying to fight the losing battle of making Mende happy, and I loved my kids as hard as I could. After a while it started to feel like it was just us three in the house. As I think back, it's hard for me to even remember Mende around. As I look back in family vacation photos, we have very few pictures with her, just enough to show that everyone was in attendance. Not the ones of everyone playing and having quality time. She spent all of her time shopping, and the kids and I were off doing our thing. The last few years of our marriage, I spent most of my time in the basement where my office was located, and now my bed.

Holidays became miserable, we forced what was necessary and got through it. I was determined to focus on being a dad and working, allowing her to do whatever made her happy. I realized I didn't have the ability to make her happy, so I gave her the space to work it out on her own, I had become content and joyful in being a father.

One day, I noticed twenty-five thousand dollars missing from one of our accounts. I immediately questioned her about it, unable to get a straight answer.

"My mom lost her house and was trying to get another house in Villa Rica," she finally confessed.

"You stole money out of our account and gave it to her without me knowing," I questioned. "Why in the world would you do this?"

An argument ensued. She knew I would have said no had she asked, so she decided to do it behind my back, hoping I wouldn't notice the missing money.

Mende's mom always had trouble with money. A few years prior, something happened that changed my desire to help her and made me realize these efforts were, and always would be, fruitless. She had been visiting with the kids and left shortly after I had come in from work. I had showered and noticed that a watch from my dresser was missing. I collected watches and the stainless and black submariner I had just taken off was nowhere to be found.

Hearing the front door close, I ran outside and caught her in the car. I asked why she was leaving without saying goodbye. She made a few comments, and as she was relieving herself of her comments, I looked into her pocketbook and saw my watch. I reached in, grabbed it, and immediately asked why she took it. She denied doing so and said one of the boys must have been playing with it and dropped it in her purse.

Mende went to the defense of her mother, stating it must have been an accident. This was not the first or last "accident" that had occurred with her and it grew to be an area of contention in the house.

I drove to get my money back and found her planting in the backyard. The money was spent, and I had no legal leg to stand on since my wife legally took it from our account. This severed the spirit and attitude of fighting for Mende's happiness. I only wanted out. I kept hearing my father say, "No one in our family has ever been divorced. It's not what we believe. You must be the husband and make it work."

This weighed on my faith. We never missed church, making sure the boys were there for Sunday School, Sunday church, Wednesday church. I was struggling because I was not having an "abundant life." In fact, I was absolutely miserable and the only happiness I enjoyed was the time spent with the boys.

Soon after that event, I took Austin and Kaedon to Disney. We had a wonderful time. We stayed in the park and I remember clearly how magical it felt for me, seeing the smiles and the happiness, the laughs. The demeanor changed for us all when it was time to go home. The boys even began to have a different temperament. This realization bothered me to the core. What do you do? Stay miserable, or seek happiness?

I remember very clearly one night it was coming a very heavy thunderstorm and you could see it for miles across the valley. As it approached, I went out to the backyard under the deck and sat in a swing. My emotions of years of pinned-up misery began to bubble out, and I asked God what I was supposed to do.

What do you want me to do? I can see the effects of this environment now impacting my kids.

One thing I have learned is that health is not contagious, if you're sick and someone healthy comes in contact with you, you do not catch health. They only catch sickness. How could I think I could make her happy, allowing her to rob me of my joy for all those years? How could I be a good father and allow them to suffer the same? I had been lied too; I had been stolen from.

God what is the answer?

A crack of lightning lit the sky and thunder so loud it made me jump. I sat motionless until the silence crept in and took over.

Chapter Six

Baa, Baa Black Sheep

"I remember feeling that something wasn't right, but I was too young to figure it out at the time."

-Austin Turner

At this point Mende had stopped going to church with us. I would gather the boys and the three of us would go together. One Saturday, we attended a youth event and went for lunch with my parents. Arriving back home, I saw a white motorcycle, dirt bike style, sitting in my driveway. I didn't recognize it. As we entered the front door, I yelled for Mende, "We're home."

I watched as a fellow church member make his way down the stairs, Mende not far behind him. This was no stranger; this was a guy that had recently gotten saved while I was speaking at a revival. He asked how I was. I told him I was fine and abruptly asked him why he was there. He said that Mende had asked him to fix some drywall and some molding in our bedroom. I wasn't aware of any wall damage, but at this point had been staying downstairs in the basement. He worked driving a delivery truck that hauled drywall to jobsites at the time. I made a mental note and just went on.

He left and I went into the kitchen. Mende came in and said, "I want to tell you something."

I thought maybe she had been able to recover the money from her mother but instead, she dropped a bomb on me. She pulled out a pregnancy test that showed positive. I just stared at her. I wasn't happy, of which she was aware. I began thinking back to the last time I had been with her. Doing the math in my head, things weren't adding up. I walked outside and the boys followed, so we picked a game of pillow fight with the outdoor cushions, mine and Mende's conversation dropped.

The next day, the boys and I returned home from church to find the same motorcycle in the driveway. I walk in to find the same guy, this time there to fix the intercom system. He left quickly as the room became very uncomfortable.

The next morning, I left for work at my normal time and dropped the boys off at school. I turned back towards the house. I pulled in at the same time as the white motorcycle.

"What did you come to fix today? Do I have a light out? Or is it some plumbing?"

Mende came outside and began yelling at me for being accusatory. The bike was started, and the guy drove away.

"Mende, honestly, just tell me how long."

"A few months," she said and smiled.

I wasn't angry. I was relieved. The Bible states that infidelity is the only excuse for divorce. I was finally free. I left and as I turned off our road, I saw the motorcycle heading back. I went to one of my business partners and asked him for a good divorce attorney. I went in that day for a consultation.

That night after the kids were asleep, I asked Mende to sit down with me. Hoping to sort things out amicably, I laid out a plan, one I felt was fair and asked for her feedback. The woman at the table that night was not a woman I had ever spoken to. Her eyes, her face, even her speech patterns had changed.

"I acknowledge I gave up on the marriage some time back," I admitted. "I am not claiming to be perfect or a great husband. I have been drained from trying to make you happy and never having my happiness considered. So, I abandoned it and gave all my efforts to the boys. We both are at fault."

We owned multiple houses and had several large bank accounts. My offer was an even split. My offer was rejected as I was told she wouldn't be happy until she saw me living under a bridge. She got up and walked away.

Eventually, while I was away on a work trip, Mende went into labor. I arrived just in time. It was awkward as neither of us wanted to be around the other. The divorce proceeded as normal.

I had shared with a handful of people at church that we had filed for divorce. I had forgotten how much people like to gossip, even the ones in church. It doesn't matter that God speaks on the tongue more than any other thing in the Bible, church people will point to other believers, never applying Biblical principles to themselves, and never feeling conviction over their actions. The news of our divorce spread like wildfire.

One Sunday during the evening service, I went down to pray for the kids, myself, and Mende. The pastor shared with the congregation what we were going through. He felt in his heart he was doing good, but I felt like we were put on display. When the service was over everyone came and spoke, some to be kind and some to be nosy.

One lady stood out among all the others. She displayed a smile so bright, something I hadn't seen in a long time.

"Hey, you," she said.

I was mesmerized by her. She was beautiful. She had on a beige turtleneck sweater, a pencil skirt, and heels. Her long hair was blonde, and perfect. She sat down beside me. Austin and Kaedon were also on the bench, holding their Bibles.

"I'm Heather," she said. "I know what you're going through. I just filed for a divorce as well and it's not fun."

She stood up and said we should get some coffee. I watched her smile, saw her joy, the happiness she had in her. Yes, I want to get coffee, my mind shifting back to reality. I guess those thoughts took too long to process.

"I meant now," she interrupted my thoughts.

The boys and I followed her to Starbucks for frappuccinos. We sat and talked, never a mention of anything negative. I leaned back and heard laughter and not just regular laughter — it was the kind that makes you bounce. I loved the moment of escape. I watched as it seemed like she moved in slow motion and beams from Heaven came down while angels lined up and sang.

Our time together ended too quickly as I had to leave with the boys. They were difficult to get up in the mornings already, so late nights out were not an option. As we reached the parking lot, Heather hugged me, squeezing tight. It was one of those hugs that you just love.

"You should call me tomorrow," she said, arms still tight around me and rocking side-to-side in a way that I found cute and would eventually fall in love with.

I opened my mouth to tell her that I didn't have her number but before I could get the words out, she pushed a napkin into my hands.

"Yes, you do," she said laughing as though she had pulled off the timing of the perfect punchline.

When we arrived home, I got the boys in the bath and ready for bed. Once we said our prayers, I grabbed the baby, Bronson, and gave him a bottle. I sat and rocked him, thinking about the evening. I watched as a train went by on the eight-foot-tall track in his room, one I had built. You could control it by remote and he loved to watch it go by. It helped him fall asleep quickly, but this was soon interrupted by Mende yelling. One of her friends from church called her and told her about our time with Heather. I hadn't thought this would be an issue since she hadn't found it difficult to move on but quickly realized it was a problem. Mende left the room, leaving me with a screaming Bronson. I rocked him back to sleep and continued thinking about Heather. I couldn't stop thinking about her smile, it was like a spell. And her laugh, like a siren calling sailors to the deep. But after Mende's reaction, should I even call her? Or am I asking for problems? With the divorce not finalized, I decided it was best to wait.

The next morning, I dropped off the boys and headed to the office. My phone started ringing.

"Why haven't you called me yet?" Through the silence came a bellow of laughter, I must admit it brought a big smile to my face.

"Well, it's early," I replied. "And I just dropped off the boys at school — but it's not smart for me with a divorce filed."

"There's no harm in talking on the phone."

Then she broke into a story about her morning that had us both laughing. In what seemed like seconds, I was at the office. I couldn't believe how fast the ride went. I was caught up in the story and the vibes that she was putting off, it felt like time sped up. I caught myself thinking about her several times throughout the day. How could I not? She was a ten and had a personality that couldn't be contained in a stadium.

Lunch time came and I decided to work through to get caught up on some things. The phone rings and Heather's name appears on the screen.

"Do you miss me already," I answered playfully.

"Yes, and that's why I'm calling," she responded without hesitation. "I know we said this morning that we were just going to talk but do you mind if I bring you lunch to your office?"

"You have no idea where my office is." At that time I had several across the state.

"Did I say I knew? I just asked can I bring it."

Without thinking I said yes and told her how to get to my office. She hung up and within 45 minutes arrived with takeout.

"I didn't know what you liked."

I looked down and she had four bags. She had picked up four unique meals to make sure I had something that I liked. She began laying out BBQ sandwiches, tacos, burgers, and Mexican salad. I just watched as she made the spread. She was wearing heels with jeans and a white button up. It looked perfect on her. When it all was set out, she paused and looked up waiting for a reply. I was so dumfounded that she went to all those places. She walked over and put both hands on my chest.

"May I," she asked and leaned in, her mouth aligning with mine.

There wasn't a need for an answer — I was already meeting her. We kissed a very slow kiss. It was the kind that you want time to stop for so you can have the moment forever. I remember her smell, Dior, and how her hair slightly blew against my face. The smell of her makeup was clean and refreshing, Bare Essentials and Mac. Her waist was small, and her frame petite, as she pushed against me. As she pulled back, I saw her dimple only on one side. She smiled big and took her hand and wiped the corner of my mouth.

"Please tell me you're starving."

She sat on my couch, and I sat beside her. She made a joke about the large amount of food and started laughing again like she heard an Andrew Dice Clay punch line. That laugh got me every time. I didn't realize how long I had been in Somber town. This change was refreshing and so welcomed.

Lunch time was up, and I didn't want it to end.

Something about her was so magnetic. I just wanted to be around her and near her energy. I had dated a lot in high school and college but never recalled feeling like this. I never got attached or fell head over heels. That just wasn't me. But with Heather, something was different. She left that day and within ten minutes I was dialing her number.

"I'm never going to get work done with you around."

And then I heard that laugh.

"Good," she replied.

Later that evening I was approached by Mende. She and I never spoke anymore, and our paths rarely crossed. But that night she sought me out and told me that she wanted me to leave the home until the divorce was final. Not wanting to leave my kids behind, I told her she could pound sand; and that I wasn't leaving. Looking back, it is clear to see that this moment triggered something inside of her. Things took a dark turn after that night.

One day, I decided to do a yard project with the boys. I bought a lion head fountain with a plan to plant flowers and greenery around it. We left early and got all the supplies we could, having the rest delivered. Austin dug holes; Kaedon put plants in them. We even brought Bronson out in the stroller to oversee the progress. We were almost finished when I was summoned to the house by Mende. When I walked into the house, she muttered something at a level I couldn't understand. I asked her to repeat it.

"What, what are you doing!?" she yelled, oddly.

Confused, I asked her what was going on.

"You spit on me," she yelled again.

"Mende, you have lost your mind," I rebutted. "I'm 20 feet away from you. What kind of shit are you trying to pull?"

She continued to yell, "What are you doing!? Don't."

I let her know that I thought she was crazy, grabbed some lemonade for the boys, and headed back out of the house. Back with the boys, I hand them their drinks, trying to make sense of what just transpired. Less than five minutes later, two Sheriff's cars turned into the driveway. I knew they had been called before I had even been asked to go inside. It would have taken them a full five minutes to get through the gate and drive back to where the house sat.

Four officers approached. I told the boys to finish their drinks in the sunroom. They headed inside and I asked the new arrivals what I could do for them.

"We were called to the house for a domestic dispute."

One of the officers excused herself. "The caller said she has proof," she called back as she made her way up to the house to speak with Mende. It dawned on me what the fiasco was. I explained the exchange to the remaining officers. One of them left to join the other inside. While there, they were given a recording. A recording. Made by Mende. How clever was she to try and create this moment for herself.

The officers eventually came back, explaining to the remaining officers that they could tell by the recording that I had to have been pretty far away from Mende. They explained that there weren't any out of the ordinary noises on the recording, certainly not any spitting or rustling. All four of them stared at me.

"Are you going through a divorce?" one asked.

I affirmed. They all shook their heads.

"Get the hell out of here until its final," advised one of the officers. "It's obvious what transpired today, but she's after you and when people start this, it can get ugly or dangerous."

My mind began to race. How could I leave home? It would mean leaving my boys behind. I reached out to my lawyer for counsel.

"We never tell the dads to leave the marital residence because it looks bad to the judge," he began. "But, with this recent display, you should get an apartment and let us expedite this. We'll file for an emergency hearing."

I had a decision to make, and it felt like a wrong decision either way I went. Seeing the hand played, I realized the point to which things had escalated. Reluctantly, I looked for an apartment, something temporary while things were being worked out in court.

I found a place and got a few pieces of furniture. I was supposed to get all three boys for a visit the day after I settled in. Visitation day comes and there is a knock at the door. I was handed a paper for a temporary TPO that states I am not allowed to see the boys or Mende. I was devastated and distraught. Why would she keep the boys from me and for what reason?

I called my lawyers, and they advised that she still had to go to court to get this granted. They told me I wouldn't be able to speak to the boys until the court date. It felt like an eternity. The judge finds the claim has no basis and tells me I can pick up the boys the same day. I'll never forget how they came running across the yard to see me and jumped into my arms.

Austin: *"We asked where Dad went. Mende told us that he left us, abandoned us. She said he left us because he liked another woman. I remember going to bed crying and missing my dad. I wanted to call him, and she wouldn't let me use the phone. She told me to draw him pictures and tell him we were mad at him. I wasn't mad, I was just missing him. I remember feeling that something wasn't right, but I was too young to figure it out at the time. I went to my room where all the model cars were lined up that Dad and I had built. We had filled up four shelves and the top of the headboard on my bead was four deep all the way across. The headboard also had shelves all the way down and the entire thing was full of the models we had built. I was holding one and crying when she came in and took it from me and threw it in the trash. Kaedon came in to see why I was crying and tried to help stop her from throwing away my model. I guess he thought his planes were next. He and Dad had hung his planes on the ceiling like they were in dog fights. She got angry and went and got a belt with ornate metal tabs on it (we called it the spike belt) and spanked both of us. I remember going to sleep that night, crying, and wondering what was happening. Dad tucked us in every night of our lives and prayed with us. But tonight, I was in bed, my shoes still on, with bruises, and missing my dad."*

Kaedon: *"When I heard her talk about Dad leaving, it just made me sad. I didn't want to talk to her about it. I just wanted to crawl under my bed and go to sleep."*

When the kids shared with me what was told to them and how they were treated, I was angrier. I couldn't even call to confront her. I was instructed by my lawyer to take notes of everything that happened and meet with him a few days before our court date. These were difficult times. When it was time for the boys to return home, they would fall apart. Our youngest son, Bronson, was too young to be affected, but Austin and Kaedon would clutch my legs and beg me not to leave them. I remember prying them off, telling them I love them and that I'd see them soon. I tried my best to hold back the tears so they wouldn't see me cry. I would get in the car, look back, and watch my children cry. Again, that silence flooded in. That deafening, high-pitch shriek of silence as I am fixated on my kids' faces, mouths wide open, tears streaming down their cheeks. I know they are screaming, but I hear nothing. It still brings tears to my eyes.

I had exactly five minutes to drop the boys off before she would call the Sheriff. This forced me to be cold to my children, to rush their goodbyes. It made each one even more unpleasant than they already were. According to the judges' order, I was allowed a phone call with the kids each evening to check in and see how their day had been. I looked forward to this time all day. I've never understood how dads can walk away from their children or decide they no longer want anything to do with them. I love my children, so these calls meant the world to me. The first few days, the calls went well. The boys were enthusiastic and eager to talk. I was allotted a timeframe, so I would call one minute before the start time. She would refuse my call until the minute our timeframe began and, regardless of where we were in the conversation, would hang up the phone the moment 30 minutes had passed. This meant at times, the boys would be cut off mid-sentence. It would be an unfair split if one of the boys went over on their half of the time and pressed into the time left for the other. This would cause a protest which eventually resulted in Mende locking the phone in a cabinet and refusing to allow any more calls. Lawyers just kept telling me to wait for mediation and finalization. There was nothing I could do.

Chapter Seven

Circus Court and a Lawless Sheriff's Department

"As I watched this, I was sickened. It made me sick to my stomach that people sworn to protect could do this to a child and allow him to be put in danger. Not only could those men have hurt him, but the mental destruction would linger for years."

The day for us to appear in court for mediation arrived. Everything was laid out before the judge; the spiked belt, a wooden spoon, bruises, the kids being told I abandoned them for another woman, throwing away their models just because I helped build them, the contempt for not allowing the kids to spend their court-ordered time on the phone with me. The Judge didn't even hear it. He appointed a guardian ad-litem.

Months pass. Things are progressively getting worse with the boys. As they share horrific stories with me, I relay them, verbatim, to the guardian. Phone calls are still not allowed.

Kaedon: *"I found an old phone in dads' desk. I turned it on, and it worked. I crawled under my bed one day and called dad. I remember him answering and I was whispering.*

'Hey dad, do you know who this is?'

'Is it the president?'

'No'

'Is it Tom Cruise?'

'No.'

'I know who this is — it's Optimus Prime!'

'It's Kaedon!'

Dad was so excited to talk to me. It sounded like he was crying. He asked what number I was calling from, and I told him. I had to hang up on him a couple of times because I heard her coming. I always called back. He said he felt good for me to have the phone in case of an emergency, I could call him or 911. I told him I felt like a spy and I was going to have a spy name. He asked what my name would be, maybe 007.

'Umm no,' I replied. 'I like the Black Anus.'

Dad went silent; I thought the phone had cut off. He finally spoke up.

'I don't think I heard you correctly.'

'I'm the undercover Black Anus.'

Dad laughed and said he felt I should pick a different name. I thought it was perfect, I would have a cloak like Dark Wing Duck. He insisted that we should work on that name. I decided I would think about it. I had to hang up. Since I was under my bed, I put the phone between the slat wood and the mattress for safekeeping. Later, I told Austin and pulled him in for some late-night calls with dad. We became Team

Turner. We used the letter T with the Superman Diamond around it as our secret emblem."

Due to the time it was taking for the divorce to be made final, there was no way I could resist Heather any longer. She and I became a regular daily fixture. She was so supportive, caring, and loving. If I was upset over the kids she would sit and rub my head and sing to me. I was addicted to the happiness! No matter what was going on, her laughter and smile made me want to smile too.

One day I was having a particularly hard day. I was worried about the boys and what they were going through, and the pressures of navigating the hurdles of court and allegations had become too much. I was mentally exhausted. As I arrived home, dinner was on the table with a candle. I thought Heather had dropped it off and left. As I approached, I saw a note and read it, I wanted you to have a relaxing evening. I know you have been stressed and worried, I want to try and help, if it's even possible. I sat down and around the corner she came with a negligee and heels on, holding two glasses of wine. I was startled at first not expecting a person in the room, but that emotion dissipated quickly as my eyes took in what was standing in front of me. This woman created a world that was magnificent and sensual. She allowed me the space to relax and forget about the everyday stresses. Then something happened that I wasn't expecting. She did a head shake on my chest, with her signature laugh, then raised up with a serious and solemn look, dead into my eyes.

"I love you."

We had been seeing each other for a few months and it had been wonderful. But as a man, we don't just throw around the "I loo.." the "I loooo.." Well, you know the words. I was speechless that this beautiful woman with so much energy and happiness had just said this, and this quickly. She smiled and said, "I know, Baby Love." I laid my head back; I could feel my heart beating in both ears. She put her head back on my chest and squeezed me tight and giggled. I hugged her back and fell asleep playing with her hair.

I woke up to my phone going off late in the night. I don't like late phone calls; they normally have bad news attached. But this time it was Austin with Kaedon, under Kaedon's bed.

"Dad, Mende is having a party and men are over here and they are drinking and dancing."

I asked if they knew who it was.

"No sir, we can't tell the voices."

I assured them that she was just having some friends over and that everything should be fine.

"Lock your doors if you feel afraid and call me if something happens."

They wanted to stay on the phone, so I obliged. They were okay and fell asleep talking. The next day I was picking them up for a trip to Six Flags. When I arrived, Austin pulled out a pink video recorder and handed it to me.

Austin: *"Dad asked me where I got the recorder from.*

'They recorded the party last night,' I replied. 'They were drinking and dancing and smoking. It's people you go to church with, Dad.'

The recorder had been lying on the coffee table, out in the open, and I wanted to see what was on it. Then I wanted to show Dad the people that we called him about. He looked at it and said he would put it up. He didn't act like it was a big deal.

I was really excited about Six Flags. Dad had promised me he would ride Acrophobia with me. It would be my first time. We love roller coasters and always travel around to find the best coasters and compare them to each other. I wanted to ride Acrophobia because it takes you way up on this wheel and you're strapped in over your head. It tilts you

*out and then drops you. Dad had ridden it before and didn't care for
the ride. He loves coasters but this one wasn't his favorite. However, he
had promised we would ride it together. As we were in line, they had
photos of how tall the ride is compared to the Statue of Liberty and other
famous buildings. We listened to it go up and people screaming and the
'vroom' of the fall and grab of the brakes. I was excited. Dad did not look
enthused at all. He got on it and we went up. As it tilted out, he shouted
out, 'Boy you better know I love you,' and at that moment it released!
We started falling and my stomach went through my mouth. And in
a second, we were stopped. Dad said, 'I'm glad that's over. Let's go ride
Superman!' So, we took off running."*

We had a wonderful day. Especially eating funnel cakes and ice
cream for dinner. Why not! I thought back to my childhood. I never
knew places like this existed. But there, my kids knew their way around
without a map.

As I pulled in to drop the boys off that evening, Mende was waiting
in the front yard.

"Oh no, she looks mad," Kaedon said.

Before I came to a stop, she was pulling on the door handles. "Get
out."

The boys filed out and I went around to unhook Bronson's car seat.
I barely had time to hug the boys before she set in.

"Get in the house, now."

I didn't say anything, just watched and got in the car. I had forgotten about the video camera.

The boys went inside and were interrogated over the camera like
they were part of the 9-11 planning, and she was in the CIA. To avoid
the usual harsh punishment, they decided to deny any involvement.
Until she decided she would just spank everyone.

Austin: *"When I heard that Kaedon was going to be hit, I told her to stop. I didn't want him to be hit for what I did, so I told her I took it and gave it to dad. She started yelling at me, calling me a thief, and telling me I was bad. I got a spanking with the spike belt, and it hurt bad. She was yelling and asked me why I did that. I told her she didn't need to be drinking and having parties and that she was keeping me from my dad. I wanted to do all I could to change that because she wasn't nice. I got another spanking and she went to her room, and I heard her on the phone for a long time. What came next has been something that has stuck with me the rest of my life so far.*

She woke me up and told me to get ready. I asked why. She said she felt bad and was going to take me to get some ice cream. I can be mad at her, but ice cream never did me wrong. I started getting ready. I went and got in the car and buckled in. I was young and didn't know how to navigate everywhere but realized fast that we were going the wrong way from the ice cream place we normally go to. I asked about this and she didn't say anything. She picked up her phone and called someone and told them we were about to pull in. As we turned a corner, I saw a sign that read 'Paulding County Sherriff's Office,' then a sign that read 'Jail.' I perked up. She pulled into the parking space way out at the end and hit the automatic open on the slide door, telling me to get out. I just looked at her. Then I saw Officer Mitchell, who was the School Resource Officer and Dare Officer from my elementary school, the school where Mende had just taken a job. He told me to get out.

I unbuckled and got out. She sat in her seat, smirking. He grabbed the back of my neck and squeezed, leading me to a door that opened on its own. As we entered, other guards with uniforms on were there waiting. They told me to put my hands on the wall. They patted me down, told me to get on my knees, then stand back up. They had me get back on my knees, only to have me stand up again. They all laughed. They told me I was going to jail for stealing. They made me march to certain places and stand, then get on my knees and yelled at me, calling me names. I had to put my hands on the wall again and kept getting put on my knees in front of the men in the jail. Then the worst happened. They took me to the cells and these scary-looking men were yelling at me. One said, 'Look at that tight little ass.'

I was scared and tears were in my eyes. The guards told them to open the doors and they put me in the cell with these people in jail. One man said, 'Oh yeah, I'm about to fuck him.'

I watched him walk toward me and I remember feeling a little bit of pee drip out as he got closer. I was so afraid. The guy took off my shoes and said, 'Dance for me pretty boy and get me ready first.' I stood there terrified, and they started screaming, 'Dance pretty boy.'

They pushed me down; I would get up and they would knock me back down, shaking their things in my face. I started dancing as they yelled and grabbed themselves. They gestured and kept saying they were going to fuck me. Finally, I couldn't contain the tears and started balling. The guards came in and pushed them back and took me out. I now stood, crying, no shoes and a small wet spot in my pants. But it wasn't over. I got handcuffed and had to march around and was told how bad I was. They took my mug shot. It would become a souvenir that Mende would hang on the refrigerator, one that would stunt the healing process from the nightmare I had been through. Finally, after what seemed like days, they opened a door and told me to go tell my mother how much I loved her. That was not what I was thinking. I was angry. What kind of mother does that to her eight-year-old son? As soon as we arrived back home, I went to Kaedon's bed and called Dad to tell him what happened.

To this day I still have not gotten my shoes back."

When I received the phone call, I was irate. The first call I made was to Mende, to ascertain what the fuck she was thinking, abusing her role as a teacher and using the Dare Officer and Sheriff's Department to mentally and physically abuse our son. She laughed and hung up the phone. I knew the Sheriff and called his cell phone. I got a voice-mail, and I left one. My next call was to the jail. The poor lady who answered got an earful until I was put on hold and connected to a Captain. When I told him the story he said, "Sir, we do not have a Scared Straight program in Paulding County, and it would be illegal to perform on an eight-year-old."

I let him know that I was on my way and that I had every intention of getting to the bottom of it. As I drove like a bat out of hell, my phone rang with Sheriff Gary Gulledge returning my call.

"Andy, I heard your message and I'll bet you my house this didn't happen. I know my jail and we do not do this."

I told him I was enroute, and he said he would be as well. I was in a Porsche and without doubt, I pulled in at three times the speed limit and locked the car down, parking right in the middle of the lot. As I walked in, seven officers were waiting, as was the Sheriff and his first in charge.

"I owe you an apology, we have the video and photos from our system of what happened," Gary said. "I'll provide those to you. I spoke with Jason (their attorney) and he said we will give you these if you tell me that you will not pursue legal action against us. We will also testify for you stating what happened here against your ex."

I said okay, as I knew there was no statute of limitations on child abuse, especially with proof, and I wanted to get the video in my hands. As I watched this, I was sickened. It made me sick to my stomach that people sworn to protect could do this to a child and allow him to be put in danger. Not only could those men have hurt him, but the mental destruction would linger for years. I asked Gary how this happened and him not even know about it. He hung his head and replied, "I'll get to the bottom of this, and I assure you people will be fired and written up."

I took the video and photos and walked out of the office. As I turned the corner, I saw a litany of officers as if they realized it would take them all should I not leave calmly. 95% of them were overweight and seemed to struggle just to stand. They looked at me as if I had done wrong. Mike Hill was standing at the door, his gaze never wavering. This would not be our last interaction.

I drove straight to my lawyer's office, I believe, as mad as I have ever been. He called the guardian, Lonnie Skipper, to give her an update on the recent events. I explained to him how seeing your child go through this at the hands of the people who are supposed to protect and serve is not acceptable. We were in agreement.

The next day I picked up the boys. I remember Austin running up and hugging me like he was never going to let me go. I had to get gas and the boys liked slushies, so we stopped at QT. I filled up and we all filed in. I looked around and found Austin down behind the potato chip rack, hiding. As I asked him what was wrong, I noticed he had lost control of his bladder. He pointed to Mitchell. I turned around and was now face-to-face with the man who was responsible for the abuse to my son. Without thought, I was in his face, nose-to-nose, chest-to-chest, asking him why he felt it was okay to abuse children. He immediately turned and went around the hotdog isle to get separation. Another officer cut off my pursuit.

"Hey, what's going on here?"

I pointed to my son and said, "I'm Andy Turner and that is my son that that motherfucker put in a jail cell so inmates could threaten to fuck him in the ass!"

The cop put his hands up and said, "Oh, I heard about this and had to sign a paper. People got written up and let go."

As he spoke the words, Mitchell left the building, got in his car, and drove away. I looked around the store, no one was moving. Everyone was staring at me like I was a crazy man. I apologized publicly for my actions. One guy spoke up and said that they deserved it and probably more.

Austin came out from behind the chip rack, Kaedon still behind me as he had been the entire time, his fists up. He was ready to throw down and defend his brothers' attackers. I felt no remorse about what I had said to Mitchell but was embarrassed that it had happened so publicly. The guy at the register told us to have a good day. I reminded him that I still needed to pay him for our snacks.

"You did sir," he replied.

I told him thank you and the kids and I left. I was choking back tears as emotions started flooding. As people came out of the store, they gave us thumbs up.

"Yea! Free chips and candy," Kaedon said excitedly.

Austin didn't speak.

At the apartment, I got the boys settled. We did our prayers together. That night, Austin's prayer stood out.

"Dear Lord, thank you for not ever hurting me and for my dad, who loves me."

Talk about a snot moment. That created one! The four of us piled on the couch and before I knew it, the kids were out like lights. I called Heather to let her know about the day's events. She talked to me for an hour, just being an encouragement, telling me that everything was going to be okay.

I'm now thinking I'm about to receive a lot of tickets. There were a lot of angry people at the Sheriff's Office. Their friends and coworkers had been let go and disciplined. I was sure to drive under the speed limit.

Boy, do I miss those days of running the same streets with a towel around my neck. Times were much simpler. Like when I could walk down the road hitchhiking, the Sheriff would stop and eat your candy, but took you back home. Times have changed from when people were innately good, and you could sleep with your doors unlocked. Now you must be leery of everyone. The ones who are supposed to be the good guys used to be the good guys.

Today you just don't know.

Chapter Eight

Legal Rape

"We have talked to the police, the interviewers at the Harbor House, we've talked to the judges and the guardians. No one ever cared to listen."
-Kaedon Turner

I received a call from my lawyer who said the Guardian wanted to schedule a visit with me and the boys. I was looking forward to this as we had a natural and loving relationship and an organic natural flow of things. Everything proceeded as normal in the home. We didn't make changes to the home like you might be tempted to do by getting out all the Bibles when the preacher is coming for dinner. The desire was for her to see us just the way we always were. We were all hanging out in the dining room playing a board game when she arrived. She suggested we sit in the living room to talk. The kids and I piled up on the couch and accommodated her questioning. She then wanted to speak to us individually. We did everything she asked us to do. She stayed to observe so we returned to the game we were playing. Not much more was said outside of her questioning.

I was informed shortly after the visit that Mende would be taking the boys to Florida on vacation and the trip was to fall during my visitation time. I questioned this with my lawyer as the day fell perfectly on my days but was told there wasn't anything that we could do. I wouldn't see the boys for a month.

The boys were adamant they did not want to go. I tried to convince them they would have a great time in Florida, maybe even go see Mickey Mouse. My efforts were met with tears. The boys were adamant that she would not be kind to them, even on vacation, and they were not okay with missing our time together. I tried my best to stay positive and keep them positive.

At this point Mende has stopped phone calls entirely and it seemed that there was always something that robbed me of precious time with my children. She had begun cheating my time by minutes. If I was due to pick them up at noon, she would lock the doors with a key and not open it until one minute after. The kids would be in the window waving, watching me wait in the car for her to release them. It felt very miserable and seemed to border on psychotic. I began to feel deep animosity toward her, not because of how she was acting toward me, but how she was treating our kids.

I kept an air of positivity for their sakes but felt tormented inside as I told my kids goodbye for an entire month. They were holding me tight and crying until it was hard for them to catch their breath. I felt like a terrible father, pushing them away from me so that I didn't overstay my allotted time. She told me the police were on their way. They immediately started yelling for her to stop trying to get me in trouble. I let them know I had to go, kissed their little heads, and turned and walked away. I got into the car and drove away. I made the first two turns and was blocked in the street by two patrol cars. They asked a few questions, I told them what was happening, and I left. That entire week the boys were not allowed to take my calls.

I spent extra time working that week, keeping my mind occupied. Each night when I got home Heather was there waiting. I noticed that I was looking forward to coming home. She had such an amazing ability to light up every room she was in. One night in particular, we had decided to go to Atlanta for dinner. I had been working on my list of cars and had just purchased a Bentley Continental GT with a V12 engine. Only two more cars left on the list!

I spent the entire drive concerned about how the boys were. I wasn't confident in their safety and worried constantly about how they were doing mentally with the mind games they were subjected to. Heather reached over and put her hand on my thigh as I drove. No one said a word, but that gesture let me know she was there, and she cared. It was her way of being supportive without trying to make me talk about it. One thing that I loved about her was the way we could communicate without words — a touch or a look, or her devilish smirk. It developed very quickly and over our time together evolved into an intricate way of communication. That night at dinner, I leaned back in my chair, and I watched her eat. It felt like I was watching a movie. Looking at her captured my every being. The way she moved. The childlike innocence in her eyes. The way she learned new things and would laugh so big. I admired how she could always be so happy. It made me want to display this same quality.

Since the boys were gone, I decided to be spontaneous and booked a beach house in Puerto Rico. I began packing her clothes, not telling her of the plan. We made it all the way to the chartered plane at PDK before she started in.

"Baby Love? Are you going to tell me where we're going or make me pull it out of you?"

I opted for playfulness, of course.

We enjoyed an amazing trip. We went horseback riding in the rainforest, zip lined, surfed, and toured the fortresses. No matter where we went, she looked like she belonged. What a unique gift! I realized what I had been missing all those years — to be loved and to see real happiness. I felt like a kid with her, the youthful exuberance she emitted was contagious. For the first time ever, she made me FEEL. The way she looked at me, kissed me, touched me had a spark.

As we left that day to be tourists in search of Mofongo, I noticed that she constantly touched me. She was always rubbing my arms, back, hair, and it was just a natural reaction from her. She was naturally affectionate and loving, and this is something I didn't realize that I craved and loved. What perfect timing for her to enter my life, after years of long face and misery, dealing with negativity and everything having to be one way without any consideration of others — living in a non-affectionate and unhappy environment. Now, I was worried about the kids, dealing with the games of calling the cops and creating an environment where my children were unhappy. My heart was breaking for my boys, and I was missing my time with them. In the midst of these heavy situations, in walks this energetic, happy, sensual, and sexy woman that has given me an opportunity to see that life can be better. I was thankful that she entered my life when she did.

The day we arrived home I had lawyer meetings. The day was spent going over financials, reviewing photos from the Sheriff's Department, the kids' interviews and statements as well as the doctors' reports. Lawyers felt with the participation in the abuse and endangerment at the Sheriff's Department, this should be an easy custody case. The group felt this was a pretty solid case and hard to lose.

Over the past year, the relationship between Mende and I was tumultuous at best. Everything was about her having control or the final say, no matter what. It did not matter if the kids were walked on or if the reasoning didn't line up if she felt she got the "win." I didn't understand the mindset. I just wanted to be with my kids and them not be hurt or miserable. That was my only wish, and I was willing to dig in and fight for them. I looked for what the boys needed and that was my agenda. I never tried to make it personal or about my wants. I fought against her trying to take them from me and not allowing me to see them, which was a common theme for the next 16 years and over 30 court proceedings which, sadly, our file is the largest file in the county to date.

Walking into court was always nerve-racking. I kept an upset stomach as anxiety and worry about the what-ifs set in. The judge had the guardian, Lannie Skipper, come up and take the stand. She was also working as a lawyer, a judge of some kind, and since she was appointed by the judge, was obviously on a friend and colleague level. She spoke first about her observations with me and the kids. All seemed to check out fine and was sounding on point until it went negative. She said that the kids and I used the same sentences and told stories the same way — verbatim. This part was true. As the kids told me things, I told it to her exactly how the kids told me, in the same vernacular. This is where she twisted it — she wasn't listening to what the kids were saying, why they were saying it, or caring about the situation they were in. She didn't care about my concern as a father or the experts who also participated. She stated her opinion, that the kids and I could only have the same sentences if they were coached on what to say. As I was listening to this, I was about to peel my own skin off.

She then began talking about her observation of Mende with the kids. She began describing events at the pool in Florida. She had observed the children playing in the pool and they seemed fine. They played like normal and were not afraid, as they had stated.

Insert a record scratch in my brain and alarm bells ringing at a deafening tone.

Wait a minute, you went on vacation with Mende? You observed the kids playing in a pool with her in Florida? You came by my house and spent about an hour but went to Florida with her? Something doesn't smell right here. In fact, something is more than off.

Through the years, Lannie gave this testimony as she became the local Andy Turner Expert if you needed a witness to talk negatively. Her story has had a couple of variations; from she was on her own vacation and took time to go and watch boys like a spy, to her initial story that she was at the pool intentionally to watch and observe. Regardless, of all the experts we have spoken to, this is highly irregular. She had watched children playing in a pool while on vacation. They were not in a situation that generated fear, they were in public and playing with other kids.

She was asked to share her opinion of the Sheriff's Department incident. Her statement was that Mende made a bad decision and she shouldn't have done that, but she was confident that she wouldn't repeat that action again. Mende denied the belt and the bruises were played off as boys just being boys. The kids went back and met with the judge. They told their story. And to top it off they had been to the Harbor House and had been interviewed by medical professionals, all separately. Those professionals testified that their stories corroborated and that kids of this age couldn't make things of this caliber up, keeping stories straight, unless the events were true as stated. The judge didn't hear anything except what Lannie Skipper said and his words were, "Why appoint a guardian if you are not going to listen to them?"

This started a long road of smear for me. I was being labeled as alienating the children from her by simply repeating what they told me. No one listened to the kids at all. This quickly taught me the courts' cookie-cutter way of doing things and their total lack of giving a shit for the truth. At no point in time did the courts ever take our plights seriously, even though things escalated because she knew she could get away with them and not be found at fault. I was drilled for 62% of my income and over the years went months not seeing my kids or being able to talk to them. They were told I didn't love them and had abandoned them for Heather.

The court system will always do the same thing. I am not a lawyer, but I can tell you the processes. Many times, over the next 16 years, I was forced to be my own attorney and, in some cases, came out well but in most was absolutely demolished and buried. Once you get behind one judge's unfavorable ruling, all future lawyers will site that judge's same ruling in their own case. This starts a snowball effect where you never get ahead because the current judge will not go against either himself or a previous judge's ruling, which is often a colleague and a friend, especially if it's in the same county, as mine all were. I had wrongly and nefariously been cruelly and inaccurately labeled; I had the "bad dad" stigma with the court system and opposing counsel.

Although it bothered me, the people that knew me best were the ones who knew the truth; and they call me Superdad. To this day, I still receive Superman logo gifts for Father's Day, my birthday, or Christmas. The system is broken and even the lawyers and judges admit it, but no one fixes it and even worse, children like mine are affected every day. Maybe it's just small-town court; I hope it's not everywhere. My kids are grown now, and they will tell you that they told me the truth and that I repeated it to fight for them but that no one ever cared to hear their cries. We were either out-lawyered or the sexist prejudice in the Courts Against Dads spoke louder than the victims' voices and the person getting smeared for fighting for them.

Mende began social media pages about parental alienation, and I was being smeared. She took to building a platform for Team Mende to raise money for her lawyers, having groves of people come to court dressed in matching Team Mende shirts, creating hate sites about me. I was doing this because my children were being abused and the only motive for all this, for Mende, was to have complete and total control. In a short amount of time, I was labeled as the "worst parental alienator ever." I shook my head listening to stories and was dumbfounded at how fast things are told and how quickly and excitedly people gravitate to the negativity. Sadly, my children are not the only statistic here that have been forced to stay in an environment that's not healthy because Moms have the power in court.

As I was trying to move on and figure out how to help my kids and balance life and work, I got a call from my CEO.

"We have been getting anonymous letters for several weeks directing us to websites that have your ex-wife talking about parental alienation. They are stating how you are mean to the kids and to her. We have got more than 20 calls this week."

They went on to say that one of the calls showed on the caller ID as Pam Cunard. Pam? That's Mende's Mother! They continued, "We don't know who all these people are but it's disrupting workflow and people's ability to work. Your personal life shouldn't bleed out into your corporate life like this, so we're going to have to terminate you."

My reviews were all stellar, my performance had grown 25% year over year. I again heard that silence. I knew they were speaking but all I was hearing was the scream of silence.

I called Mende as soon as I left. Of course, she didn't know anything about it, and her mother "would never do such a thing." Three weeks later, I was served with papers for contempt for child support even before it was late. She knew it would be. I was drilled for contempt and tried to explain the orchestration of my termination with vigor and persistence, but I couldn't prove who it was, so it was a moot point.

The time came for me to move back into my "green house" and Mende was moving into another place. The day I arrived, there was water standing two inches deep all over the hardwood floors, which are now bowing. My suits had all been sprayed with bleach. Many personal items were missing from my office, autographs, and a snowman topper that was sentimentally given to me by my grandmother, who had just passed away. That was the most painful thing to have lost.

My precious Ma-T. She was a godly lady who quoted the Bible but couldn't read it; she only had a third-grade education. She got scarlet fever as a child, and it damaged her hearing. When she went to school, she couldn't say some words as plain as the others. Kids would hold their tongues and make fun of her. She quit school and went to work in the cotton fields. Yes, my grandmother picked cotton! It was her claim to fame that she was the fastest in the county. She had little fingers and got it all out and didn't leave any behind. People would pay her $1.00 more a bushel than the grown men because of her speed. I heard this story a lot growing up. I saved every card Ma-T gave me. Birthday, Christmas, all I'd ask for from her was a card and for her to sign it. Sometimes she would write my name and the 'D' would be backward. She wrote, "I love you" and spelled love with "L-U-V." These were priceless. I had them all in a box with a ribbon around it. Ma-T passed away in the nursing home while lying in my arms. I had my hand on her chest when her heartbeat for the last time. How I loved this lady! She was always my lady and the woman in my life that I knew loved me and was there for me. All her cards were gone. Thrown away. Lost forever. Irreplaceable.

I filed a court order and we went to court. I lost immediately. Even though Mende was in the house, the house wasn't flooded and the washrag was not in the sink stopping the drain with the water running when she was there, according to her testimony. But it was when I arrived 12 hours later and while it seems obvious who the culprit was, I did not physically see her do this, have a video of her doing it, or have photos... so, the judge said she had nothing to do with it. Boom. End of story. All my things, missing or damaged, were of no concern or care to anyone but me. It wasn't her stuff, just mine. Not hard to figure out unless you're a biased court — with a long history!

I moved Heather in. I figured I might as well since she had already been cited for the reason of the divorce, and I had been accused of having an affair. She was made the scapegoat for everything. The timeline didn't matter when lawyers were muddying up the water doing what they do. This was not why I was fighting, and I didn't care, she was my happy place amid the Hell that life was becoming.

I was the victim of the toll of court proceedings as they rapidly drained everything I owned. I had very little left to sell and no nest egg or retirement funds to pull from. Eventually, I landed another job that had completely replaced my prior salary compensation but didn't tell anyone as I didn't want a repeat of the last job. I sold a car and borrowed some money to get financially caught up. I got things out of hot water.

I started to notice that everywhere I went, people seemed to know my whereabouts. I soon discovered that those social media pages were posting all of my happenings to keep Mende updated. If I went to eat, to see a movie, or took the kids bowling, she knew immediately from this created list of cronies. It was oddly intrusive. Within weeks I was called into the CEO's office and guess what? Being within my 90-day probationary period, I was let go. Same story as before and again, Pam's name came up.

We were back in court - same story! Drilled again. I am trying to figure out the motive, then I learned it from the kids.

Austin: *"I heard Mende talking to a group of her friends at the house. They were having wine and laughing and all they did was talk about Dad. She said if she got him put in jail then she wouldn't have to worry about you seeing us. The judge would give her full custody instead of joint and you would never see us.*

Every time we would come home from Dad's it was like a line-up and an FBI interrogation.

'Did your dad say anything about me?'

He never did, he never talked about Mende in front of us. Even when we were talking about what happened he would just listen and tell us to pray for her. He never said anything hurtful like she always did.

I remember one time that even got Dad in trouble with Judge Vincent. I told him in Chambers how Mom treated us and slapped me and left marks, the spike belt, the jail, the spoon. How she talked awful about Dad. He asked if Dad talked badly about her. I said, 'No sir. Not once.'"

The statement prompting the kids to pray for Mende gained me a speech at the end of a trial.

"It's alienation to tell a child to pray for a parent," the judge said. "In doing so, it makes her look like she's bad, as if in the darkness or with the devil, and promotes you to be god-like and in the light."

Pause and let that marinate a moment...

If your child says someone hit me and I have bruises and you choose not to say what you're fucking thinking and what you really want to say but instead take the high road and encourage your son to pray, that leads to the worst alienation known in this court system. Give me a fucking break! The prejudices were relentless; no matter what was presented and how we presented it, we were railroaded. I'm not sure how or why no one ever listened. Where is the right of religion for praying families who believe in prayer for every situation? A purchase, travel, a date, a person doing you wrong? The Bible tells us to, pray for your enemies and those who persecute you. But if you do, don't let the courts know about it because that makes you an awful person.

Austin: *"I told the judge about how she slapped me and busted my lip with a punch from her ring. When I tried to get away, she kicked me. I jumped the fence and ran to the neighbors and called Dad. He called the police to meet me, and he came. I sat in the car with Dad, and he took photos of my face and lip and shin. We had five police cars out. They sent DFCS out as well. People went back and forth in the subdivision asking me questions and her questions. Then suddenly, they came back and told me I had to go back in the house or be taken to Juvey for being an unruly child. For what? Getting beat up?"*

I almost blew a gasket over this one. I was screaming at the officers. They advised that she said she was using corporal punishment and he ran off. The mark on his face an hour later still showed a defined handprint. His lip was still bleeding. This is corporal punishment? And do you know what he did to get this "punishment?" He asked to call his dad whom he had not been allowed to talk to in days and she got enraged. I asked the officers if they came out and a woman made this claim against a man, with the same injuries, what would happen? I was told I was being combative and would be handcuffed. They made Austin go in to find his door removed and everything out of his room but a mattress as punishment for telling the truth.

Kaedon: *"We have talked to the police, the interviewers at the Harbor House, we've talked to the judges and the guardians. No one ever cared to listen.*

One day I called Dad on the found cell phone which resulted in it being confiscated. Austin was being beaten with the spike belt, really bad. Dad recorded the call. You could hear Pam, or 'Ga' yell to get some chains and chain him up. I told the judge about this, and the tape was played for him. No one cared, even as bad as it was.

This reminds me of a time when we were driving down the road. Time after time and court case after court case, no one cared, and we felt like giving up. Dad said to never give up hope. He looked like he was about to cry but was trying to be tough. Just then we passed a church named Hope. I yelled out, "HOOOOOOPPPPPPPEEEEE." This became the running thing to do each time we drove past. HOPE!

We all needed hope in those times and when we wanted to give up, Dad was the one we looked to for hope that it was going to be ok. It seemed the more we fought to just try and simply see him or talk to him the more she fought to make sure he was not in our lives at all. Once the phone was gone, I found that my tablet had games on it. I downloaded Words with Friends so I could play Scrabble with Dad, and we could type messages. Some months that's all I had to know he was ok, and it's all he had to know we were ok. I always was going to find a way to let Dad know what was going on with us. It was my mission!

I was at football practice one day — Dad never missed practices or games. He showed up for everything. He even came and had lunch with us at school a couple of times a month just to be able to see us when Mende didn't have him blocked with court papers and stuff. One particular practice, I went over to the fence to say hi and tell Dad I loved him, and people started filming him talking to me. Then they started yelling at him. All he said was hey and he loved me too and told me I was looking good out there today, to keep up the good work. I can't imagine that being bad for any kid. That year I led the team in rushing and touchdowns. I was up for league MVP. Mende got angry because I wanted Dad to walk me on the field to get my award. I won My Patriot which was like a Homecoming King, voted by the team. The first person out who was so happy was DAD! This caused total hell for me. I wanted to leave my trophies and awards at Dad's house because I had a curio cabinet that he had gotten for me. I had my homerun baseballs and things in it, and I wanted my trophies there to keep things together. She told me they had to be at her house, like they were her trophies. I snuck them to Dad's over time, and it later caused him problems that came up in court. She accused him of taking them when in fact I didn't want them or even me at her house. She wasn't loving or kind. She was always angry and all we heard was bad stuff about Dad — and now Heather — which I didn't understand. We loved Heather, she was kind and played games. That made Mende mad instead of being happy someone was nice to us.

My biggest upset was kindergarten graduation. Dad got me a shirt and tie and dress pants. I loved wearing suits and sometimes wore them to school. I sat looking very dapper if I may say. The teacher called every name to get their diploma. People had come to see me get mine and to hear us sing. All the kids' names were called and I'm still sitting in the chair when the teacher said, 'That's it.'

Why didn't I get a diploma? Did I not graduate? Do I have to go back to kindergarten?

I got up and ran to Dad, jumped in his arms, crying, and asking these questions. He carried me over to the teacher and asked what happened. She told him, "Kaeden's mom (who also worked at the elementary school) came by the room yesterday to get his diploma and asked that I not give it during the ceremony."

Dad asked her why. The point was for everyone to see me receive it from my teacher and get photos. She said she didn't know. Mende was in the room, standing in the corner. I knew she did this because she didn't want me to give Dad my diploma for my curio cabinet. She later confirmed this when I went to her house and was scolded for crying. She pulled out my diploma and told me she had it and that I didn't graduate. Then she put it in the cabinet. Ever so often it would be on the refrigerator just to antagonize me. It worked every time.

Eventually, I quit sports because of the way she did things. Austin quit also because she would threaten to make him quit if he didn't act a certain way or if Dad came. I never understood because we knew what kind of dad he was. He loved us and tried to protect us and just see us. No one listened to me or my brothers or even to Dad. We were robbed of time and sports under her control. But HOPE! We held on to hope."

Heather and I talked about getting married. I had finally gotten hired by a company that seemed to be a perfect fit. I really enjoyed the people and the environment, and the position couldn't have come at a better time. I had been forced to sell about all I had to get the court caught up, the contempts were steep, and if not paid, I went to jail. I sold all my watches and autograph collections. It is hard to pay anything when you don't have a job and you have active sabotage against you.

Due to the money crisis from court and mounting attorney fees, Heather and I decided to have a private ceremony. She went to planning everything as I focused on getting us on track financially, having to pay to get the house repaired from the $54,000 in damages, not counting all of my clothes and priceless things I could not replace. I remember sitting one evening in my office about my life. It seemed the Bible was correct about one thing for sure, a woman scorned! I couldn't believe how the system had treated us with no resolve. It was about money, not about serving the people who had been wronged. When the money runs out, they lock you up and go on. Legal rape! There was such a lack of care, especially with the kids, but now those kids are grown, and their voices are louder. Their voices can't be covered up with an "oh, they are told what to say." Now the kids have a chance to tell their story and be heard and set some records straight in the face of injustice. The legal system of judges in Paulding County, the police in Dallas, the Sheriff's Department, the DFCS office, the lawyers involved - they all failed my children. The system that rolls on with the cookie cutter — get a lawyer, have mediation, appoint a guardian, have a hearing, come back to have court, do what the guardian says — is all a joke. Somewhere along the way, the voices of the kids and victims should be heard outside any prejudices you may have developed. In this case, we were all dead wrong with what we thought the system was supposed to do.

EXPOSE THE TRUTH. DO WHAT'S RIGHT FOR THE CHILDREN. LISTEN.

I'm just glad that my kids survived to be able to tell you. Sadly, they are not without scars and damage from the events. Some lifelong that should and could have been avoided.

Chapter Nine

A New Hope

"I couldn't resist, laughing and falling off my horse at this sight. Hair down in her face and chicken shit dripping everywhere."

Hope! What Superman was bringing to earth the entire time. If you have never read the origins of Superman and how he mimics Christ, you should do so. He was sent by his father from another land to earth to bring hope of salvation to the people. He had powers to do mighty things. That's not what this story is about but has always been why I loved Superman over any other superhero. He represented the greatest superhero of all time. A New Hope is also a Star Wars reference of the rebellion having hope to finally come back and defeat the empire and the Dark Side. Also, a fitting reference.

We had hope that finally things were going to calm down and we could have a normal, peaceful life. We also had the hope of Heather bringing joy and exuberance to lift our spirits and that is just what she did.

There once was a country in need of new hope as they fled the tyranny of Europe for the freedoms they wanted and believed in. They settled, formed a country, and wrote a Constitution and Declaration.

In that new hope for a country is where I found myself one day while working for my new company in Philadelphia, Pennsylvania. I was doing some work at the Independence Hall Courtyard. They were building a glass top over the foundation of George Washington's homeplace that can be viewed when you see the Liberty Bell. As I was there working, I got to know some of the park rangers and officials. This led me to plan something that had never before been done.

I went home and enjoyed a wonderful weekend with Heather and the boys. They had bonded much better than I had imagined. She showed them love and kindness. The kids were hungry for that from a female since they hadn't gotten that from their biological mother. Heather played games, baked, cooked, danced, and played music and was a listener for the boy's plight. Within a short time, they developed a love for her and her for them. It was clear to me that she not only was good for me but also my family.

After the weekend, I packed two bags and put Heather in the car. We headed to the airport again, not telling her what the plan was. I enjoyed surprising her because of how she smiled and asked every ten minutes where we were going. We landed in Philly and checked into the Ritz. The next day, we rode the ducks, saw the Liberty Bell, and walked down to Independence Hall. A large line had amassed waiting to take the tour to see where the Constitution was signed. We were in the very back of the line of several hundred people. We watched as some park rangers came out with their brown uniforms on and said they were looking for a Mr. Andy Turner. She looked at me and jumped to the side.

"Why are they hunting you?"

I took her by the hand and walked toward the rangers. When we approached, they said, "Follow us."

We did as we were ordered. They led us to the front of the historic building, we entered, and they shut the door and locked it. We had four rangers and one said, "Ms. Heather, you're getting a private tour this morning."

She started smiling so big her mouth seemed to touch each ear. They took us around and showed us each area before stopping at a small table.

"This table right here is where the Constitution was signed."

Heather was wowed and turned to get my reaction. I was on one knee holding a ring. She burst into tears.

"Heather, if this spot is good enough to start this great country, it's a fitting place for us to start our family." And I asked her to be my forever wife.

"Yes, Yes, YES a thousand times!"

The rangers were taking photos. This national landmark had never been shut down for a proposal as it's not allowed. I was so appreciative of the workers for doing this for us and making this moment special.

We made our way outside to the back of the building and sat on a bench just behind the building. We were laughing and crying at the same time. Out of nowhere, as if it were planned, a horse and carriage pulled up.

"Future Ms. Turner, your carriage awaits," was announced.

"SHUT UP!" she yelled and took off running to get in the carriage. I was still on the bench. We enjoyed a slow ride past the graveyard where Sixth Sense was filmed and the building that was Bruce Willis's home in the movie. Then, after a few beautiful moments we stopped outside of no other place but GENOS. That's right the home of the original Philly Cheese Steak! The horse waited while we had lunch at the local favorite and famous delicacy. The carriage took us back to our hotel. She ran up while I took care of the driver and thanked everyone for all the help and planning put into pulling off shutting a national landmark down and having the timing of events play out as perfectly as they did. In our room, I found Heather sitting on the balcony and she was crying profusely.

"Babe, what in the world has happened?"

"I never thought that I could be so happy," she said. "Never in my life did I dream of such a magical day! And this ring? I don't feel worthy."

She looked with tears flowing and grabbed both my arms.

"I am so appreciative of you and all you have done for me. Thanks for teaching me and for loving me and going out of your way to show it."

I am looking at this beautiful woman with such humility and again I am sucked into a place of bliss. I had been in a world where I felt unappreciated, surrounded by negativity, everything was doom and gloom and was now transformed, 180 degrees, into this completely different life. The rest of the trip took us to Hershey, Pennsylvania where we spent a day riding a coaster and stole a kiss on the Kissing Tower. We ventured up to Delaware and into Maine, and after eating enough lobster to get iodine poisoning, we caught a return flight home.

As we returned home, we were met with a federal official on the doorstep. He had some questions for us. Heather had renewed her driver's license and, knowing she would be moving in, had changed her address to save the step of doing it later. In doing so, her voter registration had changed also, and a card was placed in the mail. The voter card had come before Mende moved out.

Instead of her leaving it for us, she called the state and filed a fraudulent filing, stating she didn't live there. When the agent showed up at the address, he found that she was living there and so was I. He informed us that the way it was reported meant that Heather had committed a felony.

"Sir, you're sitting at the address, and you see we live here," I explained. I then told him about our situation, he took the information, and closed the case.

We began looking around and noticed that some things were missing from the home. Mostly my things but a big screen TV of Heather's had been taken out of the garage.

"Welcome home," she exclaimed and started laughing.

I fully expected her to be mad, after all, she is a redhead. You'd never know that because she spent a lot of money making her hair that perfect blonde. As she was still hysterically laughing, she turned and looked at me.

"Bitch is going to have to do much better than that to ruin my day," she stated. "In fact, all she did was let me know that she is thinking about me, so much so that she wastes time trying to upset me while I don't think about her at all."

Moments like this made me love her so much. Instead of being mad, she laughed. Instead of being hateful, she rolled on. I needed this in my life. I have resentment, hurt, and frustration. I needed to be a little more carefree. Her attitude and approach to life helped me. We traveled often and she got attention everywhere we went. It was not uncommon for men to give her business cards, knowing I was there. She just laughed and handed them to me. Many men came up and would shake my hand telling me how beautiful she was. I never got upset or jealous, I knew where she was going to be sleeping that night. We developed a way, it was "our way." The way we traveled, just drove down the road, ate meals. I can't explain it. I had found my person.

Heather stayed busy planning our wedding. She loved details! One day, she approached me with seriousness.

"I have decided how I want to do our wedding and I want your input." She went on to explain what she really wanted. "We've both been married before and I want this to be special. No need in spending money and feeding a lot of people when we can use that money for the kids or God knows what future court costs will come up."

Knowing I was a licensed minister, she wanted me to perform our ceremony, an intimate one with just her and me in attendance. I loved the idea.

"There's something else I need to tell you."

I was looking at my feet which were crossed on the ottoman. There was a silence, so I looked up and she was holding not one, but four Clear Blue Easy at-home pregnancy tests. I couldn't see her face while trying to read if it had one line or two. This was something I needed to be sure of. As I'm trying to read them, they are bouncing, and for a moment I thought this was one of her silly games. I soon discovered the bouncing was because she was crying. Trying to be wise here, I wasn't sure if they were happy tears or upset tears, I waited for her feelings to be revealed. Finally, she wailed. I was in a paused state, still not knowing how to react.

"I hope I can give you a girl!" She went back to balling. I pulled her in tight with her head on my chest. I had three boys. When I was young, I thought of having a family, a white picket fence, and a dog. I pictured having a daughter and naming her Alexis Brianna. Heather knew this because we had this talk while sitting in the rain forest in Puerto Rico as she was washing manure off herself. We had been horseback riding and came upon a field that had a rotating arm spraying something on the field. It was a fertilizer mixture. 95% chicken shit, 5% water and chemicals. I was on a horse that was spirited named Chorables, which they told me translated to "crazy horse." He was known to rare up and take off. Heather was on an old horse named Babolinia. As we were trying to time the arm and the spray, Old Chorables took off and was in a full run. I felt like I was in the Kentucky Derby or a Kevin Costner movie chasing "Tatunka." Well, Heather and old Babolina didn't have the same relationship, here giddy up was more like a senior slow poke and she didn't time the sprinkler arm very well. The arm didn't just spray her once but covered her three times. I couldn't resist, laughing and falling off my horse at this sight. Hair down in her face and chicken shit dripping everywhere. It didn't stop ole one-tooth Jimmy, the tour guide, from making his move. Even covered in shit she had a magnetism. He caught an iguana and gave it to her.

We sat by the river as she tried her best to get the smell off. I couldn't stop laughing. It was like the punchline kept coming back. Out of the blue she asked, "Would you want any more kids?"

Then she asked what baby names I liked. I had shared my youthful story with her, and it was what was on her mind at this moment.

"If it's a girl, I want to name her Alexis and we can call her Lexi. The name you always wanted."

I am still processing the information. We did this backwards. I was raised in church; the church people will be on gossip central. What a shame that that is a true statement today. I absolutely love church and love to worship. I enjoy the music to ready myself for the message. What I don't enjoy is the people. I used to. I used to love being around people so loving, supportive, caring, and helpful, like church was supposed to be. Now people gossip in the prayer requests.

"Please pray for Ken, you know he has not been feeling well. He has that addiction to porn and lust, and I hear he has an STD. We sure missed him in Sunday school. Pray he recovers soon."

I know you've seen it, too. The Christian Army is the only army that walks on its own wounded. Of all the people, the ones deserving of Hell, but grace has stepped in, and The Blood has been applied. They don't stop and think of all the sins they've been forgiven of, but instead talk about other sinners and the areas they struggle in. This is the reason churches are empty, but they blame God for it.

As I am holding Heather, she's crying and has already named our child, one that I found out about just minutes ago. The shock is setting in. She pauses and looks at me. I'm looking back and no words are spoken. Just looking into each other's eyes.

"I'll make you a great wife and be the best mother to all four of your children, if you'll let me."

Four. Four. That sounded foreign at that moment. She leaned back and rubbed her stomach, then started crying again. I was still in shock, to the point I was thinking, am I asleep or is this real? Ironically, she said, "Honey, you're awake. This is happening," like my thoughts were in a bubble above my head.

This brought me to a different state. She could read my face, that's how well she knew me. In a year she could tell you what I was thinking. How amazing was this woman? A girl. Humm. Maybe I will get that daughter.

Heather fell asleep on my chest. I picked her up and carried her to bed, tucked her in, and kissed her stomach as I covered her up. Lexi's first kiss. I went downstairs and fixed a glass of Angel's Envy and was sitting on the deck trying to process the information. I was still there when the sun came up. By this time, I had steadied my mind to the reality of another child.

Heather had taken to writing a lot on social media. We had quickly grown to 18k followers. We weren't sure why; we were just posting simple life events. We got so many questions from couples about our relationship, we started a couple's coffee to share our lives.

Our friend's list grew daily. I posted about sporting events; Heather posted the photos sessions and funny stories. It dawned on me, happiness must be transparent, and people could see it. They were inquisitive about it. I felt like the luckiest and happiest man alive, my only worry being the negative connection with Mende and the constant court battles, having to worry about the boys' well-being. Outside of that, things were just perfect.

I looked through all that Heather had posted. Family photos, vacation photos. She hadn't let the secret out. My gaze was broken with the door opening onto the deck. It was Heather bringing me one of her green bark smoothies that I wish didn't exist.

"Here, Baby Love. Got to get healthy so you will live forever for this baby girl."

"How do you know it's not a boy? Seems I only make boys."

"This time it's with me!" She laughed that big Heather laugh.

We had a doctor's appointment coming up and hoped we would find out the sex of the baby. I had already started getting the nursery ready. After the shock had settled, I found the thought of a daughter exciting. A Daddy's girl who would work on cars, go fishing and hunting but look as beautiful as her mother in an evening gown.

I had a hard time believing it wouldn't be another boy. That is what I produced: all boys, all big babies. It was easy to spot my kids in the nursery. The nurses would come to me and say, "your son is the big one, correct?" I'd smile and nod. They all were healthy and heavy baby boys. I can only imagine this baby being the same. It would be odd to see pink in the house.

The morning of the appointment we were anxious to find out if her instincts were correct. On the way she wanted to stop and get a chicken and cheese biscuit from Martins. She said she had been craving this for days, and pickles. Of course, I stopped and obliged as I do enjoy the peace, because a hungry, pregnant Heather is not as happy and jovial as the regular Heather, for some unknown reason. As she takes that first bite you begin to see the real Heather emerge, the smile, the laughter, and the silliness. What a powerful tool breakfast truly is!

As we made our way to the OBGYN, I could see a look of anxiousness on her face. She reached over and took my hand, and we just rode. Not speaking. She wanted assurance that the baby was healthy and ok, but she also wanted this baby to be a girl.

We arrived and met with the doctor and midwife. They discussed the care and what to expect from them moving forward. Then it was time for the sonogram. The lady doing the procedure asked if we wanted to know the sex of the baby. Like a barbershop quartet we answered in unison.

"YES!"

She smiled and said we would have to see if the little one would cooperate. I stood there looking at the monitor, Heather holding my hand squeezing her eyes shut. Then we heard these words.

"Oh, there it is, look at this, do you see this little hotdog bun on the screen? You have a baby girl!"

I don't know what force hit me at that moment or where it came from, but it took my breath. I couldn't talk. Literally I could not get a word out. I looked at Heather and my eyes filled with tears.

"Your girl! I'm giving you your baby girl!"

I tried to muster some words, but they would not form. I looked at the lady doing the sonogram. She was crying too. I let go of Heather's hand and walked out into the hallway and into the bathroom to try and gather myself. I looked into the mirror and saw an absolute mess. I washed my face with cool water but could not get it together. When I rose, the emotion flooded me like a tidal wave and started over all again. I realized I needed a moment for this spell to wear off. I walked out of the bathroom and went to the car. In just a few moments, Heather came out and joined me in the car. She leaned over and kissed me on the cheek, and it made it worse. What was wrong with me? Sure, I wanted a daughter but I'm not an overly emotional person. Where is this coming from?

Heather asked if I was Ok. I still could not get a word to form. I drove. I drove straight to Kids-R-Us. I grabbed a buggy, Heather did as well. I went in and the first thing I saw was the words I Love Daddy on a bib in pink. I picked it up and cried and put it in the buggy. Beside that one was one that said Daddy's Girl in pink. In the buggy it went as well. In fact, everything that was pink and said Daddy went in the buggy. I ended up on the aisle with pacifiers and I see a juice cup with the name ALEXIS on it. In the buggy it went. My buggy was overflowing, and I decided to try and find Heather. She was in the crib and baby bed section loading her cart with what she had picked out. Together we picked out a car seat/carrier/stroller combo.

It had been hours and I was still crying. What is wrong with me? Heather had picked up an outfit that said Mommies Shopping Mate. That was a scary thought. Finally, I started to get a hold of myself. We were in the middle of the store with two buggies full and a flat cart and I paused and looked at her and her stomach. She smiled and rubbed the side of my head. I looked in her eyes and mustered up the words, "Thank you." Heather grabbed me the tightest I ever remember her doing so and hung on for the longest time. And with tear filled eyes she yelled, "I LOVE YOU ANDY," then "WE'RE HAVING A GIRL!" Everyone in the store was already looking at us as we were making a spectacle and did not care. She decided to open this spectacle up to the world. The store erupted in clapping and people saying congratulations. The manager came and gave us 20% off our purchase, which was much appreciated with three full pushers!

For the next few months Heather lived on pickles, apple juice, and chicken sandwiches. She had the audacity to bring me the green bark shakes every morning since she wasn't drinking them anymore and would tell me how being healthy was important. I'd roll my eyes and drink them, then get a biscuit every time I left. You know, pregnant sympathy eating! Even into the third trimester, Heather still looked amazing. She had just a bump in her belly. I on the other hand looked like I was having triplets and for some reason my jeans wouldn't button, so I often just opted for the grey sweatpants look. Don't laugh at this, it wasn't very funny! I was tired of hearing people ask which one of us got pregnant. I decided to join the gym.

I booked a vacation for all of us at Disney for five days in July. When the boys came to the house, we told them we were going to Disney in Florida! Everyone was excited and yelling, jumping and screaming. Wahoo!

I looked over at Miss Thang who had been poking fun of me, calling me pregnant. She was looking at me with a definite smirk.

"You think you're funny. Taking me to Disney in the hot right near when I am due to deliver. That's OK, I'll outwalk you since your carrying triplets."

Ouch! She was laughing so I let her have her moment. I knew she was right though, I needed to hit the gym to get ready. I spent the next few weeks at the gym running on the treadmill. I cut 20 pounds before the trip and was back in my jeans. She on the other hand started to blossom. Baby girl had kicked in the growth. Heather was struggling with her body change.

"I don't feel sexy anymore."

I tried my best to reassure her that she was still beautiful. Out of the blue I'd get drilled with questions like, what if I get stretchmarks?

"Babe those would be stretchmarks from carrying our baby and giving life to our daughter," I would assure her. "That alone is beautiful. I see no shame or flaw in that."

One night she was fed up with the transformation. She wanted to feel sexy, so she lit candles all over the bathroom and put on a negligee, which didn't fit and left her belly sticking out of it. She was beautiful, and that belly was our created life. I walked over to her and leaned in to give her a kiss.

"I don't look sexy," she said with frustration and blew out the candles next to me. She had blown so vigorously that hot candlewax went airborne and hit me in the face and chest. What you don't know is I have a hairy chest which got covered with drying candlewax. To make matters worse, my right eye sealed shut with wax. The cackle I heard coming out of her sounded like a wicked Disney Princess. As I stood there, the laughter rose and became uncontrollable for her. The wax now had me sealed like a letter from the 1800s.

"Well, I feel better now. Thanks, Baby Love," she said once her laughter had subsided.

"So glad I could be of assistance my dear!"

Do you know what a pain it is to get candle wax out of chest hair? Of course, you don't, but maybe good ole Lannie Skipper does, I'm confident of this.

Disney bound, I was driving, Heather was shotgun, Austin and Kaedon and Bronson were all strapped in the back with their Mickey, Donald, and Goofy shirts on. Everyone had high energy. I like to leave for trips around 3 a.m., so the kids sleep most of the way and won't fuss, fight, have to stop and pee every two exits, or tell me how much they are starving. And I like to see if I can get there faster than on the last trip! But this time, the boys were wide awake and pumped. They had their Game Boys, and the TV was playing Disney movies in the car. As soon as I pulled out Heather said, "I'm going to stay awake to keep you company, so you don't fall asleep." She was out not even ten minutes later, snoring.

The boys on the other hand were in for the ride. As we approached the turnpike a song came on the radio that everyone knew but me. Let me explain something. I grew up in the 80s and graduated high school in '92. I stopped listening to the radio shortly after that. My music is 80s and 90s rock and Frank Sinatra. The radio played a song from Nickelback called Rockstar. We all know that I cannot sing. I'm tone deaf, however I never let that stop me from singing! I didn't know the words but that was not a deterrent either. So, I tore loose with what I heard and had liked and was yelling, yes yelling! When you're tone deaf, the louder you get, the better you sound! So, stick it!

We all just wanna be big rock stars, living, 15 cars, girls come easy, drugs cheap, skinny just won't eat. Hang out in the coolest bars, hey we all want to be big rock stars.

These were about all the words I knew, so I kept yelling them. I was rocking the car, doing an amazing job, but I woke up the Princess. She tried to roll over, which ended up looking more like a flop, and looked at me. The pause was messing up my singing. Then, out of the blue, she started singing the same words as me! The kids joined in, and we had a band! It was magical! When the song went off, everyone started laughing. I kind of felt like the laughter might have been aimed a little at me.

We spent three straight days at the parks, Magic Kingdom, Hollywood Studios, and Epcot. Then a day of pool time, Universal Studios, and then home. I must say, Heather was out in the 100+ degree Florida heat kicking it like a champ! I was so impressed with her. We would ask constantly, "Do you need to sit? Go cool down?" She was like a machine! Marching and going. I was secretly asking with the hope that she would want to sit down because I was hot and wanted to get an ice cream. But no, she was all about getting her steps in. Not many women have this kind of drive or personality. She didn't whine, complain, and was never negative. I thought she needed a cape!

The boys were amazing on that trip as well. I had so longed to be able to have this time with them and was eating it up. We piled up and watched movies, rode rides, but what made it for me was being with my kids and seeing them smile. I got hugs every day and we had ice cream and bacon for breakfast! The "I love you daddies" made me melt.

It was almost midnight when we left for home.

"Hey Dad?" I heard Austin speak up.

"Yes sir?"

"Thank you for taking me to Disney. It meant a lot."

"You're welcome son, I loved doing it."

I heard another sweet little voice,

"Dad," it was Kaedon, "Thank you for my stuffed animal and for taking me to have fun."

I'm swelling up inside and I hear another voice,

"Dad, fanks for bringing us, it was fun, and I loved the ice-cream." As soon as Bronson spoke the last words, he mustered all his strength and fell asleep. This is what I craved. Those sweet moments of being a dad that make all the shit-times worth it. I looked over and Heather was asleep. Within moments they were all out. As I drove home, I looked at each of them and pondered a verse I had read. Psalms 127, verses 3-5, "Happy is the man whose quiver is full." Meaning having a lot of kids. I must say my happiest moments are being a dad, seeing life through my children's eyes and watching them experience things for the first time. Everything I do and have done has been for my family.

As soon as we arrived home, it was time to start packing for a work trip. I had never packed a bag since Heather came into my life. I traveled almost every week and each time, she packed my bag for me, hiding notes everywhere — in suit pockets, shoes, in the bag. She made the trip special. I crashed for the couple of hours that I had and when I got up, she was waiting with my coffee, my medication, and my packed bag. She met me with a kiss and told me how much she would miss me. The executive car pulled up to take me to the airport, I kissed her goodbye and I left. I immediately missed her and the boys. I could feel it in my bones. I had a ritual when I traveled. I would text her when I got to the airport safely and in and out of cars. We would Facetime when I got on the plane. Then, I would put on headphones to stop my neighbor from chatting, and I would play Michael Bublé, I Wanna Go Home. This trip was a long one and a hard one. West coast to east coast.

The week seemed to creep by. In L.A., I met up with my friend, Jeremy Miller. Many of you know him from Growing Pains or the voice of Linus on Charlie Brown. We had lunch and caught up a few minutes before heading to my hotel. Then in Seattle, I got to see my buddy Thomas Janes. He and I played football together and were hometown friends back in Cedartown, Georgia. Even with the company, I was lonely for my family. Leaving Seattle for New York, the week was almost over, and I could go home. New York meetings went long and delayed my flight into Atlanta. This caused me not to arrive home until one in the morning. I got all the bags in, trying to be quiet. I was exhausted. I grabbed a quick shower and slid into bed and of course, was suddenly wide awake. Right as the sun started breaching the high post of the bed, I was dozing off. Heather's alarm went off indicating it was time to get up. It was Saturday and the boys had football games, so I put on my Dad New Hope shirt that had Kaedon and Bronson's numbers on it. We head out to watch our favorite football players play. Both boys had great games. Kaedon scored two touchdowns and Big Ole Bronson got put at quarterback and they ran the wildcat with him about every play. Those little kids had trouble trying to tackle him, it looked like the 85 bears putting the fridge in the backfield. After the game we took the winners out for pizza. Then they had to go back to the Lair.

Following this, I was in contact with a childhood friend that I lived next door to when we owned the store. Brent and Gary Huff lived in the house behind Ma-T and Pawpaw which was only two houses down from my house that burned down and the store that was attached. They had a cool story about the house they lived in. The house was ordered from the Sears and Roebuck catalog. It came as a kit and was assembled. It is still there today, painted blue. I loved going to play with Brent and Gary. They liked Star Wars and always had cool Star Wars ships and men. Their mother's name was Lynn, and she was always kind to me, she worked at one of the hospitals. Gary was in the area, and Heather and I were going to meet him at Red Lobster for dinner. Gary was working as a pastorate at a church and working a full-time job. It was good to catch up with him and hear how his family was doing, and to tell stories about how we played as kids. Gary was always a solid young man and good person. As we ate, he asked the blessing over the food and shared how God was using him in the ministry. I was very proud to hear this and see the excitement in him as he spoke of this and his family.

When we finished dinner and got home, it was late. I went straight to bed since I had been up essentially for about 48 hours. I went down hard and was sound asleep, the kind of sleep where you slobber on the pillow. Out of nowhere, I felt an abrupt tapping on my shoulder. It was like a big bird was having a seizure, causing me to bounce on the bed. I heard, "T. Wake up, T." This was another name that Heather called me.

"What is it?"

"I think my water broke."

"If your water broke you wouldn't have to think, you would know it."

I was lying on my left side with my back to her. She stood up and I heard something splash on the hardwood floor! It felt as if an outside force grabbed me and hurled me to the closet where our bags were prepacked. I had them in my hand and was in the garage before my eyes opened. I hit the garage door and hopped in the Porsche. Wait, shit, where's Heather? I got out and back inside the house as she was coming around the bannisters. I grabbed her under the arm and helped her to the car. I was born at Cobb General Hospital, as were all three of my boys. I peeled out of the garage in that direction, grabbing gears. We arrived at the hospital in 17 minutes. They came out with the wheelchair and took her from the car. They gave her an epidural and began checking her progression. At 12:00 in the afternoon, on the dot, Alexis Brianna Turner was born. They let me field and help deliver. I cut the cord and held her, then walked up and laid her on Heather's chest.

"This is your mother." Heather kissed the baby's head.

The nurses took her to do all the APGAR and weight and whatever else it is they do. I looked at Heather and across the room at Lexi. Wow, what a moment!

In a little while they brought her back and we held her, counted her fingers and toes, and examined her. She was perfect, no scars or cuts, or anything wrong. I held her in awe, and she held on to my finger. They wanted Heather to feed her to see how Lexi would latch on. Immediately she did and was eating. I sat and watched and couldn't wait to tell her the story of the day I found out she was my little girl. It was August 12, 2009, and life had changed forever.

The next days I brought the boys up to meet their sister. They were excited. Kaedon put on a suit; Austin had a stuffed animal for her. Bronson was skeptical.

"Does she like to play Mario party?" he asked.

"Not yet son, I'm sure she will over time if you teach her. Right now, she must learn pretty much everything." His eyes got big.

"EVERYTHING?"

"Yes sir."

"Girls are not that smart then." This got a laugh from everyone. I explained to him that he had to learn as well. What a beautiful day. With this new baby girl. I had such high Hopes for her.

My mother arrived at the hospital the next day to meet Lexi. Heather said that her father, Billy, had called and wanted to come to the hospital. I asked her what she thought about this. He had not been a stable figure in her life. He was in and out for whatever reason. Heather had shared some stories that for a while he was trying to make it in rock and roll. He also had struggles with substance abuse, and life took him to Texas for an extended period of time. Her "Pops" had always been the stable male in life that she referred to. After my mother left, Heather broke her silence suddenly and said, "I'll call him back, but I want you to have a talk with him. If he is planning on seeing Lexi, then I don't want him to be a grandfather that's in and out. He needs to be consistent and better for her than for me."

I listened and nodded, knowing if he was still battling demons of addiction, we wouldn't be able to let him come around.

"Ok babe, I'll gladly honor your wishes."

She called him. It seemed like a nice call. A few hours later he arrived at the hospital, and I met him outside. I recall we sat down on the curb and had a nice conversation. I explained I was coming at the request of her and in good heart. He seemed to take it very well and reciprocated nicely. Our exchange had laughter and he openly agreed that he could have done better for Heather in her younger days. My response was that it was water under the bridge, today was a new day, and we should make the best of the time we had. We went upstairs and he spent time with Heather and Lexi.

The next morning doctors said we could go. I had already put her car seat in the Tahoe, had taken it out and put it back in three times. I was so paranoid that I went to the fire station to ascertain from them if it was correct. It was, and I had my conscience eased.

A wheelchair emerged from the front doors, a nurse pushing Mom who was holding Baby! I took Lexi and put her in the carrier and turned and help Heather in the car. I double checked Lexi again and pulled up the sunshade that we had customized for her to block any light from her eyes. I had bought a mirror that was attached to the seat behind Lexi and a long mirror that went over the driver's mirror that double reflected so I could see her little angelic face as we drove. I got fixed in the driver's seat and finally we were off! Headed to take us home.

Chapter Ten

The New Frontier

Then came the one that made everyone quiet, "Thank you for never
hurting us."
...Silence.

We were getting settled into life well. Lexi was growing and perfectly healthy. The court cases had slowed down momentarily, and things felt like they would level out. The boys loved their little sister and the transition from three to four children went very smooth. Then Christmastime rolled around.

Anyone who knows me knows I live my life as an open book. I steer clear of drama and I'm not a locked-phone, has-secrets kind of man. I prefer to live my life in a manner that I don't have any reason to do these things. Until Christmas. Then I have secrets. And I am always planning. I usually start my Christmas shopping in September and think through every family member to plan to the highest detail how their Christmas will unfold.

I have been fortunate enough to have been friends with many of the kids from the famed movie "A Christmas Story," which is one of my favorite movies. I learned something from that movie that I have implemented into our holidays ever since Austin was little. At the end of the movie the lead character, Ralphie, thought he wasn't going to get his most wanted gift, the official Red Ryder BB Gun with a compass in the stock. The "Old Man" played by Darren McGavan, whom to me was the star of the movie, had hidden that present and he waited to point it out and let his son know it was hidden. Every year I hold out big presents for the kids, sometime all the way through the day till bedtime, so that Christmas lasts all day.

Oftentimes, one kid had the "Big Year," like if one of the kids were fifteen and it was Christmas prior to their sixteenth birthday, that kid always received a car. That way they could drive that car on the learner's permit to get comfortable with the car, then they would use it to take their driver's test. I always found different ways to have the most unique and special reveal for them.

With Lexi now with us, Heather and I were in great spirits. We decided we would make this the best year ever, a Christmas that the kids would talk about for the rest of their lives. While on a business trip that Heather joined me for, we found a kind mall Santa. This Santa was an absolute master at the craft of playing the Jolly St Nick. We discovered that he was from our hometown, and we knew right away that he would be perfect for our unforgettable Christmas memory. I found a reindeer farm nearby that would be icing on the cake and things were in motion.

On Christmas Eve, Santa would arrive, along with his reindeer, and surprise the kids. We had a lot of traditions that made our Christmas Eves special, and this year was no different. We baked cookies together, we called Norad to see where Santa was in the world, and we all laid under the 25-foot Christmas Tree and gazed at the lights, talking about past Christmases. Then, like my brother and I always did, we piled up in one bedroom and told our favorite Christmas memory, then our favorite gift, no one wanted to go to sleep. And on this particular Christmas Eve, they didn't have too.

At midnight, when I normally threaten the kids that Santa will fly over if they are not asleep, they heard a noise. Kaedon was the first to hear the bells. He flipped over and with a whisper so loud that you could hear it in a saw mill he said, "Did you hear that? It was Santa's sleigh bells!"

I smiled and kept going with my story as if he had lobsters crawling out of his ears, pretending I didn't hear anything. Kaedon was on alert as he knew he had heard something. He had crept over to the window and was now looking down at reindeer tied to a sleigh full of presents. He was jumping and pointing. They heard bells again, but they were inside the house this time. Kaedon bolted and dove, doing an army belly crawl out the door to a hallway that went to a banister that overlooked the living room below. When Kaedon bolted, Austin and Bronson went as well.

What to my wondering eye did appear? Santa putting presents under our tree. At this point, we were all laying on our stomachs watching. I looked at my children's faces. Their eyes were as big as basketballs. The smiles on their faces went from ear to ear and all were open mouth. For a few moments it seemed time was suspended. Then Kaedon could not stand it anymore, the itch was too much to bear, he had to scratch it.

"SANTA!"

And over me he jumped and went for the stairs. Like a stampede, the Turner kids were gone. I watched as Santa turned appearing startled, and said, "Kaedon, is that you?"

As Kaedon was now turning the banister at the bottom of the steps, he said, "Wait. You said my name."

Santa laughed with that beautiful big shaking Santa laugh. "Of course, I know you, and Bronson and Austin, and Alexis."

The kids were like deer in headlights frozen in front of him. Bronson went in for the hug. Santa said, "Gather around quickly for I don't have much time. Tonight is a busy night you know. I want to tell you some stories."

He pulled a chair beside the fireplace. He read them the Christmas story from the Bible and taught them that every good and perfect gift comes from God, and that Christmas was to always be remembered as a birthday celebration. He told them how Santa got started as Santa and let them know that he worked for Jesus.

Bronson never left that hug and had now fallen asleep in Santa's lap, missing one sock and wearing Santa's hat. We have the most memorable photo from that night of Santa with his finger over his lips as to say "SHHHH" while holding little Bronson. He finished putting out gifts and had to go. When he opened the door, the kids saw the sleigh and bolted. I was in fear for the deer and wasn't sure if they were about to be tackled or not. Proudly the kids pulled back and acted like they had been raised indoors. Santa gave them some reindeer food to feed the deer. Then we had to hurry back in so he could make it around to all the other kids before sunrise. As soon as we got back inside, Bronson fell back asleep on the couch, still with one sock, no idea what happened to the other one. Lexi was curled up asleep in the chair, Heather was laying in front of the fireplace on some pillows with coffee in her hand, asleep. Austin made it to his room, but Kaedon was wide awake.

"Hey, Dad. I told you I heard some bells, you didn't hear them, but I heard some bells. Don't you remember when we were coming home, I saw Rudolph's nose in the sky and I said Dad, Rudolph, Santa's coming to see us, and Dad, I saw Santa and he was putting out the presents under the tree, and Dad...."

I smiled as the "and Dads" kept rolling off his tongue. He was hyped up like a high school cheerleader on Red Bull and Pixie Sticks. The excitement was over the top and amazing. When Kaedon was smiling and excited, he was the cutest little guy. I sat with him for over two hours before he came in for a landing and went to sleep.

The next morning, the kids had a lot to open. When the time had finished, the living room looked as if it had vomited Christmas. After cleaning up paper and ribbon, I went and picked up Ma-T from the nursing home. Mom came by to see the kids. It was a perfect Christmas Day, but the surprises weren't complete. I called everyone into the room to check out one last Christmas card that hadn't been opened. It was a letter, to Heather, from Santa. It told her to pack everyone up and drive to a location, which happened to be the location where we spent our first Christmas together. As soon as we pulled up, she found a wrapped gift, tickets for the entire family to see Wicked at the Fox, as well as a note leading her to another location.

The second location was where Heather and I went on our first date. There she found another present, a musical globe of the Wizard of Oz, and another note, with yet another location. This location was where we first met and this time the gift was a pair of Ruby earrings, and you guessed it, another note with another location.

The last location was where we often go to get crappy pizza. The lot was empty, except for something with a very large bow on it, a red and white skunk stripe mini cooper, and tickets to fly out to LA for a live filming of Dancing with the Stars! Accompanying the car was a card that read, "Merry Christmas! Thank you for teaching the boys to tie their shoes, for all the sandwiches you have made, for all the laughter you have created, for the love you have given to the children, for the fun we have had and for the fun we will have forever. By the way, we named her DORTHY. Love, Your Husband."

Heather broke down crying as she read it aloud. The kids chimed in and started naming all the things they appreciated about her. Some of the shouts were playing tackle football in heels, making up parody songs, always playing games, dance-offs, hugs, kisses, being my mom, grilled cheeses, trips...

Then came the one that made everyone quiet, "Thank you for never hurting us."

... Silence.

This had me choked up because not one kid said it, but it was two, in unison, unrehearsed. Heather looked back at our children. "I love you all and I'll never hurt any of you."

With those wolf grey/blue eyes filled with tears, she turned to me and said, "Baby Love, thank you for the greatest Christmas ever."

Looking at all of the things that Heather did day-to-day, she deserved an amazing Christmas.

Chapter Eleven

Mike Tyson Marriage

"I looked at her and saw that smile. Hell, if I can land a wife like this, anything else would be far less of a challenge. I had hit the jackpot."

The new year brought with it the hope of a great year. This would be shattered by a phone call, another job dismissal. Again, anonymous calls and letters had flooded in, even an accusation that the business trip I had taken Heather on was using company money. This meant personal life was interfering with corporate life and the only answer was to let me go. The timing was terrible. Child support, a mortgage, car payments, a new baby...and now no income, again. This had to be illegal!

The house payment fell behind a month, then two. Car payments were late, including Mende's car that I was still paying for. I couldn't pay my lawyer, so I was dismissed as a client. I was forced to file for bankruptcy. As provider of the family, this hurt my pride.

One night, while struggling with how things had taken such a drastic turn, Heather grabbed me and held me, a long, much-needed quietness between us. Eventually she spoke, "Baby Love, don't let them get you down. I'll live with you under a bridge if I have too. All I care about is that you and the kids are healthy. Things do not matter. We may be knocked down, but we are not knocked out." She suggested that we get married the next day! "We will show the whole world they can't stop us."

That next morning, I put on my tux, and she put on one of her gowns. In our living room, I spoke my promise to love, protect, honor, and cherish — traditional vows. When it came time for her to reply, it was anything but traditional. It was 100% Heather. I'll never forget it.

"I promise to always have your back and love you like Ma-T did paw-paw. I promise to not only be your wife but your best friend. If you're healthy, sick, skinny, fat, poor, rich, living in a mansion or in a box. I don't care. I'll listen to your old music and love it. No matter what, I'll cherish our boys and baby girl and never let them down. They will know what a mother's love is from me because I love them and I love you, Baby Love, Mr. Andy Turner, my husband."

We exchanged rings, kissed, and went and fixed dinner together. We didn't even have the money to eat out. Nothing was going to stop us. As we prepared dinner, she hopped up on the counter with a glass of wine and asked what I thought of her vows.

"I thought they were perfect, which means you must be the perfect woman."

She smiled and said, "Only the best for you."

I couldn't sign my own marriage certificate, so we decided we wanted ed Gary to do it since we had a sentimental connection with him. The next day was Sunday, and I got a lead for a job interview and booked a last-minute flight to Texas leaving Monday. Heather said she would call Gary and meet up with him. My mind was focused on trying to get some income to help our situation. I flew out, not thinking much more about the signature.

I spoke to Heather on the phone, and she confirmed that she had spoken with Gary, who was honored to sign our certificate, and she was to meet up with him to get it signed before filing it at the courthouse. I thanked her for handling it and we talked about what a great team we make. I got back home and started the waiting game from the interview process. In the meantime, my cabin in the mountains was foreclosed on, and we had to move out of the green house. This hurt my heart to lose two houses in the same week. They repossessed the car the next week. I am calling everyone I know but no one is hiring. I finally got a call from the job in Texas. They promoted someone within the company.

The same day as this call, I had court. I was dreading this. I was way behind on child support, and I had already been raped in this court. Mende's lawyer presented me as a deadbeat. They were looking for incarceration as I hear them spouting totals from left field. They are citing debts from a previous judge that have already been paid and stating it is contempt. Here I am with no lawyer. I got absolutely railroaded. How can you say it's willful contempt when it's not willful, it was the result of inability! Did anyone listen? Did anyone give two shits? Not at all, they said they have a history and kept on. Now, I had more money to pay through the court within the next 90 days than I made in total the previous year. And if it's not done, I have a new address. How is this right?

It looked like she was finally getting what she wanted. I had lost everything, was in bankruptcy, and the judge didn't care. It was like they had worked this out over cards the day prior. I decided I'd go and talk to my father figure, who educated and mentored me. He made a phone call for me, to some friends of his and it opened some doors. I had a private jet taking me to Canada for a job interview the next week.

Heather packed my bag, including the only suit I had left since having about fifty tailored suits sprayed with bleach. I would be applying for a VP of Sales and Marketing role and hoped to appear corporate enough. You know how feeling good in your clothes creates a sense of confidence? Well, I was wearing an off-the-rack suit and I am not a typical body type. The suit did not fit and did not look good. It wasn't at all comfortable, and I hoped that the lack of professional appearance would not hurt me.

Once I arrived and made it to my room, I Face Timed Heather. She asked about the flight and drive, as she always did. She could see on my face that I was troubled without me saying anything. Out of the blue she said, "I want you to know you're the smartest, most talented man I know. You look amazing in anything; you are going to wow them."

I looked at her and saw that smile. Hell, if I can land a wife like this, anything else would be far less of a challenge. I had hit the jackpot.

Heather had been a Godsend for the boys to feel loved by a mother figure. They had all three gravitated to her and on their own started calling her mother. They felt such animosity toward Mende. While I approached that biblically at first, not by telling them to pray for her, I learned my lesson there, but by trying to help them understand how to keep their chins up and have an attitude of respect and honor for her. Eventually I realized that how they felt was a direct result of how they had been treated. I learned to allow them to feel however they needed to feel without influencing them. I had to let them work through the emotions they were left with.

After witnessing the decline of what the boys needed in their lives and now seeing Heather willing to step in and love them for no selfish reason, it made me appreciative. I knew that the kids were in good hands, and I didn't have to worry about them being taken care of, which was a load off of me. Heather also went by the nursing home and checked on Ma-T. We had a routine of going every evening and being with her during dinner. When I was gone, Heather still went and took the kids. These were priceless acts of love to me.

I looked at myself in the mirror, remembering Heather's encouraging words. Almost getting angry about my tailored suits, I tried to shake off the negative thoughts. That's spilled milk, Andy. Let it go. I was grateful they had missed one and I still had it, even if I hated the way it fit. I had no idea that God would use that one suit, left behind untouched, to bring me from ashes. I folded my handkerchief and put it in my chest pocket and tied my tie in a Windsor. I looked in the mirror and smiled. This suit never fit so good.

I walked out to see my car picking me up. It's time, focus!

I took a deep breath and remembered Joshua 1:9. "Have not I commanded thee? Be strong and of good courage; be not afraid, neither be thou dismayed: for the Lord thy God is with thee whithersoever thou goest."

At that moment, I felt the Holy Spirit speaking directly to my heart. "Dummy, haven't I commanded you already? Did you forget this? Be Courageous! Do not FEAR! Do NOT WORRY! Because I'm your corner coach and I'm your audience cheering YOU on. I am your strength now GET FOCUSED. I'VE GOT YOU!"

When I arrived at the office, I was sent to a holding room. I surveyed the room and see six other guys all looking sharp, their suits on point. The fellow I sat by was what I deemed the sharpest-looking in the bunch. He was a West Point graduate, served in the military and upon returning, obtained a masters from Harvard. Oh man. What a pedigree! And he has the look. I leaned back in my chair and scanned the room. Every guy there looked like a clone to this fellow.

I must admit that the confidence, and Rocky theme music I was hearing, faded and I felt my heartbeat in my ears.

For some reason I pictured an episode of the Flintstones, the one where they had some new neighbors move in that were all monsters. Their house had a raincloud above it all the time. I felt this heaviness, like I wasn't good enough or didn't measure up. I grabbed my binder to go over my notes one last time and saw a piece of paper sticking out of the business card section. I pulled it out. It was one of Heather's hidden notes. It said we love you daddy, and we believe in you, signed by Heather and each of my children. It was then that I was reminded of what I'm fighting for and against and that I have no option. I cannot lose this! I watched every man go in the room for the interview. I was the last to be called in. Alphabetical order — the Curse of the T.

I walked into the beautiful office and placed a copy of my resume on the large desk. A gentleman approached and a massive hand wrapped around mine, what felt like twice. I looked him in the eyes and thanked him for having me out. He offered me a drink and upon noticing the resume on his desk, he informed me that he already had a copy but had no desire to talk resume.

"I want to know about you," he said. "What makes you tick and who you are. Why are you here today?" He went on to explain that he didn't want a corporate answer. One thing I have learned from psychology education is that if a man asks a question so precise, he more than likely already knows the answers. On his desk was a thick folder with my name on it. What could be so thick in that folder? Bankruptcies are public records and so are civil cases.

I handed him the photo of Heather and the kids. "This is why I am here," I began. "This is my family, my wife and kids. Nothing in this world means more to me than them. It's my desire to work and provide a life for them that they deserve. I want to do the best I can as a father and a husband to provide for them. But I am also here to be a help to grow your company, I have a stellar track record of growth and profits everywhere I've been—," he put his hand up to cut me off.

"Please tell me why you had very short tenures in your last jobs and had to file a bankruptcy."

I had not listed those jobs on the resume, so he did some serious homework on me. I was very honest about the letters and calls and that it had nothing to do with my performance but with the unfortunate hand I was dealt. He leaned back and, in my soul, I felt that drama was such a negative. It felt like garbage coming out of my mouth. I was embarrassed having to explain it to him.

"I believe in family," he continued. "A man with a family will come to work each day to make sure they have food and a roof over their head. If he loves his family, he will be at work even when he is sick to make sure they have insurance and the things they need for school and sports. A family man will be hungry and will fight to hit numbers and make my companies successful because he needs to provide. Mr. Turner, ironically, of all the men I interviewed today, you are the only one with a family."

I saw a shadow fall across my face as he had walked right in front of me. He had his hand out, with a piece of paper on it with a written offer. It was double the salary of my last employer and use of the company jet and a car allowance. He offered to pay me a sign-on bonus in lieu of the first year's commission as he knew about the court order.

"That way you won't have any worries and can focus on work."

Joshua 1:9 Why did I doubt? Why was I worried?

He had a plan for the calls and letters that would inevitably be coming as soon as word of where I was working hit the street. He wanted to help fight for justice and end the defamation.

I quickly learned that he wasn't kidding about the importance of family. He wanted to meet everyone. I flew Heather and Lexi up to meet him, but the boys were not given permission from Mende to go. He flew down at a later date to watch them play football.

As soon as I was back in Paulding County, I got everything paid up. It wasn't long before it was time for the "checkup" hearing to see if I met my order or go to jail. Everything was paid up on par.

"Your Honor," I heard the opposing council say. "It's amazing how hidden money becomes available when you tell Mr. Turner he's going to jail."

Wow.

When I die, what my children say about me will mark what kind of father I truly was. Not what was thought by lawyers and judges. And the same goes for mom. You can file a vault of court cases... they mean nothing. The truth lies with the ones who know it.

IRON MIKE TYSON MARRIAGE is what we are building.

Chapter Twelve

Who Are We? The Turners!! And we're closer than a brother.

"...you will ask yourself who are these people??? THEY ARE THE TURNERS."
-Mark Stocker

The kids huddle in like a football team at the park. We have been running pass routes for a couple of hours and just enjoying each other's company. Mende now has a court order that no one can pick up or drop off the boys at her house. We now swap at the park in front of the courthouse. Yes, I had to drive to the gates of Hell to pick up and drop off the Heaven in my life, but at least the kids are not having to deal with the doors staying locked until the last second.

"Who are we? TURNERS! Who are we? TURNERS!"

We all hug goodbye, and the boys begin dragging themselves to the parked car where Mende sits with her mother. Pam will drive the boys home, as Mende will stay and so will I. We will walk back into the gates of Hell yet again. On this occasion, it's really the same thing. Her agenda is to do everything she can to keep me from the boys. On this day, she would be dealt another hand of success, one that would create a wound for the kids that they will never forget or stop talking about.

I was awarded two consecutive weeks each summer to take the boys on vacation. We had a cruise booked and paid for. My two weeks were to be the two weeks following Father's Day. Mende did not want the boys going on a cruise with Heather and me. We had gone on one the previous year and the boys had an amazing time. She was determined this year was going to be different. Her council brought the most outlandish things to the fight and threw so many noodles against the wall hoping that one might stick. It did. I could not believe the ruling.

The judge did not stop the kids from going on the cruise, he only blocked me. So, Heather had to take the boys and Lexi, without me, to foreign countries. This was a huge backfire to Mende's plan and both parties ended up with a deal they weren't planning for. This only fueled the flame for Mende. She began telling the boys that Lexi wasn't their sister, she was only a half. She bashed our home and how we raised our kids. She never saw what a mistake this was in their relationship, leaving permanent damage.

But in our home, we spoke love and respect. We didn't bash her in our house. We just lived our lives and were only worried about the kid's safety and well-being.

I protested the ruling. Not only did it not make sense and was unfounded, but it also created a safety risk to the kids and my wife. Mende had used her lack of a relationship with the boys and blamed me for causing it. Eventually, the visitations supervised by Buddha, maybe I am bitter, ended and she was replaced with someone who had a Harvard education, someone who was an expert in the field and highly acclaimed. She would later testify that the children's problem with Mende were, in fact, a direct result of Mende.

Back to the cruise. I could not get my money back, but I was able to transfer my ticket to my mother's name. The boys were devastated. We always have an amazing time on vacation. Because it's about the TIME! Quality time laughing, playing, being silly, having ice cream and bacon for dessert. Loving and sharing the gift of family.

Austin- *"I was so upset at Mende for this. I overheard her on the phone with her friend saying she was not going to let us go on any vacations with my dad and "HO-ther."*

She always told lies about my dad, trying to make him sound like he was an awful father. What made him a bad father? He worried about our safety. He knew we were being mistreated while phones were locked in cabinets leaving us without a way to call 911, should that ever had been a need. We had watched Mende's dad flee to California to escape the constant attacks from Pam. Our dad didn't do that. He stayed and he fought for us.

Now she was robbing us of a vacation with Dad, and blaming him for being the reason we didn't want to have a relationship with her. I am 21 years old now as I write this. I'll tell you the reason that I am not close to her. It is 100% due to her actions and how she treated me directly. And yes, she disrespected my father for years when he did the best he could, and I am bothered by that. He had to fight to be in our lives and be a father. In my eyes, he is Superman. No one should have to go through the Hell he has had to endure and miss out on so much.

We all had a tough time missing Dad on the cruise. Heather did her best to make sure we had a good time and tried to brighten the mood. But despite her efforts, there was still a resentment there that I just couldn't shake."

Kaedon- *"I had a particularly hard time on the cruise. I missed seeing the different side of Dad. On vacation, he was more himself, free, like he had no worries in the world. It was just us and him. Vacations meant no phones, computers, work, Mende, or school. Just Family. The T-Fam!*

I had a hard time with him not being on the ship. Every night at dinner I brought a framed photo of Dad and sat it in a chair and ordered his favorite foods and made them put it down. I cried every time I saw that empty chair there and Dad was not chewing his food with his eyes closed, savoring the moments. We made sure to go to the shows he enjoyed and to the piano bar to listen to the piano man play and sing. I could feel anger growing toward Mende for doing this.

I thought back to the running track a few months ago. Mende had gone to a doctor and said I wouldn't mind her and had me put on Prozac. She was trying to make me a zombie, so I wouldn't ask to talk to dad or rebuttal her bad talk about him. Dad came to see me at track, and I normally run a couple of miles without stopping at a fast pace. I ran one lap and was doubled over, throwing up. Dad carried me into the bathroom holding my head. I told him she had got these pills and I refused to take them, but she was hiding them in my food. He was furious. He yelled at her and she called the police. Dad went to the doctor who prescribed my medication and talked to him. You see, with Mende being a teacher and a teacher of special needs kids she knew what to say, and doctors treat the symptoms. She got me put on drugs. Dad told this doctor that I do not have behavior issues and explained that I was extremely well-behaved at his house, at school, at church, and everywhere. The doctor revoked the prescription and called her and told her not to administer it anymore. She was mad and continued to put it in my food.

I stopped eating anything that I hadn't made myself, or that Austin hadn't made for me.

She took Dad to court again, and it was always over money or just her being mad. You see, Mende loves Mende and money more than anything. It has shown in life. What we saw was her trying to sabotage Dad then taking him to court for money. And now she had ruined vacation. Every morning on a cruise, Dad and I would get up and have coffee and watch the sun rise. It's been our thing. This time, who was going to do that with me?"

Bronson- *"I was very upset about the cruise. I cried not being able to see my dad. I was so angry and never understood why she would want to take us from the person who loved us the most. I just hoped that one day it would stop, and we could live normal."*

I was very bitter at how this game of using the courts to get her way was playing out. It seemed she had learned and been able to have police, jails, lawyers, and court systems help her with everything she devised. I had no choice but to press on. I couldn't quit. It was all about my kids and what was best for them. There were many times when I almost lost faith, but God never left my side. I was reminded through my kids and their unwavering faith that He loves us and cares about us.

Austin has performed doing concerts by himself since he was very young. By middle school, he had songs that involved his brothers and sister, and some that Heather even sang with him. We would travel all over to different churches that invited him in to minister through song, but I was ministered to every time I listened to my family singing. One of my favorite songs to hear my kids sing is called, Even in The Valley. If you've never heard it before, you should look up the lyrics. The words are beautiful. Who better to deliver that message than my children? Already my heart is open and full of love just because they are singing. But the words of this song have come to me many times, right when I needed it the most. Even in the valley, God is good.

Boy have I been through some valleys. But through them all, my God and my kids have always been by my side. I can't say this for the Church. We are to be salt and light to the world, to go to the world as Christ did when He came to seek and to save. But all too often, it is easier to walk away, forsaking our brethren. This is where I stand now with my kid brother. He has been a pastor for the past several years from Georgia to Kentucky, back to Georgia, and now in Texas. I have seen my brother a hand full of times in the past twenty years. He was my best friend growing up and the person I was closest to in life. Unfortunately, I lost him somewhere along the way. His wife was a close friend of Mende, and he was put in the middle. Cody and I had a falling out. I take ownership of that. It was very difficult to see the dynamic of our family change so suddenly, a wedge driven between two brothers. In a moment of weakness, I acted in a way that was unacceptable. This ended my relationship with my only brother.

Proverbs 18:24 says, "A man of many companions may come to ruin, but there is a friend who sticks closer than a brother."

Why do you think Jesus said He sticks closer than a brother? Why would he choose this over a parent or a sister? It's true that brothers are supposed to be close, but in biblical history, we can see that many do not honor family love and loyalty very well. The heart is softer with people you love, and this is true for me with my brother. I have gone to him multiple times, apologetically, to express love and care for my baby brother. Even after twenty years, he isn't ready to accept it. His desire is that I continue to grow close to God and maybe one day, I can have a relationship with him. How can you possibly know someone's walk with God if you aren't around to assess it? This argument is one of Swiss cheese to me and this mentality from church leaders is why churches are empty today. We need more shepherds willing to leave the 99 that are healthy to help the one in need. We are taught that brethren should hold each other accountable. Iron sharpening iron. How does iron sharpen iron with only one iron? And just as my kids minister to me better than anyone else can, so it is with family. I expect more from family, including my church family.

How often do we see this same behavior playing out in our churches? I by no means am church bashing, I am a strong supporter of the church and believe in gathering with the body. But I also believe the church has the power to turn away souls due to their own actions of not being truly Christlike. We have churches on every corner, and most are empty. If you want the real love and compassion that Christ taught, where do you find it if it's not brought to you? Most people were not looking for Jesus, He went and found them. This is the responsibility of the Church. To seek the lost, the hurt, the downtrodden.

I have a Doctorates Degree in Theology; I am highly educated in Bible and religion. Not once did I need to hear someone tell me what the Bible says, that I am already aware of. What I have needed so many times throughout my lifetime was someone to live out the Bible, as Jesus did.

Yet I am disappointed in how I witnessed the church in many opportunities fail in ministry to me and my children. What I found was the church was just like everyone talking to Jesus in John Chapter 8 and failing to see what He was teaching at this moment. What is the role of the Church? Once you bring people in for salvation, then what? Everyone perfect? Will people fall, fail, be like Peter? According to some pastors, we must separate from them and let them figure it out. One of my favorite stories in the Bible is when Jesus healed the leper. Indulge me a moment here. I think even if you're not a biblical believer you can glean something from this.

Think of the leper in the Bible in the first chapter of the book of Mark. A leper had to announce himself to anyone crossing his path. "Unclean, unclean," he would have to yell. Others would move to the opposite side of the road to avoid him. He would be forced from society and made to live alone. Then enters Jesus, who healed him. Do you know how he healed him? With His touch. How long had it been since anyone showed him love and compassion? He sat alone, miserable, dying. But Jesus moved with compassion, put forth His hand and touched him, and said, "Be thou clean." He didn't tell the leper to clean himself up and maybe one day, he could have a relationship with Him.

How many people do we know who are hurting, struggling, or really going through something? We cannot leave them unclean, alone, and miserable. We are the Church, and we have been commissioned by God to encourage, love, restore, and uplift.

How will people ever turn to God when the Church is the cause of people not walking back through the door? I am grateful for my children, the ones who have kept the faith, who have ministered to me in my lowest of times. They have helped me keep my eyes focused.

Who are we? The Turners!

And we are grateful for a friend in Jesus, that sticks closer than a brother.

Chapter Thirteen

Boobs in Hell

"Wait a second. You removed what? Just cut them off and—"

My job in Canada was going great. My boss held his word and stood up against the comical calls coming in against me. He asked the caller to identify themselves. Once they refused, he asked if they were concerned with identifying themselves and having to pay restitution for the lies and trouble that were caused. No other calls or letters arrived after that. I was so thankful for him and the stand he took believing in me. It made me want to push to do more to take the company to all new heights, just for what he had done for me personally.

One weekend I flew back home to catch one of the kids' games and Heather picked me up from the airport. She wanted to go to dinner and asked me to drive to one of my favorite restaurants. Then she dropped a bomb. She needed to talk to me. I'm thinking I might be in trouble. She is dressed up and looking stunning and wants to talk. I knew anything she might ask for, she was gonna get!

Her face dropped as she began to tell me she was unhappy with her body. She had breastfed Lexi and it made her feel insecure about her boobs. She had started working out extensively and I thought she looked amazing, but I listened, wanting to hear her heart.

"Have you done your research about this?"

She handed me a folder. It contained documents with prices, reviews, references, and even photos. Yes, my wife handed me pictures of other lady's boobs!

She then went on to tell me she also wanted to discuss her going to work. This was more of a shock than the boob conversation. We had discussed and agreed that her place was in the home, but she had had a change of heart and wanted to get out, contribute, and feel like she was being helpful. I thought she was incredibly helpful with all she did for the kids and in the home but she was adamant. While I felt conflicted about both topics, I ultimately knew that her happiness was what mattered most. I would do whatever it took to support my wife.

The next week we were at the doctor, and I was trying to make the best of this situation. The doctor brought out some sample implants and left the room for us to decide how big we wanted to go. I began goofing around, playing with them quite vigorously, and ended up poking a hole in a ten-thousand-dollar implant... oops! I froze. Ms. Cackles almost fell off the paper sheet she was sitting on. We decided that was probably not the brand for us since the durability was not up to the testing. In comes the doctor and my sweet wife blurts out that her husband, "was playing with those fake titties, and one didn't hold up." The doctor's face turned beet red. How hard is it to embarrass a plastic surgeon that deals with boobs all day?

He looked at the implant and explained that shouldn't have happened. He was going to notify the manufacturer. The way I view it is that I may have saved many a woman from having leakage. I'll take the credit.

We paid for the procedure, and she was scheduled for the following week.

Surgery day rolls around, she was excited and ready. I was anxious. They took her back and I was left to wait in the waiting room. It felt like all day had passed when finally, the doctor came out and sat beside me.

"Surgery went fantastic. I decided to remove the nipples and insert the implant, so she wouldn't have any under scar," he continued as if this was a normal, everyday conversation. "So, she has some drainage tubes in and it will look rough until it heals. I think they will look fantastic."

"Wait a second. You removed what? Just cut them off and—"

He laughed. "Of course, I put them back on."

He went on to explain how he made the incision exactly on the areola so you wouldn't see a scar. I'm trying to wrap my mind around this and he's so nonchalant about just hacking off body parts and putting them back on.

Here I am thinking that if I dig a hole and fill it back up with the same dirt, the hole almost always ends up overfilled or with not enough dirt, but either way the hole is never the same. I'm all concerned about what he has done. I'm thinking Dr. Hack-em-off has ruined her. She woke up and I took her home. She was required to keep the girdle on tight for 24 hours. I did not mention to her what the doctor said to me. In fact, I just tried to forget it myself. When it was time to remove the girdle, he was correct, it didn't look so great. But in a week when everything healed, they started looking like she had hoped. In a month she was completely healed and happy, sporting new bras, and smiling bigger than ever.

Everywhere Heather went she got a lot of attention. We started working out together and planning more cruises. We loved going places. The back and forth with my job did start to wear on me. It was difficult running an international company and keeping up with the family. One thing that I will never sacrifice is the family time that I have fought so much for.

Heather talked to Mom about an opening at the courthouse. My mom worked for the Probate Court at the Paulding County Courthouse. She was a clerk and entered traffic tickets. We knew the judge for many years, a good, Godly woman. Heather got hired to be a clerk and worked alongside mom. It was a tough transition, as we didn't have the flexibility that we had prior to her starting work. This was an adjustment. I noticed I needed to fly back and forth more which was a great company expense. I was missing practices for the first time, and I felt conflicted about this. But this company had been so good to me, and I absolutely loved the people. With the coming football season just a few weeks out, I was anticipating major heart/brain conflicts ahead.

Heather loved the job. She came home each evening and told us all about how much she was learning and what her day had been like. She shared stories of what it was like dealing with the public and started gathering stacks of business cards of men leaving them for her.

She was definitely shopping more as she has deemed "her check" as her shopping money, since it was extra income outside the budget for the year. Packages started coming every day, and she was working out all the time. She looked amazing. Her focus and ability to stick to goals was amazing. She was putting on lean muscle and able to run solid for several miles now. I noticed that she really started working out a lot when Pops was diagnosed with cancer and was told that he didn't have long to live. That was her way of dealing with it and it appeared it became something she loved.

One evening at dinner, Heather started laughing hysterically out of the blue.

"I have got to tell y'all about this guy that works in the office. He is so weird!"

She went on to tell us about her coworker and his doll collection.

"He has them on his desk and he said he has a lot more at his house." The boys were looking at her in disbelief. I asked her if they were collectibles, like porcelain dolls. She shook her head, still laughing.

"These are not fancy dolls, just cheap ones that he likes."

Periodically throughout dinner, she would burst out laughing and we would look up, she would just nod.

"Yep, still laughing about the doll guy!"

After that dinner it passed, and she didn't bring it up for quite a while — five to six months at least.

One evening Heather came home and started cooking dinner. We would be going later to work out before going to Austin's chorus performance. Heather was unusually quiet all evening.

"Hey, Babe, everything ok? You seem like something is bothering you."

She said she did have something bothering her, but she wanted to talk about it later that night.

"You remember doll boy? He has started creeping on me pretty heavy."

I asked her for some details.

"Well, at first, I thought it was just him being work friendly. But then he started making comments that have made me uncomfortable several times. Then he progressed to giving me sticky notes and now today to top it off he gave me a movie and said he wanted me to watch it at a certain time, so I'd be watching it when he was."

"Have you asked him to stop?"

"Yes, but he just continues, and I feel harassed. I don't know what to do about it."

I asked Heather if she had mentioned any of this to the judge. Surely, she could put an end to it.

"No, I don't want to do that," she explained. "I don't want her to think I'm not capable of managing myself or work relationships, and it would feel like I'm running and playing tattle tale as an adult."

That was a fair answer. She handed me what looked to be a pirated copy of the movie La La Land with a sticky note attached telling her what time to start watching.

"So, a grown man gave you this DVD and asked you to start watching it at 7 p.m. so you would be watching it at the same time he is?"

"Yes."

I assured her that her feelings were warranted; this was definitely weird behavior and well outside the boundaries of normal work cordials. She told me she thought I might know the guy because our families were friends. I did know who he was and was bothered by his behavior. I was more upset when she started telling me some of the things he was saying that were making her uncomfortable. They were statements thrown into casual conversation but were not appropriate things to say to someone. And after a strange comment about what he enjoys about a blow dryer, I was done listening.

"These are fireable offenses, Heather. Something needs to be done."

She didn't want to get him fired, so she asked if I would call him and ask him to be professional around her. I told her I would and started planning how that uncomfortable call would go.

The next morning Heather was up early. Her perky mood had returned and she was busy making biscuits & gravy, sausage and eggs. We had breakfast with the kids and when the table was clear, she said she had the guy's cellphone number and wanted me to go ahead and call him. We stepped out on the back patio, and I dialed his number. No answer. I waited a few minutes and tried again. This time he answered.

"Hey, Robbie. This is Andy, Heather's husband."

I made sure that I chose my words carefully and spoke to him in a respectable tone.

"Look the reason I'm calling is Heather told me you have been out of line with her on comments and being aggressive. This has made her uncomfortable. You know she is married. I know how you were raised; I know your dad raised you right. I expect you to respect Heather as a worker and as my wife. And I expect that we won't have to have this conversation again. Frankly what I have heard is disturbing."

He was quiet for a moment and then said, "You're right and I respect the bonds of marriage, I meant nothing by it, and I'll make sure this never happens again."

I told him I appreciated it and so would Heather. That was the entire call.

My mom was at work when he arrived that morning. He threw his keys down loudly and said to her "That son of yours, how can you be around him? He just called and threatened me."

He began flailing his arms, talking loudly and stomping. He talked with coworkers about the call, telling them a way different story than the mild interaction that actually took place.

He created a false sense of endangerment and someone suggested he file a report.

I was told at one point that the judge advised that if I showed up, I should not be allowed in the building. I have never been able to confirm this but I do have the incident report.

4/12/17 around 2130 hours, I spoke with Joel Herbert who works in the probate office and goes by Robbie. I spoke to him at this courthouse in the probate office. I advised him we in court security had been advised of a

phone call he received from Heather Turner's husband. I advised him
that I came to see if he wanted to file a report about the incident. Robbie
stated he did not, because Heather wanted to file a report and he would
write a statement. I then spoke with Heather Turner, who also works in
the probate office. She stated she did not wish to make a report at this
time, because she did not want to make her husband mad. I advised her
if she changed her mind to contact us and we would make a report.

-Deputy Baker

In true fashion when rumors start being spread, the shitball of misinformation grows as it rolls down the hill. The story was quickly blown way out of proportion. One version had me at the courthouse yelling and making threats until I was escorted out by security.

How boring would your life have to be to sit and troll social media for gossip sites to have something you feel a part of. And everyone has an "expert opinion," as if their field of education could back their brainless statements. With this incident, people were calling the courthouse requesting open records and asking for video footage of what went down. Even after being told there was no video footage as I had not even been in the building, they continued conjuring up bizarre, half-witted, injudicious tales of a good man gone bad.

"There must be a big cover up and someone has gone in and deleted video footage of this one..."

"Someone has deleted the incident reports..."

"And I bet they had to pay, or blackmail, all the people involved to not say anything."

It's all garbage. But I digress.

That night following the call, Heather came home energetic and happy. I asked her how it went at work; she advised me all was great, and it was a much better day. She gave me one of those one-leg, one-foot-up kisses with her arms around my neck and she was bouncing. She told me he kept to himself, and all interaction was strictly professional. We had a wonderful dinner, and she went and packed my bag. That night as we were having our talk, Heather got emotional.

She thanked me for being the type of husband that was willing to stand up to protect her. I was taken aback by this. "Isn't that what a husband should do?"

She nodded and laid her head on my chest and with her finger traced her tattoo on my chest. It's her handwriting, and says, "Andy, I love you with all my heart."

She told me a story from her past marriage that broke my heart. She wasn't used to being with a man that loved and protected her. This made her grateful for our relationship. I told her I was sorry for the days she ever felt unloved or unappreciated and made it my goal for her to never feel that again.

The next morning, I was flying to DC for work. Heather had my bags ready and waiting by the door. When I left, she sent me a photo of her in red heels and she had written hurry home across it. Always the little things.

We kept a tight routine anytime I was away. I would check in with her to let her know I had made it safely. We would talk every evening. I would always FaceTime her before getting into bed. One night I asked her if doll boy had given her any more trouble.

"Absolutely not. I think he hates me now since you called him, which suits me just fine. I'd prefer him to stay in his dollhouse."

I returned a few days later to an empty house. The boys were at their Mende's and Lexi was with her grandma.

"I believe I have a scheduled T-time," Heather said playfully. I had grown well-accustomed to the new boobs, and it seemed everything was going well.

Chapter Fourteen

If I Had Only Known

"I was there! I know what happened, I know when the noise came exactly where my father was."

-Lexi Turner

Heather called me on May 3rd. She was putting together a grocery list and wanted to confirm what we already had. I asked her what she had in mind and she said she was going to make her man his favorite dinner. I knew right away what this meant — fried Salmon patties, homemade biscuits and gravy, and a cantaloupe. I know it's a simple dinner and doesn't sound like much to many, but it is hands down, my favorite.

Growing up, there were many times when we had beans and corn-bread for days, but my mom could make some killer salmon patties. It was always a treat. And I loved them with biscuits and gravy. When Heather learned to make this meal, it was a game-changer. My dad had come for a visit and spent the day teaching Heather how to make homemade southern biscuits. The first time she tried they were hockey pucks but before long she mastered it. I was excited that tonight she would be cooking my favorite dinner! I made sure we had everything gathered up and ready for when she arrived.

Lexi wanted to ride her bike that day as the weather was beautiful, so we went outside in the front yard. Lexi would ride down the long drive and cut up through the yard, peddling hard and fast back up to me. She kept the same path and pattern for a while. Then she wanted to throw the football. That's my girl! We were throwing the football when Heather pulled up. She got out and ran around right for me like a safety coming in for the stick hit. Lexi threw the ball in my direction, and Heather jumped on me for the tackle. Here we are in two-day, fresh-cut grass. She has on heels and dress clothes, rolling in the yard with grass clippings. It didn't take long for Lexi to add into the tackle and pile on. We played like this until it became too itchy, and we decided to sit on the porch couch. Lexi wanted to show her mother a trick she could do on her bike.

Heather leaned over and said, "You're going be happy. I'm not going to be working anymore." She said they had been harping about no personal phone calls and no personal emails during company time. "The emails I've sent you and all my personal ones have got me in trouble. The judge told me I was going to be let go, that I needed to come in tomorrow prepared to decide if I want to resign or be fired."

I questioned this, knowing in the corporate world if someone violates a policy, they are terminated. Heather said she believed that they wanted her to quit so she wouldn't be able to file for unemployment.

"Well, that's okay, I am not upset about having you home all the time," I said to her.

She replied, "Me either, I miss the freedom and seeing my girl."

Lexi- *"It was a nice sunny afternoon; I was out riding my bike and my dad was watching me from the porch. We had a long driveway that I could ride my bike down and when you're small you feel like you're flying. I remember my dad always telling me, 'Don't go past that last crack!' The last crack in the driveway was where the road started. I would ride down that hill always telling my dad to watch and when I reached the bottom, I would throw my bike around and could be inches away from the 'last crack.'*

That day when I was through riding, I asked my dad to throw the football with me, he happily said yes. We stood in the yard throwing the ball around. A little while after we started, my mom pulled up. She got out of the car as fast as she could in her high heels 'running' towards my dad. Now with her heels on, her 'run' was more of a slow stomp. I watched as she went to my dad and tackled him in the grass. They started rolling around laughing, of course I ran over there and jumped in the pile.

Eventually, we went inside so me and my mom could start dinner. We went into the kitchen to make my dad's favorite meal, salmon patties and biscuits and gravy. She got the ingredients out for the salmon patties and put them in a bowl, she always let me mix everything up cause that's what I loved to do. I mixed it up and she started preparing the biscuits and gravy. I watched as she made the dough, she saw me glancing over and said, "come over here and help me little miss." I was excited because I enjoyed rolling the dough and putting it in the pan, and she always let me keep a little chunk to play with. I had flour all over myself and on the floor. It was like making a mess was part of cooking. At least when I was cooking with Mom that was how it was. She put Crisco in the pan, and we placed the biscuits down, then she popped them in the oven. I always got to have the last bit of extra dough and I would make a crazy-shaped biscuit and we would name it something silly. I watched her as she whipped up her gravy and we started cooking the patties. The food finally finished cooking and we made plates for each of us. We sat at the dinner table and my dad looked like he had seen Jesus himself. He looked at the food and was so excited. We prayed and finally got to eat. We ate quickly and after we finished my mom jumped on my dad's back and he started giving her a piggyback ride. I pulled out my phone and started taking pictures. They were so happy; my mom always had the biggest laugh, and my dad has a smile that could make any person's day better. I loved watching them as they laughed and had a ball. After dinner we sat down to watch a movie, I ended up falling asleep on the couch right across from my parents' bedroom door. My mom and dad didn't wake me as they got up after the movie and went to their bedroom to go to sleep."

Lexi remembers this day exactly as I do. I have stood many a day and replayed the images in my mind of them at the stove cooking. The sounds of the oils and the kitchen looking like it had a covering of fresh snow. Heather was her true self; they were singing songs. They had this one song by Shawn Mendez, called Treat You Better. Lexi would mess up the lyrics and during one part of the song she would sing, "what a funny cat." That's how she heard it, so Heather also joined in with the cat lyric and changed the words, both singing their hearts out.

I sat at the table and watched, admiring as they spent time together doing something for Dad. Heather always made my plate, it made me feel special for her to do it, and she was smiling so big. She leaned over and kissed me. Lexi brought me a glass of southern sweet tea and like she learned from her mother, leaned over and kissed her daddy. What a blessed man I am.

Lexi started the prayer, Heather finished it. This was something they did a lot. The meal was amazing, they had outdone themselves. We ate and talked and laughed, and of course, I wanted seconds! How could I not of my favorite? I had another portion and leaned back, feeling fat, and my pants getting snug. That is a common feeling I'm afraid.

I stood up and grabbed the dirty dishes and was taking them to the sink when out of nowhere, like a Ninja, Heather leapt on my back and yelled, "Giddy up!"

I dropped the dishes into the sink and began to prance around the island with her.

"Faster, my valiant steed," she yelled.

Lexi was giggling and she took out her phone. She was taking photos of her parents being silly and playful. We made several laps like I was a rodeo stallion then ran out into the dining room and into the living room, gaining speed. We then made a barrel turn, heading back for the kitchen, all along, I was being spurred and whipped and told to giddy up. I was giddying all I could giddy! With these old knees and back... but I was not about to let her know that. As I made the final turn she reached up and almost like a chokehold, squeezed me very tight.

"Ahhhh," escaped her lips as she exhaled. "I love you so much."

I stopped and raised up and Lexi took our photo.

I had no idea this would be the last photo we would ever have taken together again.

If I had only known.

I would have ridden longer, played harder.

If I had only known, I would have never stopped no matter how bad I was aching.

If I had only known, I would have just kept riding. I would have had her hold that choke hug forever. I would have paused that, "I Love you."

If I had only known that this was the last meal that I would ever eat with my wife and best friend, I would have gotten thirds, and kept eating. I would have talked more.

If I had only known.

I remember thinking how wonderful it was and I was soaking it up. And now I look back.

If I had only known...

After dinner, Lexi decided to create a masterpiece on her pottery wheel. Heather and I sat at the table and shared some wine. She snuggled up so close as we watched Lexi and the faces she made as the clay spun. She was the cutest thing. Heather turned to me and said, "We did that, that's our little monster."

It was so memorable.

After a while Lexi was over the wheel, so we decided to watch a movie. We all went in and piled up on the couch. I had both my girls; it was wonderful. Lexi was stretched out with her head on my leg, Heather was behind my shoulder with her head propped up. It felt like time stood still. She was rubbing the back of my head and I was enjoying this, but Lexi had worn herself out. She fell asleep as we watched TV. We put a cover over her and left her there so she could rest and not be disturbed.

We got up and headed to the bedroom. I pushed the door closed softly to not wake up Lexi and when I turned around Heather was right there pushing up against me. She kissed me softly. I remember how the look in her eyes was so intense and sensual, the moonlight reflecting shadows and light across her body.

She said she wanted me. I picked her up and carried her to the bed and laid her down easily. She was so beautiful and sensual and so perfect. She had such a way about her, I recall thinking many times over the years how blessed and lucky I was. Everywhere I went people would tell me, "You out did yourself with that one," or "you out punted your coverage." What I kept hearing was God showed favor and chose to bless me. How many men have such a beautiful woman, one that loves his kids, takes care of him perfectly, packs his bags for trips, cooks, loves him, and is crazy about the family while doing everything right? Probably not many. God showed me favor.

Our night together was different. I can't say it was any one thing, but it was different. I fell asleep with my head laying on her back. It felt like everything in the universe was perfect and nothing else existed.

Lexi- *"I heard a loud noise, raised up, and realized I was still on the couch. I jumped up and took off running toward my parents' room where I heard the noise. As I went through their bedroom door, I saw my father coming around his bed. They have a big bed with a canopy top on it. We got to the bathroom door and both my hand and dad's was on the knob, we turned and pushed. I saw half of my mother's body from the waist down. My dad saw everything before I could, so he grabbed me and jumped back, we both fell on the floor. I heard my father moan like I have never heard and cannot describe it in words. He screamed out, 'Nooooo,' then he picked me up and ran and sat me on the couch and said to me, 'Mommy is hurt, don't get up, don't move.' I was confused on why he told me this at the time because I did not know that my mother was dead. He called my grandmother to come sit with me, because he was afraid I would get up and see all of what happened. His voice was breaking, and he had tears streaming down his face. After he called my grandmother, he went back into the bathroom and called 911. I couldn't hear his conversation. I was confused and wanted to know if my mom was okay. Soon after the 911 call to the police, ambulances started to arrive as well as my grandparents. I was watching the police swarm my living room. My grandmother took me upstairs to sit with me and keep me away from what had happened. When the coroner came upstairs, detectives were talking to my grandma and the coroner took me to my room and asked me what happened. In my parents' shower they had a rack that would fall regularly, so at the time when she asked me this,*

I had no idea what had happened and the first thought in my mind was 'the shower rack fell' or 'Mommy fell.' The detectives and coroner went downstairs, and I was now left with my grandmother again. I was sitting and noticed my uncle Johnny had come in the living room, my grandmother's words began to go silent as I was listening to my dad and his conversation. I heard my father say, "I tried to save her." Right then everything went silent. I knew my mother was gone. Did I know how or why? No, but she was gone. I started crying and placed my head on my grandmother's chest as she held me, we were both crying together."

Startled, what was that noise? Did I dream it? Was it real? As I'm thinking this, my body is in autopilot getting out of bed. I'm sure many of you can understand this in my inability to describe it properly. My brain had identified a noise and was telling my body to wake up and move but all the senses were not fully operational yet. As I got up heavy-footed and rounded the bed, I caught a motion in my peripheral. It was Lexi coming through the door. The door was open, the room was still dark except for the light coming around the cracks and underneath the door leading to the bathroom. Lexi and I emerged together at the bathroom door as I opened it.

Life changed forever.

There was a counter that held the sink on the toilet side of the master bath, where Heather's body had fallen, I could see her upper body. Thankfully that counter was there and blocked Alexis's view from seeing the entire scene. My initial reaction was to stop Lexi from going in. I cannot even say it was a conscience thought, as the next hours of my life are the hardest for me to contemplate or describe. I grabbed Lexi as simultaneously what I had seen was fully registering in my mind and now being processed. I remember the shock, the pain, the disbelief, all hitting me like a tidal wave. When I grabbed Lexi, I jumped back, and it took us to the floor. I do not personally recall the noise I made as Lexi and I went down, which she describes as one of agony. I picked her up and ran to the couch, sat her down, and instructed her not to move. The last thing she needed in her memory bank was to see her mother in that capacity and have that memory forever etched in her mind. It's devastating enough for her to have seen her mother's legs laying there lifeless. What I did next has ever since obtained me great scrutiny. I called my mother! Mom, who also gets up early to go to work at the courthouse, was up and ready for work and walking out the door when my call came in.

"MOM! I need you to come here now. Heather has shot herself! Come sit with Lexi."

So many people have crucified me for the decision to do all that I could in a moment of crisis to try and protect my daughter from more harm and devastation.

I want to pause and address this issue because; I have heard countless people on social media, streaming tv and podcast, YouTube, media outlets, television, documentaries, sadly even in person, who have felt so empowered to state what they would have done and what they felt was the "right" thing to do. I will tell you; you have no idea what you would do until you're in that moment dealing with grief, pain, shock, and a parental innate sense to protect your child all at once.

One person in particular even appeared on television to state that he was owed answers. You are not owed anything. My family and I have the right to privacy and to mourn. Sadly, we have been denied this opportunity because people have taken to social media and chosen to harass, lie, slander, and defame our family, all while acting as if they are owed something from us. They are then appalled when we are not obliged to the total disrespect and evil we have endured. This same person also stated, "If it was my wife, I would have called 911 first." Well, I hope you are never faced with the nightmare that I endured, but frankly, no one gives a damn what you would have done. I decided to protect my baby girl from the mental trauma that she would never have gotten over. I stand by that decision and if I had to make it over today in slow motion, I would make the same decision.

I ran to the bathroom, calling 911, and when I entered that room again the amount of grief that hit me was indescribable. I knelt beside my wife, my best friend, the woman that I was just laying on, hearing her heart beating with mine and thinking how great life was. She had no clothes on, blood was everywhere, and I am trying to do CPR with her mouth full of blood. I turn her head to try and clean it out so I could breathe for her, but it wouldn't stop.

The next moments were fleeting. I remember speaking to the 911 operator. I don't remember the words I spoke. Many of you have heard the 911 tape of that morning. I hear my voice on the call but have little recollection of saying those words. I don't remember if I was counting out loud. I do remember that there was just so much blood and I couldn't stop it from flowing. I tried with a towel, and I tried to breathe for her, but the blood was just consuming. This is a woman that I know every inch of her body, but there are some things I should never see. This was horrifying and words can't express the shock, dread, heartbreak, and desperation I was feeling all at once. I wish I could pick which moments of that morning my brain remembers and which ones it doesn't. I'd much rather remember the 911 call rather than the still-shots, like a collage of pictures that are etched in my brain, creating endless nightmares and sleepless nights. I'd choose much differently if I could run the program in my brain.

But why, Heather? Why? I remember screaming this and watching tears fall on her as I did chest compressions. Baby, why? I remember the lady on the phone asking me where the gun was, I looked around and recognized it. It was the 38 that I had gotten for her.

Heather no, Heather no, Heather no, please no. Baby no, Heather no. Why? Wake up Heather, wake up, talk to me, Baby please, talk to me.

I was now breathing two breaths, then giving 25 compressions. I breathe and blood hits my face and eyes and goes in my mouth. I can't give up. Compressions. Come on ambulance! God, please touch her, you have raised the dead, healed the lame, you created her body, God it's nothing for you to heal her, God, somebody...

I kept hearing the operator and the phone is cutting out really bad. It's in and out, I hear her speak four to five words before it glitches, and then she's back. I don't know if she hears me well, I feel vomit about to come up. I'm trying my best to hold it together, but it feels like eternity in Hell waiting on someone to walk in and wake her up. Finally, I heard something, and my dad and mom enter the bathroom. They had met the ambulance going the wrong way and motioned for them to turn and follow them. Dad grabbed my arm and said, "Son, stop." I didn't want to stop. I didn't want to give up. I wanted my wife. I wanted my partner and best friend. I couldn't give up. I remember him saying to the operator that she was beyond saving. I leaned and hugged her and pulled her to me. No was the only word I could form.

I was holding her and looking at her when I saw brown pants in my peripheral. I have no idea who walked in first, I know in moments many deputies were in my bedroom and a couple in the bathroom. One squatted down and said, "Sir, I need you to step out." I was holding my wife — I didn't want to let go. I just wanted to hold her, and for her to wake up and say, Baby Love. I kept looking at her, then the guy got loud and forceful. I didn't respond to him. Then he reached for me.

"I will walk out, just give me a moment." He went to say something, and another guy interrupted him and took his place, this deputy having more sense and understanding of the situation said, "Sir, I can't imagine what you have gone through. We have a job to do now, and we need you to finish up and step out please."

I laid Heather down. I kissed her forehead still in disbelief of what had happened. I stood to my feet and as I looked at the mirrors, I saw notes of I love you everywhere. As I walked to the door deputies had formed a semicircle and I'm now in the middle.

"Stick your hands out, sir."

I'm surrounded, two men, one on each arm. They hold my arms out as a lady starts touching my hands all over with what looks like an ink blotter. I made eye contact with one of the officers. I have just lost my wife. I have just witnessed the most horrific thing I could have imagined in seeing parts of my wife that I should have never been able to see, and I'm being treated as a criminal. The blots on my hand, I was told after asking four times, were to test for gunshot residue, one which gave immediate results.

Every time I asked questions, I was ignored until I repeated myself over and over. Then I was answered in the most smart-ass tone, as if I was bothering them or being an inconvenience to their day.

"There's nothing," I heard the tester say. Some smart-ass guy behind me tells her to check again. So again, my arms are grabbed and here comes the blotter. My entire hands and arms this time, every square inch, like they were expecting something. After checking I was told to strip naked. As I began to protest, I was threatened with being taken down. My daughter and family are in the other room and my wife is laying behind me. What the Hell is going on? They take photos of me, make me spin around. I asked what the purpose of this was. I received the response that they were looking for scratches. What? A defense wound of any sort.

"It's protocol to check, sir," someone else answered.

"Defense wound for what?"

Someone behind me answered, "Sir, if you were attacking your wife, you could have scratches on your body. We look for this and check her nails for skin."

"Hold on a second guys. Just pause for a second, please," I'm looking around, obviously dazed and confused.

"You mean to tell me, after all that's happened this morning, I must be subjected to being treated as a dirty criminal?"

"Yes, we have no choice on any gun death, we have to check other members in the home."

"Okay, let's just get this over with." After all I had nothing to hide. I'm just in shock and dealing with assholes who needed to learn some sensitivity for moments like this. I kept having moments when tears just burst out uncontrollably. I'm trying to hold myself together and be strong through this.

Finally, a man named Christopher came in. When he did, people's actions changed. They were not as big of an ass in front of him. He spoke very kindly. I remember when his phone rang his ring tone was a siren and it was loud, it made me jump every time he got a call, and he got a lot of them. I started to feel very sick. I asked if I could go out to the front yard, they followed me, and I hit all fours and started vomiting. I felt hands on me, and it was the paramedics. They hooked me to a heart monitor and were checking me. I have a history of Myocardial Infarction and I'm on heart meds.

I was then told I could wash the blood off my arms and hands. In the kitchen, I notice the coffee pot is on. My coffee mug was under the spout, not hers. This is out of the norm. She always puts hers in and takes it with her and I make my own when I get up. Why would my cup be under? I looked around and didn't see her coffee cup. Heather is a coffee lover, especially in the morning. Then I spot her cup, it's in the garbage can. Why is this? I took it out and put it in the sink.

My uncle Johnny arrived. Uncle Johnny is a great man, loves the Lord, is a pastor, and a Chaplain for the fire department. He knelt down beside me and put his hand on my arm. He said, "I'm sorry." I saw the tears welling up in his eyes and he hugged me and said a short prayer for comfort for me and the kids. I appreciated it so much and it did calm me some. Uncle Johnny didn't leave my side until that night, and I am extremely grateful for that to this day.

People were in and out of the house nonstop. They were photographing the entire bathroom and bedroom inch by inch. I am thinking how ridiculous this is, but I understand they have a job to do, and I'm trying not to take it personal.

As they are working, two familiar faces come walking in. Lyndsey Eberhart and Thomas Cole. The coroner and assistant coroner. I know Lyndsey from being kids, playing at her father's funeral home and Thomas Cole has been a pastor in this area for many years. I heard him preach some good sermons at Pumpkin Vine Baptist Church many years back. When Lyndsey came in, I saw her and said hey.

"Hey Andy, please tell me it's not Heather."

I nodded and tears appeared. She walked to the back room. In the meantime, Christopher pulled up a chair with several other guys and surrounded me. He was very respectful and talked to me with ease. He needed me to tell him exactly what happened. I did. He asked me why she would do this? I genuinely didn't know. I would have told you she was the happiest, kindest, silliest person I know. And that is what I told him.

He asked if we had had any fights or disagreements. We hadn't. In fact, in all our time together, we might have had two disagreements.

He asked if there was anything going on in her life that was upsetting.

"Well, yes, her grandfather had just passed away and that was very tough on her. Pops was the closest family that she had, and we went to visit him regularly. She took that hard, but she hadn't mentioned it in the past couple of days."

I thought of the conversation we'd had the night before.

"She did say that she was getting fired and that she had to make a choice of resignation or termination, but when she told me about it, she was laughing. I do know she enjoyed working there and seemed to be doing a pretty good job.

"The only other thing I can think of was her former husband had called out of the blue. She hadn't heard from him in a long time, and he was going to be doing some things that she shared were troublesome. To my knowledge those were the only things. I can't tell you anything that would ever warrant this."

He asked me if suicide ran in her family.

"Yes, her mother. She overdosed and Heather was the one that found her. That anniversary is coming up, I believe, but I am not certain. I'm just trying to brainstorm."

Now at that moment something hit me, and it hit me hard. What had I missed as a husband? I took pride in knowing my wife and taking care of her. What had I missed? Surely, she had given a sign, and I failed her by not seeing it. Surely, she had some cry for help and I let her down by not answering it. Think, Andy, think. How in the world could this have happened in my family? Did she give hints in any way? I thought and thought. I absolutely could not come up with anything. Not one thing. I felt that I had let her down, that I failed the kids.

"Lieutenant Christopher, I can't think of anything. I feel like I have let her down."

We heard an officer say there was a note. I had not seen one, maybe it would explain things to us. Where is it? I want it! They wouldn't allow it to be moved. Christopher got up and said for me to follow him. We walked into the bathroom, everything still on her sink as it had been from the morning. I had not seen anything on that side as I was so preoccupied with her on the other side. On my travel planner she had opened a page and simply written, "I'm sorry, I love you." This does not give me what I need here. It's still no answer. What demons were you fighting? I can't imagine anything being worth this, I always felt we talked about everything. Did we not? Obviously, we didn't. I would have bet that we did, I did, and I felt like she did.

Lyndsey came out to talk with me, and Christopher went up to speak with Mom, Dad, and Lexi.

"Lyndsey, do they have to do a full autopsy?" I hated to think about what they did to the bodies during an autopsy. Lyndsey said yes. She said they would be taking her out and suggested I go upstairs so I wouldn't have to watch. I didn't want Lexi to see, and honestly, I didn't want to watch her leaving our home like that either.

Christopher spoke with everyone and was on a lot of calls. He came back to me and said, "Mr. Turner, on behalf of the Sheriff's Department, we offer our condolences. This is an open and shut case of suicide." He told me to call if there was anything I needed. He said the same words to my parents, even in front of Lexi. He spoke to my dad and uncle and told them that they were finished with the photos and all they needed in the house.

I needed to get to my boys to let them know what had happened. Dad and Uncle John, with permission from Lt. Christopher, went back that evening and cleaned the bathroom so I would not have to see it again and so the kids would not have to see it. I appreciated what they did. I know it was hard on them. It would have been next to impossible for me.

By the time everyone left, I had been questioned for almost three hours. Uncle Johnny offered to drive me to pick up the boys. We went to the school that Mende worked at and had her paged to the front.

"Mende, I'd like to get the boys please and take them with me," I'm standing with my uncle, which was out of the ordinary.

"What's wrong?" She pressed.

I mustered up the words, "Heather passed away this morning."

Mende looked shocked, she stepped up and gave me hug, and said she was sorry. She gave me permission to check them out and keep them. I appreciated this from her on that day. We left the elementary school with Kaedon and Bronson. They could tell something was wrong, but they were not asking. We drive to the junior high and pick up Austin. When he saw Uncle Johnny, he was inquisitive. I just put my hand up to signal, wait. We drove back to my parents and went to the basement where we had everyone gathered. Uncle Johnny's granddaughter had arrived, she was trained in how to handle grief and trauma and is amazing with children, such a wonderful young lady.

With everyone together, I said, "Guys, I need to tell you something. This news is going to be difficult."

Lexi is already buried in Grandma. Everyone's gaze is fixed on me. I'm trying my best to put words together. I look up at my children's faces staring intently at me. Very broken, I uttered, "Heather passed away this morning."

In unison I watched my children fall apart. Kaedon, Bronson, Austin, and Lexi. We had family there to help hold and comfort my children during this time. I felt so helpless knowing this was a hurt that I could not help or heal in any capacity. The look on their faces broke my heart in a completely different way than this morning. The sounds of their cries and yells still hurt me to this very day.

I had told Lexi that morning her mom was hurt, she found out through a conversation that her mom was gone. I was hesitant in telling the children how until I had some direction. When they asked, I told them we would talk about it later. I never wanted to implant in my children's minds that suicide was an acceptable way out.

I lined up counselors for the children through the Harbor House. This was actually part of the Sheriff's Department. The kids had been in counseling there for years and we did family counseling. I wanted the kids evaluated and in therapy until deemed okay to stop. I had no idea how important of a decision this would prove to be later on.

Lexi- *"After everyone had left, me and my dad went to pick up my brothers from school and take them back to my grandparents' house. We got all the boys and arrived at the house, and everyone went to the basement. My dad told my brothers that Mom had passed away. The room got quiet and then all you could hear was the sound of people crying. My brother Kaedon was sitting beside me and put his head on my shoulder. We, as a family, were sitting there heartbroken, wondering what's next. We knew we had to stick together. Family is most important is what dad had always taught us and we realized it on that day. Having family there to comfort and support each other means more than words when you're hurting."*

Austin- *"It's difficult to discuss this day. It's one we rarely talk about. My mother died on this day. She may not have given birth to me, but she was Mom. When I found out what happened, I was blown away. All I ever saw were smiles and her and Dad loving each other. Just a couple of days before she passed, we were all playing and laughing. Tragic day."*

I had no plans to go back to the house. The kids and I made a pallet in the floor and piled up where we could all touch each other; we slept that way. All connected like a chain, loving, supporting each other, and grieving. I woke up screaming in the middle of the night because I was having a night terror of what I had seen. Austin was right there beside me. This happened every time I went to sleep for some time. I just couldn't shed the images I had seen. I wasn't sleeping much, and Austin was sleeping less as he stayed right beside me worried about me not resting.

If I had only known what she was thinking.

Chapter Fifteen

Finding a New Normal

"Holy shit, Mighty Mouse, tuck it back in. Do not corner my daughter,
she's been through enough."

The next morning came, and we had to go to the funeral home to
plan arrangements. I dreaded this with every ounce in me. We had
known Sam Clark for many years, and having considered him a friend,
we agreed to use his funeral home. He met us, gave his condolences,
and handed us over to a guy named Ken Fields, who would be helping
us write up the service and final plans. Ken led us to a small room
where he and I, along with both of my parents, all four children, and
my Uncle Johnny packed in. The entire ordeal was overwhelming and
difficult. The questions were hard to answer. I knew Heather wanted
to be cremated but beyond that, we hadn't discussed anything about
songs or scripture or anything else he was asking. What would Heather
want? Suddenly grief hit me.

Why am I making funeral arrangements? This is not something I need to be doing. Why am I having to do this? Heather, what the hell?

The interactions with Ken were awkward and uncomfortable. He insisted on touching me while he was talking, laughing and cutting up like we were old friends catching up. My parents assured me that he was just trying to be nice and that I was on edge. I was on edge. I was making end-of-life arrangements for my wife.

The kids and I picked out a casket for her viewing, several bible verses, and some photos. At that point I was just going through the motions to get this over with. I needed a moment of solitude and to get out of that small room. I found a dark, quiet room in the back. It was much cooler and offered a reprieve. I sat down and tried to decompress.

About the time I started to relax, Ken appears out of nowhere. Where the fu— Where did this guy appear from? Here he is, beside me telling me a joke about a guy and two prostitutes. I just stared at him expressionless. He repeated the punch line again like maybe I missed it. I was biting my jaw to keep from being the asshole I wanted to be. I just looked, didn't speak. As if he didn't get the hint, he looks me dead in the eyes.

"Andy, that Heather was a beautiful woman."

Knowing I am on edge, I sat quiet. Something is not registering right with this guy. Something, I just can't put my finger on it.

He continues to tell me how pretty my wife was and how when he had to go to the courthouse to get death certificates, she always looked so beautiful and was dressed so nice.

"We used to fight over who was going to go to the courthouse just to see her."

At this point the on edge took over. I arose so I would be over him.

"Oh yeah, so what I just heard was you perverts used to fight over who was going to gawk at my wife. I bet she hated seeing you walk through the door."

It finally registered, and he hurried down the hall. I got myself composed and walked back to join my family. As I entered, he and I made eye contact.

"I'm sorry you are here today."

I nodded, hoping those would be the last words he would speak that day. I was ready to go. I felt closed in and wanted to get out. I was frustrated, upset, and I hated that place. It was sad.

"Why did she do it?"

What? Why do people ask surviving families of suicide this question? Really, how do we know what someone is thinking? We can speculate. We can wonder. I am looking forward to the answers as well. I need some closure, too. All I knew was she was upset over her grandad's death, and she was losing her job. That's all I knew.

I stopped and looked him in the eyes again. I could feel my ears heating up. I walked out and went back to the car. I did not want to return to that house, so I went to my parent's house. The kids and I grew accustomed to falling asleep in a circle, each person touching the next. In fact, we couldn't fall asleep any other way. We all had to be touching. We gained comfort from being together and from physical touch.

Things were different and I began to be affected by things that I wouldn't have normally given a second thought to. I could no longer watch movies with gunshots in them. As soon as I heard it, it would send my brain in a whirl. I cannot explain this. I did not want to hear it or anything resembling it. I have always been a hunter, now I am not interested. When the kids played Fortnite, the same effect. I sat thinking what's wrong with me. I am so broken and messed up.

Bronson's birthday is on the same day Ma-T was born, May 2. Heather died the morning of May 4. That weekend, we had a big birthday party planned that was cancelled. I remember Bronson saying to me, "Dad, I don't think my birthday will be right now, from now on, this is what I will remember for my birthday."

"No son, we will make sure you have parties, and everyone honors and celebrates your special day."

He dropped his head. I wanted to help him, to affirm him, but that year, I just had to survive. I had to find a new normal. I had no idea what to do with myself. I was good at being a husband, I enjoyed doing that. I liked the routines we had. On weekends while Heather got ready, I'd make her a cup of coffee and watch her get ready and we would talk. This is what we did every weekend for years. Weekends now, what would I do? What would my night routine look like? I looked down at my wedding ring and got a call. It was the funeral home. The medical examiner released Heather, and we have her here.

"I am coming to see her."

I wanted to see if we could have an open casket or if it had to be closed. I drove to the funeral home and when I arrived, I saw a lot of new faces. Who are all these people?

I've known Sam for a long time. He wasn't a man for a lot of turn over, he would run lean and be cheap to save money, but have a lot of new people. They had a guy I had never met to escort me back.

Someone I had never met escorted me to a prep room where Heather was. She was wrapped tightly in white towels. Her hair was still stained red from the blood. She always took such great pride in her looks. When I saw her face, I wept. The whole left side of her head and eye were drooping down. It did not look like her at all. I knew that she would not want anyone to see her like this or to stand and gawk at her. I decided on a closed casket with lots of photographs.

I looked at her, laid my head on her chest for a moment, remembering how just a few days ago I had done the same. Heather, why was I not enough? Or the kids? What was so heavy that it took you from a husband that loves and adores you? And your baby girl? And our boys? What was it? Oh, Heather.

I gave them my decision and walked out.

The line for the viewing went out of the funeral home and wrapped the building. The kids and I were stationed around the casket. We had set up photos and some of Heather's favorite things around her. Red bottom shoes, Jimmy Choos, her pocketbooks. For three hours solid we had people in front of us. I tried to keep a steady eye on the kids. All the kids had a big turnout of friends and teammates. They were surrounded by their friends, receiving love and support. When the kids would have breakdown moments, their friends would huddle around them and just love on them. It was touching. I saw people I had not seen in years. They came by and said things like, "We're here if you need us, we love you guys and we're here to support you." Then there were people who would ask, "What happened?" How do you answer that? I didn't have an answer.

My friend Tony from the Briar Patch catered lunch for the family. It was such a kind gesture. Heather loved eating there.

The next day was the funeral. All the boys and I wore yellow shirts and black pants. Lexi had on a yellow dress. Heather would have loved this.

On my first date with Heather, I gave her a single yellow rose. Every time I sent her flowers after that, each bouquet had a yellow rose mixed in. It held significance for us, something that was important between us. My Uncle Ray made the casket arrangement and made sure to add yellow roses.

On the way to the funeral, everyone was emotional. We rode in total silence, no music, no talking, nothing. My phone rang and I answered it. Looking back, I shouldn't have. It was a friend who was living in California. He had a hit TV show in the 80s, but was now struggling to keep food on the table. Heather and I had wired him some money in the months leading up to that moment. The kids really enjoyed being around him and I thought maybe his condolences would bring them comfort.

"Hello, Jeremy."

"Andy, how are you buddy?"

"I'm holding up, we're driving to the funeral now, the kids and I. You're on speaker."

"I know the last few months you've helped me out. Do you think you could wire some money today? Because we're already late and, I must admit my wrongs here and own them—"

On edge Andy won again.

I spoke to him like no human should ever speak to another. It was probably the worst I have ever spoken to a person. He hung up. My kids were looking at me.

We arrived and before we stepped out of the car, I spoke to my children. "Hey guys, I apologize. Dad was wrong."

They tried to assure me it was okay, but I knew I had not displayed the heart that I should have. His timing was bad.

At the funeral, the family was given time to spend with Heather alone. We opened the casket to see her for the last time. All the kids had written her notes they wanted to give her, and I had written her one as well. We stood and viewed her. I still couldn't believe it.

Why would God give me a perfect life, then strip it away? I couldn't get used to not having her every day. Life without her was just not what life was supposed to be.

We all put our notes in her hands and said what we needed to say. I leaned over and kissed her for the last time. We closed the casket and Uncle Johnny said a prayer. The family lined up and we all walked to the chapel.

I started the ceremony with a story. One day after speaking at a church service, Heather began asking a lot of questions. When we arrived home, she sat at my feet and told me she felt she was under conviction.

"I need to be saved," she said to me.

I prayed with my wife to accept Christ as her Savior. I later baptized her. This funeral was not goodbye that I was saying to her, but I'll see you in the morning. Uncle Johnny did the service, and he did an amazing job. His words were heartfelt and encouraging and then we played a recording of Austin and Heather singing *Through the Fire Again.*

When the service was over, I was completely exhausted. I was tired of talking to people. I just wanted to be with the kids and try to find this new life that I was going to have to live now.

That night the kids and I decided to go back home. We all slept on the living room floor together. I woke up constantly screaming out from night terrors. The kids missed school the next day, we decided to get back to our routine the next day. That was the day that changed our lives again. The boys got up and got ready. Lexi wanted her hair braided for school. I had never fixed Lexi's hair. She had a mother who was a master of hair. Not able to go into the main bathroom, we stood in the guest bathroom, and I watched a YouTube video on how to braid hair. I was trying my best and Lexi sat so patiently. I started over a couple times and finally I thought I was doing a good job, until I was done. She looked up in the mirror and at me. I started crying. "Baby, you look like a homeless person."

She said she was fine with wearing it like that. I knew better. I called a friend of mine to come do her hair.

I dropped the kids off at school and was headed back home when I got a call from the school nurse. Lexi didn't feel well. I turned the car around. Her stomach was hurting.

Back home, I search the house for some Pepto. As I passed by the front window, I looked out and was stunned by what I saw. There were so many people in our yard, it looked like ants. Cops were everywhere, going around the house. I called for Lexi to come to me. There was a bang. Not a knock. I know some of you know exactly what I'm talking about. I opened the door to find about 15 officers standing there.

"We have a warrant to search the home."

"For what?"

"We've had several phones calls over the last few days which have led to speculation that Heather's death may not have been a suicide."

They pushed past us.

"What kind of phone calls would lead to such," I asked.

One of them spoke up and said he was not at liberty to say. I recognized that guy. Short. Familiar. And then it hit me. He was the guy that stood and watched as I left the Sheriff's office with photos in hand the day Austin had been abused by the government officials. This little twerp had been there.

"Hill, Mike Hill," he said. "I am the lead on this."

They went through our house. Cabinets, cars, dressers, underwear, everything. I sat at the table with Lexi and called my lawyer to tell him what was happening. I was tired, I was weary, and I wanted to rest, yet I had to read a warrant while they were going through everything hoping to find evidence of murder.

Mike was a smart ass every chance he could be like he was looking for a reason to be. I was getting pot shot questions and they eventually cornered Lexi.

"Hey Mike, I realize you have a job to do," I said as I pulled Lexi back to where I was.

He cut me off, "Oh and I'm going to do it too, and I'm going to do it very well, and you will be disappointed."

My response was not well thought out.

"Holy shit, Mighty Mouse, tuck it back in. Do not corner my daughter, she's been through enough. This is bullshit and the way you're talking is not appreciated."

"I couldn't care less, Mr. Turner. We are here to get rid of people like you."

Lexi heard this and started in at her dad's defense. I picked her up trying to calm her.

Lexi- *"All of the cops who I knew had done my brother bad were now in our home being mean to my dad. They were looking through everything and throwing things on the floor. I was there! I know what happened. I know when the noise came exactly where my father was. Why are people trying to lie and take my only parent from me. This guy was so mean."*

The GBI Agent was dressed sharp. He was respectful and at least had some training. Or maybe he was just raised better than some of the others as he had common respect and communication skills. He never exhibited the need to be an ass in any capacity. What he said to me next, and the following conversations led to a world of discovery that I wish I had never known. You have heard the phrase ignorance is bliss? That is a very true statement. If you don't know things, they don't hurt your heart. Some things I had rather just not known and been a fool about.

The agent pulled out a folder.

"Sir, how was your marriage?"

I replied," I'd bet you that we had as strong and good of a marriage than any that exists."

He paused, Lexi showed him the photos she had taken of our last night together, her cooking and riding my back. He asked if Lexi could play in a different location. I asked her to go over to my chair and play games on her phone.

"Are you aware that your wife was having affairs?"

"Not a chance of that sir. We were very active, always on the go, and she always had the kids."

He asked if I had heard of Robbie. I explained that I knew about the harassment, but I had spoken with him and, even though Heather thought he probably hated her, he had left her alone after that.

He handed me some emails to read. I couldn't believe what I was seeing.

"I just can't believe that these are real, where did you get them?" He didn't answer me.

He pulled out several more stacks and asked me if I had heard of any of the names listed? I had not. I glanced over the emails and saw words that were shocking.

I enjoyed seeing you last night. Can't wait till your husband leaves again. Your photos looked amazing.

I still didn't believe these were conversations with Heather.

"She told some of these guys you were a bad husband, that you guys fought, and that she was hit and held against her will."

You have got to be kidding me.

It was clear in text messages and emails between her and me that these things could never be true. I was so taken aback that I remember thinking at one point this might be a game the police were playing to try to trick me into a false confession.

I have since been told by close friends that I confided in that this is pretty normal. People who have affairs will often tell lies about their current relationship to get sympathy from who they are dating or talking to. They will say things like, "My spouse doesn't have sex with me, or I'm verbally and mentally abused," and then the details are added for believability. I still had a hard time accepting this of Heather. When I was told I should take off the rose-colored glasses and stop looking at her as the love of my life and look for what really happened to cause this, I got upset at the person who told me. At the time it was too soon, and hearing it angered me. I learned later how correct that statement would be.

I looked up from the pile of emails, the personal Hell that had just been placed before me, and I see a pile of electronics on the floor. Computers, Xbox, laptops, desktops, Alexa's, Dots, tablets, Gameboys, cell phones — all piled on the floor. Not neat. Dropped and piled on each other.

"We're taking all of this into evidence to have it analyzed."

Mike enters. "I need to take your daughter's phone."

"Are you serious? Can you tell me the purpose of this?"

"You could have searched, texted or called from her device something that would be useful to the prosecution."

"To the prosecution for what?"

He grinned.

Calm down Andy, don't play into his tactics.

I looked outside to see all our car doors and trunks open. I saw people I knew, guys I played ball with, and went to school with. It was embarrassing, invasive, intrusive, and unnecessary. They handed me a sheet of paper that listed everything they had taken and finally left.

Lexi- *"I was sitting and playing games on my phone like my dad told me to do. In the middle of me playing my game, a short officer walked over to me and jerked my phone right out of my hands, he about jerked my arm right off my body. My dad jumped up and shouted at him. A different officer walked in and yelled at Mike, and told him to go away from me and my father because he was only causing problems. The officer that had told Mike to go away apologized to me and my dad for the way he was acting and that it was totally unprofessional. They proceeded to talk with my father and left shortly after."*

They were gone about 15 minutes before I received a call from an unknown number.

"Hello?" There was only silence on the other end.

"Hello?" Still, silence. So, I hung up.

I immediately got a call back, again from an unknown number. And again, there is only silence.

"Hello?"

Just before hanging up, I hear, "You murderer, it will be your turn soon." I hung up.

I wondered if it was a neighbor who saw all the police cars outside. I called the GBI and let them know about the calls. I was told they would look into it. I never heard back.

We continued sleeping in the floor together as that was the only way we had peace. And each night you could hear the sniffles and weeping from the kids. It was a hard scene and the only comfort we could find was in togetherness.

One morning, we were awakened by that awful banging. Again, it was the Paulding County Sheriff's Office, this time with papers for an emergency custody hearing.

On the day of the hearing, the courtroom was filled with an entire staff of attorneys and a bodyguard. Yes, a bodyguard.

"Your Honor, we're asking for full emergency custody. We are not saying that Mr. Turner is a murderer, (that mention just put it out there, though it lacked subtlety) but what we are saying is that in his home was violence. Violence that resulted in the death of his wife. We don't know if he did it or she did it or if it was an accident, but we want to ensure that the children are safe until this is figured out. My client is worried for the kids and herself."

I leaned to my attorney, "Where is this coming from? It was an open-and-shut case of suicide. She left a note. Why is the word 'murder' coming out of people's mouths like this?"

Eventually, we learned that websites had been created touting a conspiracy theory that maybe it wasn't suicide. This is not a new concept, but rather a way for people to gain a following while harassing others without consequence. It happens all the time. And this time it was spearheaded by the same team who had perfected the art of stirring up trouble using parental alienation sites. I was ordered to pay more money, which was what always happened, and why she continued to run back to court every chance she got, because she would win and get money. This time it came with an odd order, I had to take the money to the Sheriff's Department instead of depositing it to her. I have to take a large check to the PCSO, and they will give it to her. Seems like unnecessary steps, and a very odd order from a judge, but you know how they are, he speaks and you jump through the little hoops like a circus doggy, or you go to jail or pay even more money. I had just lost my wife, and now here was Mende, trying to take my kids.

I had left my job in Canada for a job in DC so I wouldn't be gone so much. The calls and letters started immediately. This time they said something differently. Now they asked, do you know you have a murderer working for you? That would get anyone's attention and make people feel uncomfortable. Then guess what. Yep. I was let go.

Multiple social media outlets began to slander and defame. People called me an outright murderer and threatened me and my family.

One day, when I came home my garage doors were spray painted. 'Murderer lives here.' I didn't want the kids to see it, so I tried to clean it, but it wasn't coming off. I remember clearly being out there late at night so people wouldn't see me and I was scrubbing and crying, but it wasn't coming off. Finally, the emotions became overwhelming, and I yelled, repeatedly punching the door, crumpling it. The next day I had to get two new doors installed and I didn't have the money to do that. Calls were coming regularly.

The kids and I had a cruise booked that had been paid for a year prior. Heather was supposed to be on it. With all of this going on, I wanted to take the trip, after all, it was paid for. That came with complications. I couldn't do Lexi's hair, for one, and we always did formal photos on vacations. There was also the concern of going into restrooms with a little girl. We had plenty of time to plan, and we were all looking forward to the time to escape the craziness. I began looking for a nanny to go and help take care of Lexi. I called around and was recommended to talk to a young lady named Christy Chupp. I called her and asked if she would be interested in getting paid to take a vacation and help me with my daughter's needs.

I had a friend who was the CEO of a company in Atlanta. He was able to get me the job of VP rather quickly. I started going by a portion of my middle name "professionally" to hinder them from finding out where I worked. I wasn't sure how they were doing it so efficiently, but I tried desperately to protect my family and survive.

The following Sunday was Mother's Day. I asked Lexi what she wanted to do. She crawled up in my lap and sat still, very unlike her. She looked up and both eyes were full of tears, "Dad I don't have a mom." She buried her face in my chest. "Baby Girl, you do have a Mom, that's how you're here! She is just no longer here with us, she's in Heaven now." Lexi decided she wanted to spend the day with

Grandma, and we would release balloons to Heaven with notes for Mom. It was a quiet and heavy day.

I had gotten a loan to pay the money I was required to pay at the Sheriff's Department. I walked in the door and spoke to the lady behind the glass.

"Sir, we are not allowed to accept checks or cash. I can't take that."

"Ma'am, let me explain, I have a court order that says I must pay this here, look, signed by the judge. I have no other options."

"Sir, I'll be fired if I take this. I can't handle money. It's against our policy."

Suddenly I realized what this was all about. The lobby door opened and about twenty people entered the vestibule, and there stood Mike, all three feet of him, chest poked out so far, he looked like a mini–Johnny Bravo. He introduced me to the new GBI representative, the other guy had received a promotion. I could see why; he was the only professional one I'd seen in the bunch. It took a moment for it all to register. The odd order to send me there was not a coincidence, I was sent here just to be harassed by these mindless idiots, again.

"Mr. Turner," Mike began.

I'm counting now, there are 8 of them, 9 of them, 10 of them…he broke my thought of counting idiots to look down at him.

"We need you to come back here with us and answer some questions."

"Listen, Mr. Wonka probably needs you to help with the fizzy lifts. I have answered more than four hours' worth of questions and based on your actions, motives, conversations, past, the child abuse, the child endangerment, trying to question me without an attorney, I am not doing a damn thing with you or for you and if you keep harassing me, I'll go ahead and file suit against the Sheriff's Department for all of the above. Now get your orange ass out of my way."

He stood directly in front of the door to block it. With purpose, I started towards the door with every intent of moving him out of the way. I was willing to take the gamble knowing that the cameras surrounding me would obviously show the harassment and bullying from the Sheriff's Department. As I approached, he stepped aside, and I walked out without incident. I took the check to the courthouse to the judge's chambers and told them of my issue. They accepted the payment and had it transported as he instructed.

All these events were really starting to take a toll on me. I noticed that, even though I used to never drink, I was now drinking regularly. In fact, I was drinking too much. I was trying desperately to stop the pain I felt, pain that would worsen at night when things slowed down and that damn silence started to get loud and deafening. I was trying to dull that noise and ease the pain of loss, loneliness, despair, and now the concern of why people were trying to create a conspiracy. The concern that all the mess would gain traction, that it would move outside of Mende's circles and the corrupt backwoods cops. Tiny moments of liquid escape became better than constantly living in the Hell Heather created.

Chapter Sixteen

Firing Squad

"We never know the private and public hells that people are going through. Some more than others."
-Mark Stocker

One night I had Mom watch Lexi for me, and I spent the night with a fifth of something. I woke up and my phone blew up. I had voicemails of people breathing and making noises, mumbling, calling me a killer. I took these to the Sheriff's Department. I might as well have sent them to weasel. About the same amount of care or follow-up would have been done.

One call I received was from a cheerful voice. "Andy, this is Daniel Wilkerson."

"Hello Daniel, I don't believe I know you."

"I am a reporter for Channel 46 in Atlanta. I am doing a story on suicide and am looking for someone local who has experienced this."

I asked about the purpose of the show, hoping it would be to help deter someone from making that decision. He affirmed.

"We want you to share your story so that maybe someone struggling might see it and get the help they need and not put their family through what you are dealing with."

I was hopeful about the content but felt it was too soon for us to participate. I thanked him for calling and we hung up. He called back that evening.

"Have you given anymore thought to what I said earlier?"

I hadn't but told him I would talk to the kids, and we would consider it. I did talk to the kids who all liked the idea of helping people, and I thought maybe it would get out there what we were dealing with and quash some of this conspiracy garbage.

He called again the next day at 7 a.m. I told him we would do it and he was sitting in our home that evening. He asked us questions about suicide and how we dealt with it. He asked the kids a lot of questions. He wanted to see the bedroom where the ashes were. Then he asked to see the bathroom. As soon as he asked, I noticed his camera man made eye contact with me and very lightly shook his head no. I hadn't even gone back in there yet, so I told him no.

We went outside and the kids took photos with the news van and Daniel. He later called us and said the story was going to air the next night. We all gathered around the television to see what he had put together. The kids were all excited to see their parts as each had a good bit of individual camera time.

Here it comes, the lead story! All of our faces flash onto the screen but wait a minute. The headline reads, Was It Murder or Suicide? Here we were thinking we were putting ourselves out there at a very vulnerable time to help people who are struggling and possibly prevent a family from going through the hell we were going through, but this guy had flipped the entire story and completely lied to us. The interview was edited highly. I can see my phone lighting up like the

Rockefeller Tree. I felt numb. The kids were crying, every one of them. Then here comes another caveat. We had been working closely with Lexi's therapist as she was trying to gently educate Lexi about suicide. She had learned about suicide and learned that her mom had chosen this, but we had not crossed the how yet. No one at the house had mentioned a gun. She was young and we were trying to protect her as well as make sure that we do not have a continued cycle, Heather's mom, then Heather, so I am taking every precaution here. Daniel said she was shot with a gun. Lexi starts screaming.

"That's what that noise was. That's what that noise was, Dad! That's what woke us up. It wasn't when she fell, it was a gun."

Damn you, Daniel. You are a lying motherfucker. I'm tried to call Lexi's therapist for direction when I saw Daniel's number pop up on my screen.

"Hey, what did you think?"

I damn sure told him what I thought. He laughed and said, "Hey man, it's just journalism."

"Daniel, this is not journalism. You lied and have hurt our family, and this is how you seek to try and promote yourself? You're a sorry s—" Click. Well, I'm sure he knows anyway.

I look down and my phone is walking across the carpet. Messages, calls, social media. I need a big rock to crawl under. I look up and the kids' faces are pale.

"What is it?"

"Dad, some of my friends are calling you a murderer."

Kaedon looked sad. "I had a friend say my mom didn't love me, so she killed herself."

"Let's take a break from phones."

All the kids' phones were still dinging. I took them and put them on my bed. It sounded like R2D2 with all of our phones sending notifications.

Um, okay...let's play some Madden, or Mario Cart.

"Dad, we can't. Paulding County took all our Xboxes."

Well, damnit! UGH!!!!

"Come on, get in the car. Let's go get some ice cream."

We went out for yogurt at our favorite spot. As we were sitting there, the TV that's always on cartoon network is on the news and now it's on replay and yes, it's Channel 46. I'm not a person who whines or complains. Never have been. I normally get frustrated, find a solution, and get to cranking on making things move forward. Right now, on the verge, I watched my children's faces. My heart melted into my shoes seeing them hurt.

"Let's go kids."

We get in the car and the kids are in heavy protest. I am sitting silent. The silence again is taking over. I'm staring through the glass at the TV in the distance and all I hear is the hum.

The silence was broken when I got a notification from a tag on social media. It was from someone I thought was a friend but ended up only being a friend until he was no longer able to use me for his benefit. He had written an entire rant stating what a disgusting piece of shit I was and how he knew Heather didn't do it. Jeremy had only met Heather a few times, but I guess that made him an expert on her, so much so, that his wife headed a webpage against me. You see people's loyalty and who they really are in moments like these. But for someone to champion a stranger, and a stranger who didn't even like her, is bazaar. Heather was never friends with her. They never had any type of relationship. The extent of their time together only consisted of her inviting Heather to go out to clubs with her, but after telling her about how she liked to flirt with other men to make her husband jealous, Heather kindly declined her offer. Now this lady is leading websites for Heather. I sat back and shook my head. When you do things for attention, so others will come to you and tell you how great you are, it feeds the ego and is why these actions are committed. I removed myself from the tag. I really didn't care.

I arrived home and saw the GBI car in the driveway. "We need you to unlock Heather's phone." I laughed. What a technologically advanced bunch you are.

"Ok, but there's a photo on there I want."

They perked up like they had something. I shook my head. They reminded me of those late-night CSI shows where someone goes and tells exactly what happened at a crime scene and they go back to the officer in charge and he says, "That's good old-fashioned police work there." No, dumbass, you did nothing. People gave you what you needed.

"What photo do you want there, Mr. Turner?"

"Our last night together, as we were lying in bed, she was holding my hand. She reached and grabbed her phone and took a photo of our hands clutched. I have never seen that photo, I want it."

I open the phone and they pounce on it like a grizzly on some salmon. They opened the photos and began going through them.

"It should be the last photo she took. Please send it to me."

"We will have to email it from the station. We can't do it from here." They left. To this day, I still have never seen that photo.

That night I decided we were all going to go out to eat at Longhorn Steakhouse in Hiram. I enjoyed having time with all four of my kids. I told each of them individually that they were my favorite, "just don't tell the others." We go in and sit in a circular booth near the back, close to the restrooms. I'm on the end and Austin is dead center in the middle. They brought out bread and our salads and a man walks up and is standing over my left shoulder.

He said, "I believe I know you."

I looked up and said, "Sir, I offer my apologies, I don't recognize you. Do I know you from work or church?"

"You're that guy that killed his wife!"

As I processed the words, I saw Austin coming up and putting his foot mid-table and leaping. I was shuffling and caught him. Austin and Kaedon are trained boxers and know how to hit, they are also young, full of vigor, and not afraid to fight.

"Austin! Austin! Look at me. We cannot do this."

"Dad, he deserves it! And he's about to get it."

Austin- *"At this moment I had heard enough. I was tired of hearing people talk bad about my dad. I knew he and Heather loved each other. I knew she was never leaving, and all seemed happy, even if she was living two lives, she was living them very well. With my anger, I was thinking I'd be tried as a minor for kicking this guy's ass, which would be worth some Juvey for me. That was enough. If dad hadn't caught me, that man would have slept in the middle of Longhorn."*

I finally got my son to hear my voice.

"We can't do this. I agree he deserves it. I want to turn around and kick his ass right now. But that will make them right and breed more of them. It will feed their cause of what they are saying I am."

I turned around and looked the man in the eyes.

"I'd suggest you get the fuck out of here before I change my mind." He decided that was a good idea.

We sat down. The entire restaurant was silent and looking at us. The manager came over and comped our meal, but we couldn't even eat. We all sat there silently looking at each other and holding back the emotions that wanted to escape.

One day, I dropped the kids off at school and got busy trying to get some work done, hoping to feel normal. That afternoon when I picked up Lexi, she got in the car and said she had been taken out of class by cops and a lady with Children's Services. I wheeled back into the school where Heather's cousin served as principal.

"Why did someone take my daughter out of class and question her without my knowledge? No one called me at all. What's the meaning of this?"

Lexi- *"I was pulled out of class. As a matter of fact, that was the first day of seven days in a row that I was pulled out of class. We had over 150 calls to child protective services in one day. I had been called up and walked into the office where my principal was standing, along with detectives and police officers, they told me to have a seat. I sat down, and they started asking me the most insane questions I have ever heard, such as, if my father had ever hit me and they asked me where he 'touched me.' I looked at them with confusion and shock on my face and said 'my dad has never laid his hands on me. Why are you asking me this? You need to call my dad.'*

They refused to call him and continued to question me.

'Well let me ask you a different way—'

I said 'No, I already answered your dumb questions.'

I went back to class and waited for the day to be over. As soon as I got in the car, I told my dad what had happened, he was shocked and angry. He turned the car back around and parked, and we went into the school. My mother's cousin was the principal, my dad went to her and asked her why she would ever let me get pulled out of class and be questioned, especially without him being there. She said when they come, she has to let them question me, and that she can't stop them. My father replied, 'somebody should let me know if something involves my daughter.' She just shook her

*head and we left. The following days it kept on happening, them asking
me if my dad had ever touched me or made me feel uncomfortable.*

*I was small, and I was wild, so I fell down a lot and had bruises.
When I wore shorts to school, they would ask me if the bruises had been
caused by my dad. They tried to put words in my mouth to try and
get me to 'confess' to their lies saying, 'we know your dad touched you,
just be honest with us.' I was being honest. I told them I was tired of
them pulling me out of class just to ask me the same absurd questions.
It was embarrassing, and I told them that. I couldn't even complete my
schoolwork because I was constantly pulled into the office. One day I got
fed up. I called my dad myself and told him they kept doing it. He finally
pulled me out of that horrible school and put me in online classes for my
safety."*

Lexi was being harassed at school, yet no one had called me or come
by the house. I finally loaded her up with my attorney and we drove to
the DFACS office. We were told they had gotten a lot of calls flooding in, all at one time. Each caller was saying the same thing, nearly
verbatim. She said the calls were coming from all over — Indiana,
California, only a couple from Georgia. All were anonymous. As we
were sitting there my attorney was hitting up the websites created
about me, and he found a post that instructed people to call DFACS.
It even listed in the post the very stuff they were supposed to say in
the post. Here these people are calling thinking they are helping some
poor girl and they have no idea that they were being used as a pawn by
people to harass and try to destroy an innocent family. I still haven't
put together all the pieces of what was happening. I just know things
were happening and I was not happy at all.

We showed the post to the DFCS workers and the detectives in the
sheriff's department. Yes, the same one. Do you think I ever got a call
back? DFACS did come to the house to make sure we had food, water

and to look at the house. I was so put off at this. People can call and say anything, and then your life has this intrusion. My biggest anger is how the damn sheriff's office was trying to bait my daughter, telling her she had been harmed. This was the lowest bullshit I had ever heard of. I was about at my breaking point. I withdrew Lexi from school and put her in a Christian school, where I knew they would do right by her. Pastor Martin, a solid Christian man, was over the school. He played football at Alabama with Bear Bryant. He had that old-school way of doing things that I relate well to. His kind daughter, Laura, helped me get Lexi enrolled and transferred over. Amid it all, anytime I called, she was there to help. She made sure Lexi was safe and got the education she needed. It felt like a win. But, as soon as I got one fire beat down, another one started.

I pulled up to our house and our street was lined again with assholes. As soon as I got out of the car, they looked like ants getting out of their cars walking toward me. What now?

"We are going to luminol your house."

"For what? You took the photos of Heather in the house, you saw the blood, you know that was contusive to the injury."

"Mr. Turner, we are going to luminol the house."

I guess they were not making Wonka's chocolate that day, so making my house glow was what they wanted to do. They sprayed every inch of the entire house. I asked why. They handed me the coroner's report. Lyndsey had just started as coroner. I believe that Heather was her second call ever. She was green. She had written something that now the sheriff's office was using to come back. She now said she had observed the wall and one part appeared to be washed. Dear Lord. If you look at the wall around the toilet the wall has a base coat of paint and for an architectural look, it has a brown sponge-over in spots. If she had paid attention when she walked in, the very first wall seen at the front door looked this way and the entire laundry room was done the same way. Obviously, her lack of not seeing wallpaper, or seeing some homes that tried to spruce up a little had thrown her off. This little comment now fed the drive and my house was getting sprayed. Fabulous. I had zero worries over that, they were wasting money, material, manpower, time, and hope for their desire, outside of creating evidence, which I wouldn't put past them. After spraying the entire house and going over every square inch with their light, do you know what they found? Not a Damn Thing. You know why? Because there was nothing to find! This obviously pissed off the Oompa.

"Mr. Turner, make sure not to touch any of this stuff, you see our guys are wearing protective suits. It's toxic, you don't want your children to touch it either."

Wait a minute, you put this shit all over the place, on the kids' stuff, all over the food areas, then tell me it's poison.

"You clean it up, you should be responsible for this. Hey, hey—"

The ants left. And left me with a toxic mess that I had to have a company come in and clean. Since this was considered a toxic cleanup and the house needed to be in negative air, it cost $10,000. They treated it like mold and took everything and washed it, scrubbed walls. It was lovely, thanks for that.

The social media crowd was growing and the people hitting it were becoming familiar faces. People I went to school with. People I had known for 30 years. People I had helped and been friends with. It was amazing how fast people turned for drama and negativity. The outlandish lies I was reading. I am still trying to put all of that together. What led Heather to all of this? Grief? Living double lives with several different men? Pops? Her job? What was it? And now they have some lady doing spiritual readings to foretell what happened. Her prediction? I didn't do it. It's amazing what people will accept if it agrees with them, but if it disagrees with them, it is rejected.

One day I really fucked up. I went to get my medication at the pharmacy and this guy walked up behind me. He was so close I could feel the heat of his breath on my neck. I have avoided trouble this whole time and not fed into their bait. I stepped forward in line. So did he. I turned around.

"What's up man? Why are you all up on me, breathing on me?"

"I don't like guys that hurt and kill women—"

He never got to finish that sentence as I forced my entire weight and body mass into a punch that went into his throat and sent him flying right into an end cap filled with bottles of pills. The entire shelf came down and every shelf on that aisle. I watched as what looked like thousands of Tylenol and Advil bottles rolled on the floor and this guy was down and out. Shit. I knew I had messed up, I reacted without letting logic go first. Now I would be arrested for knocking this guy out, there were cameras everywhere. I put my hands on my knees. Damn it. Mende is going to have a field day with this one.

The manager came out, "Andy, what happened?" I told him. He told me to go home. He said he knew the guy and that he would take care of it.

"Man, if I go and he calls the cops, they will come get me and then say I fled."

"I know him. It will be ok. I promise," he reassured me. The guy started coming to. I apologized for the mess and went and sat in my car. I sat there a while not really knowing what to do. Eventually, I went home and never heard anything about it again. I did run into the guy, about a year later, and he just nodded and went on. I was so thankful God spared me that day. I had so much frustration, anger, hurt, and emotions I couldn't even identify. He just chose the wrong day.

I received a voicemail one day from a guy in California who wanted to question me. He planned to make a movie about Heather's life. I had a lawyer send him a letter and immediately went to the Screen Actors Guild and certified the rights to the story of our lives. I would get this call four more times over the years, each time referring them to the rights and sending a letter from the lawyers.

It felt like we were in front of a firing squad. They kept firing all they could at us, they still do. One thing after another, it's nonstop. I'm lonely. I miss my friend and my wife. I hate this. Why are people turning on us, people who should know better? Why are church members talking bad about us on social media? And then quoting Bible verses in the middle of their sins. We're trying to survive. God, was Heather feeling like this? Was her pressure heavy like this? Was she feeling something on all sides that she had hidden so well but couldn't hide it anymore and gave in? I want to know why. I am tired now too. This is a lot for any person. And this much. Let me have some sleep medicine and rest well tonight.

Chapter Seventeen

Jethro Bodine

"At some point with me, niceness will dissipate. I will try that road first, but you can go too far."
-*Bronson Turner*

I f you have ever watched the Beverly Hillbillies, you know Jethro. He had a goal of growing up and being a "Double Naut Spy," but he was just the show's idiot with the brawn. I have been amazed at how many Jethros I have met. You know the type, a complete and total idiot, but in their minds, they see themselves as an expert detective and spy. One Saturday, I walked outside of my home and was met by reporters waddling across my lawn like racing ducks. I stopped and waited for them.

"We would like to get some statements from you."

"Okay," I said. "I have a very important one for you. You're trespassing and about to be thrown off my property."

As they were walking away one started in with questions, "Was Heather right or left-handed? Have you heard about the emails she was sending? I heard she was tied up and shot execution style. Is that true? Do you know she was offered keys to a lawyer's house during court in front of people? Do you know she was seeing some of the deputies? Can you confirm how many men she was seeing? Have you seen the photos she sent them? We just want some statements."

Even off the property, the shouting continued. I went back inside and sat down. I started thinking about what they were throwing at me. Some of that was outlandish, some of it repetitive. I had heard some of it before. Could it really have truth behind it? Did any of these things play into why she did what she did? Or are these just idiots repeating what the fools on social media are saying, believing it to be fact because Facebook said so? The statements all sounded the same. These were some of the same comments that were coming from online followers who had been used as pawns, instructed to call DFCS. Now, there were media parrots regurgitating the same garbage on my front lawn. How could I tell what had validity from all the crazy BS? Did I even want to? I did want to know what Heather was thinking.

I went to her closet and sat down. I opened one of her pocketbooks, looked in the zippered section. She had handwritten notes from different guys. Different handwriting. Different guys.

"I love you, too," one read. I had to pause when I saw that. Not, "Hey I love you," but as in a response, "I love you, too." Do I want to even keep looking? There were more, a lot more. And poems. One note had apparently been attached to something and it read, "I am going to ram this in your cooch." What the hell was this attached to? And what kind of weirdo says cooch? My guess is that it had to be a guy who collects dolls. I found things that let me know people were at my house when I was gone. How could I not have known this? How did she hide this so well? Who are all these men writing these notes?

Then I found something that shook me to my core. Three at-home pregnancy tests that showed positive. She had the Essure procedure done. She wasn't supposed to get pregnant. I started looking up information on failure rates. They have had some failures, but it was very rare. I read the autopsy report, it said that she was not pregnant and had not been. Had she had an abortion? A miscarriage? Maybe these were someone else's, and she was holding them? Why did I look in here and even start this? Ignorance is bliss. That statement had never been truer than in that moment. Before I knew about these notes and her doings, I was better off, in my ignorance, just not believing these things were ever a possibility. Now, I not only felt the loss of a spouse, I felt deceived, and it was the ultimate deception that I couldn't go and ask her about or yell or hear an apology...

An apology. Like the note she left behind. Was her I'm sorry an apology for the things she knew I was about to find out? Was she afraid it was all coming to a head in her life? Were some of those guys getting too deep in the feels and threatening to tell me? If she was fired, was she afraid all her emails would go public, and the kids and I would find out about this other life she had been living?

I thought back to the note she left. I'm sorry, I love you. You can't truly love someone and treat them like this, but I'm thinking logically and not where she was at the time.

I found burner phones, three of them. My mind was racing. Did she buy these or did someone give them to her? Were they all for different guys, to keep them separate and not get mixed up? Damn, Heather. Just damn. How could I have been so crazy to think we had a perfect marriage? How could I be such a fool to think that you loved me like you swore you did? Why would you deceive me like this? And with so many? I found stacks of cards that came with flower deliveries. Where were these sent? Notes talking about naked photos, sexting, or video sex calls. I read these and cried, because I thought my marriage was sacred. It wasn't at all. I looked at all that stuff and was more heartbroken and angrier and bitter that she would do those things.

And now, I will never have an outlet to ask why, to get out my sadness and frustration.

I stopped looking, because every time I looked in a new place, I found more. That alone is taking advantage of me being a trusting husband. Shame on her for taking advantage of it and lying about it. Shame on me for thinking that our postcard marriage was just that.

I got a call from a guy who identified himself as a reporter, although I didn't catch which one. His first question, "Did you kill your wife?"

What kind of lousy reporter are you? Did they teach you how to ask questions in school? Did you even go to school? I lit into Jethro. It was all played back later that night on 11Alive.

"Don't you think her family needs and deserves answers?"

I yelled at him, "We are her family mother fucker, and yes, we need answers. Are you striving to get them for us? What are you doing to help Heather's family? That would be her husband and children." But that wasn't who they were referring to when they said, her family. They completely dismissed her husband and her children, the ones who were with Heather, day in and day out, the ones who depended on her, who loved her. Rather, they chose to focus on some drunk that she saw three times in 15 years, who suddenly emerged to get the news and tv shows to give some relevance to her life because it was a miserable existence as it was. They were choosing to listen to the people who were creating the drama, telling the lies. They created more problems and danger for Heather's family in their process. The interview ended with a cynical laugh from the reporter just before he hung up.

Atlanta 2, 5, 11, 46... I can't recall how many out of state and national networks I had received calls from. And the questions all came in the same vein. LISTEN TO ME CLEARLY. You never know when life may have you on this side of these Jethro vultures. When they are asking questions like this, they do not care about your story at all. They already have their story. All they need you to say is something they can creatively edit or twist.

Stay away from them. Wait to find the time and place to tell your story with someone who cares and believes in you and the truth, and not sensationalism to try and get ratings. Don't get caught in their web. Everything is negative. There's only crime and garbage. That's why so many people have stopped watching it. It's no longer a kid selling lemonade and donating all he made in a summer to a charity. It's how many people were shot, arrested, drugs, rape, robbery, wrecks, politics, and we find very little that is positive in a community. Why doesn't one station push for a change to promote positive things, happy things, encouraging things? I bet it would go number one in the ratings and set a trend.

In fact, every one of the stations' reporters were rude. They had no care or concern about what our family had endured. They had no regard that this continually stirred the vipers and encouraged them and created danger for my children and for me. They didn't care that they grew doubt and hate and helped incite violence against a family who had only tried to survive and stick together.

After WSB Channel 2, WXIA 11, and Fox 5 aired their initial sweep, it created a lot of unrest for us. My family had been in danger for a long time resulting in me having to hire personal security for not only me, but the kids. If I had not done so, my kids would have been harmed by the sensationalism of these people trying to create falsehoods, because they didn't like what Heather chose and refused to accept that answer. Guess what? We, as her family, didn't like her choices either, and we were trying to deal with them and had all of that compiled stress to deal with.

My middle son was working at a local restaurant when some people came in and asked if he was my son. He nodded, and they refused to eat there, storming out, creating a scene. Later, when he left, he called me. "Dad, I'm being followed. I watched them pull out behind me, and they are changing lanes and speeding up with me." I have educated my kids on paying attention to their surroundings to a minute detail. The security vehicle got between them and allowed him to get out of sight. This happened several times, to the point that they finally stopped the car and the people inside tried to create an altercation.

A few weeks later, I heard his Jeep pull in and heard yelling. I yelled for the other kids to stay inside and as I looked out, four grown men had surrounded his jeep and were beating on the glass. I exited the house and with force removed one guy from the side of my son's Jeep. In moments, Austin pulled up with his best friend, Christian, that helped de-escalate the unnecessary situation. The people fled.

Austin- *"It was rare that I ever went out with my friends anymore, to minimize separation from the family in case anything was to happen. Sometimes people decide they're brave for five minutes, and you never know when that will be. The occasion that I'm about to explain to you really puts it into perspective and shows why I tried to minimize that separation. My buddy, Christian, and I were pulling up to the house and as we rounded the curve, I noticed that there were scattered golf carts, people on our grass, people in our driveway, and lots of screaming. So, probably like you'd expect, I rolled out of the truck with every intention to solve that issue in the most Mike Tyson fashion. I walked up the grass trying to gather my bearings of the situation when I heard a commotion from one of the scattered carts in the street. A big Humpty Dumpty looking dude with no hair and his overly drunk wife were screaming out that my father was a murderer and he deserved to be in prison. At that point in my life, I was past all of the logic of being nice to save image, so I marched down into the street and stood in front of that cart and begged both of those sorry excuses for people to slide out so I could execute the plan I had made in my head — to curb stomp both of their faces until my leg got tired. But that liquid courage ran out quick as ole Humpty put that cart in reverse and got out of my way. A real man would have gotten out, especially with what I was saying to him and his, all but dainty, wife. Now, it probably wasn't the right thing to do, but I was prepared to accept all consequences of my actions if they'd decided to grant my wish to release all of my anger. After he backed up, I addressed the people in the yard. They all reeked of cheap alcohol and weren't able to make full sentences that made sense. Ole Humpty Dumpty and his wife gained some more courage as they drove off and again screamed out that my dad was a murderer as they sped away. Pretty cowardly if you ask me. By now, my blood pressure was through the roof and I was just ready to hurt someone. The people in the yard were the next target for whatever was about to come out of me. I guess they were starting to decide that it wasn't a battle they were going to win, because they started to retreat, until Ms. Drunk-a-lot (Humpty's wife) decided she was angry about what I had called her in retaliation to the situation that she had been a part of starting. She came up out of nowhere and got close enough that I could see all the blackheads on her nose.*

'What did you call me?'

I responded without hesitation the exact words I had proclaimed before, because I definitely wasn't in the mind space of backing down from the drunkard who grew the balls to come back. I'm sure that those "balls" were just an extra shot of the bottom shelf booze that she was throwing back.

People are really brave when they have a crowd. I've seen them countless times when they weren't surrounded by buddies and I've waited for that bravery to surface again, but it never does. I'd say it was because they were ashamed of how they acted, but they'd have to have the mental capacity greater than a rock."

Bronson- *"One day I was at school, just having a normal day. A kid got brave and started to smart off to me. At first it started like any argument in school but quickly escalated. He began taking shots at personal matters.*

'You're the reason your stepmom killed herself.'

Everybody has triggers and that one was mine. At school, I would put on a persona that I was young and naïve, but when someone said something like that, it hit a level of dignity. I proceeded to beat the piss out of the kid. I got two days of In School Suspension. At some point with me, niceness will dissipate. I will try that road first, but you can go too far."

Lexi- *"It was Christmastime and my family and I were riding around on our golf carts looking at Christmas lights. We entered a cul-de-sac and there were people out. They had obviously been drinking heavily. They were being loud and slurring their words. As we were going around, a woman looked at the cart I was on and saw our family logo printed on the side. It is a diamond with a capital T in the center. It resembles the Tennessee football logo.*

She yelled out, 'Tennessee! Woo Hoo!'

We just looked at her and smiled and continued to ride away, no one spoke. My brother, Austin, was on the other golf cart behind us. I was looking forward when suddenly I heard his tires squeal. I looked back and my brother was walking towards a woman that had said, 'Is that the murderer guy?' A bald, fat man named Larry started to scream at my brother. He was drunk out of his mind. He was yelling, 'get on your cart and roll away.' My brother, not saying a word, unbothered, was standing there looking at him with a small smirk. My dad got off our cart and ran over to my brother making sure he was not about to get into a fight. I got off the cart and kept my distance, listening to everyone yell, trying to make out what people were saying.

The woman that had asked if my dad was a murderer started to apologize. She said, 'I watched a documentary on him. I forgot his name, so I just said murderer guy. I wasn't accusing him. I'm sorry.'

People started flooding the streets watching what was going on. A tall, skinny woman walked out of her house, and I looked at her. She was talking to someone about my dad. She said, 'He murdered his wife!'

At that point, I could not bite my tongue any longer and I looked at her and yelled, 'Are you serious!?'

Her attention turned toward me, and she yelled back saying, 'You need to watch cable TV.'

Obvious from this comment, she didn't know who I was and didn't know that I had been the one living through all of this. The man she was with took her inside so she wouldn't continue to run her uneducated mouth. My attention turned back to my dad and brother. Larry, getting in my brother's face making a fool of himself, starting calling my brother fat and all of the childish insults he could come up with. People finally got Larry back inside his house before he got hurt very badly, but even from the streets you could still hear his voice yelling from inside. Things calmed down after my dad talked with people, telling them what was going on and people apologized to him even agreeing that the woman should not have said that. We went back to our carts ready to drive away.

Before we could drive off, a kind man approached us. He said he was sorry about what happened, he looked at me as I had tears in my eyes trying not to let them roll down my face, and he said, 'Don't listen to them, they are rude and don't know what they are talking about.' He said he was sorry we all had to go through this. I thanked him, my dad talked to him a little while longer before we all got back on our carts. After that we just went home, not in the mood to be out anymore, our night was ruined by people that had no idea what they were talking about."

Anytime I had someone over to help me with Lexi, with her hair and clothes and general things, they would appear on social media. Others would identify them as having been with a 'killer' and social services would get involved. They would be questioned about their ability to raise their own kids since they were putting them in jeopardy. And then the social media rumors started that I was sleeping with everyone I saw. I lost friends over this. They would call and tell me they loved our family, but the intrusion was too much to handle. They were being called or contacted privately on social media being 'warned' that they would be next and 'who' I really was. Why had no one stopped and really thought about it? Why had I not been named a suspect, arrested, or worse? Has anyone stopped to think that if less than 1% of the total shit told on these media sites were true, I'd be under the prison?

One Jethro dumbass said that Heather would have had to have used her thumb to pull the trigger. This particular person didn't even know which side of the head she was shot on but felt qualified to make statements like that. Others heard it, fed into it, and validated him, so then he repeated it as if it was factual, posting it all over the internet. That is what is wrong with social media! And just like the reporter who said she had been tied up and shot execution style, Jethros were everywhere! Once something was posted, all the other Jethros would believe it and then spread it as facts. And if you contact Facebook, you will learn that it's not against their community guidelines to slander and defame and bully and harass. I have paid lawyers and services to stop it and have had small success but failed miserably in the long run. Due to that, it created a growing following that created more violence towards us. I have been amazed at how ignorance breeds ignorance, and they act like they are geniuses. What I will never be able to get accustomed to is how they do this and then quote the Bible, claiming to be Holy. Of all the people that should know better!

Currently we have had over 40 nails hammered into our tires. We have had tires slashed, cars keyed, people run us off the road, notes of death threats mailed to us, calls of death threats, physical altercations for myself and every single one of my children, harassment and bullying on social media. Some of the messages we have received have been heartless and crude. Others, again, think they are that spy detective who has it figured out. Eight jobs lost, many, many court cases, all while dealing with loss and mourning, and I still haven't told you the worst parts.

I have also been ear raped by the uneducated who are willing to open their mouths and show us all exactly how they know everything. They say things like this, "No woman would ever shower and shoot herself naked." Well, I know one that did. I'm guessing she's not the only one in the world. Do I know why she did it that way? No, no clue. Only she does. Maybe it felt like a cleansing or washing of her sins. I can speculate all day but the Jethro statements that people post as if they are authorities and know all, are ludicrous. In my opinion, no one in that state of mind is thinking that clearly, obviously. Why would you try and put logical thoughts or even patterns of what the majority would do to fit this person? We are all different. I wish I had all the answers to the questions I've been asked.

How about the Jethro that asked why Heather would use her non-dominant hand to shoot herself? I'd love to sit down with that dumbass and ask him what her dominant hand was. Seems they are all experts in the matter of my wife and seem to know her better than her family.

Take note that the people making those statements had not spent any private time with her, they only knew her from photos and from passing at work or church. I can't help but be frustrated at all the Jethros who have taken it upon themselves, without the self-awareness of what an idiot they are making of themselves, to try and look relevant, and then they lead others to believe what they are saying when they have no clue. They have no idea what deviant person might read their statements and view them as fact. On almost every post it ends in proclamation of me being a psychopath, narcissist, sociopath, killer, murderer, or piece of shit, most posts which began with scripture or a biblical comment.

I heard lawyers say how hard it is to win slander and defamation lawsuits when people post you're a killer and murderer. I have the screenshots and can show how this has contributed to lost jobs and wages and harm to my family. And yet when I sue, they file bankrupt, and so it continues. But now we have TV shows and the sheriff's department that are guilty. They can't avoid the penalties that they will have to pay for their actions. Those people have wrapped it all up with a beautiful bow, making it easy for me to prove.

Speaking of Jethro Bodine, I saw one of the documentaries. I hated watching it, because I liked the host and I had been a fan of her husband's acting career. Sadly, she didn't want to hear the truth or tell the real story. She had already interviewed men with whom Heather had affairs, family members we didn't even know, family with whom Heather didn't associate or even like. She drank the Kool-Aid, like so many others. They do well at spinning lies and creating doubt. They are great at being judge, jury, and executioners. With all of their 'facts,' things seem to blow their minds as to why they have not seen what they want come to fruition. I wish I could spit and call it gold and sell it for gold prices, but I don't know that formula, however I have seen it done, successfully.

The biggest spinner I saw recently knew he was doing just that. He was so happy to be on TV and feeling important that he kept one-upping his story. He refused to show his face, stayed in the dark. It was obvious seeing the silhouette, looking like a Volkswagen with both doors open, that it was Ken, the guy who wouldn't shut up from the funeral home. Now, he was in fear for his life, because our family has powerful people. Well, okay, if I was so powerful then I'd think the court cases would have gone a little differently, and my son wouldn't have been abused and endangered at the hands of the sheriff's department. I could go on; however, I am sure my points have been made. You have been reading a book about how powerless I have been, so back to the story. He was shaking and terrified, so scared that he had to be recorded in the dark.

John 3:19-21 tells the real story of why he was in the dark. He remained in the dark because his deeds were evil, and the darkness helped him cope and feel more apt in the lies he was spewing. Do recall that this was the guy who stated he would fight to go to the courthouse to get the death certificates just to stare at my wife. Same creep. Let's keep going through what he was willing to say. He wanted to be seen as an expert. I wondered what a non-expert would look like. Let's focus on his next statement — in all his years this was the "worst he had ever seen." Let me allow this to just get real for a moment. Heather used a .38 caliber revolver. That made the worst victim he had ever seen? In all his years he had claimed to have been doing this, I'm guessing he didn't serve in the military or do any tours. How much experience could he really have with that kind of statement? I will tell you from my point of view it was awful, it was life altering, it was horrific. I was looking at a wife and a person I loved. He also said he had never seen a death certificate say cause of death was undetermined. According to the medical examiners I spoke to, that was fairly common and was explained to me. To know the cause of death, gunshot, they could not with clear certainty speak to the mindset of a person. With no witnesses, they had a hard time determining a cause of death, because it left some unknowns. Did she pull out the gun and it go off by accident? Was it malfunction? Did she do it on purpose? Or did someone else do it? Without strong evidence or a witness, they cannot just make it up. So, in those cases it's ruled undetermined.

This guy was supposed to be a professional, been doing his job for years. I think you can already see the onion peeling at how full of shit he really was. Let's continue, what did you hear him really say the most? How beautiful she was, how talented. He went on too much about that, didn't he? Did he sound professional? Did he sound creepy and lustful? Do I think he was inappropriate when her body arrived back? I sure wish I had camera access to verify. In my mind that is the perfect profile of that type of creep. Remember how he asked me why she did it? What professional would do that to any widow, widower? Then, he didn't know what side of the head she was shot on, but makes the claim it had to have been done with her thumb. Holy molly. Let's stop and think about dumping truck loads here. Sounds like he's getting his information from websites, not the medical examiner. If you don't have facts, why are you TV dumping the fertilizer?

Double Naut Spy!

Once the show aired, social media lit up. Amateurs were posting photos of a mannequin head with stickers labeling where they say the entrance and exit wounds were. Come on, seriously? And those same people were the ones accusing me of taking the bullet from the scene and cleaning up a wall. What was ridiculous was the people commenting on the posts, as if somehow everyone was a damn expert on forensics and ballistics.

Here are the facts, Heather shot herself from the left side. She used a soft tip hollow point, which was originally purchased to protect her and keep her safe. These bullets spread to inflict the most damage to an attacker. It also keeps the bullet from exiting the body in a way that could harm an innocent bystander. We threw away every box she had after her death. It made us sick to look at them and to think of how they worked on our precious wife and mother, rather than an attacker that they were intended for. The majority of the bullet never exited her body, but rather became shrapnel and stayed inside. One small part of the shrapnel had an exit, but not a solid bullet. That caused the entrance to be larger than the exit where the small piece came out.

Does our family owe anyone this information? Not at all. The people who need to know it, have known it. Do you think this is easy to relive and reflect upon? I'd rather slam my manhood in a car door than ponder this detail and be forced to relive that day over and over. People feeding into the outlandish Jethro theories which are not based on facts or even real information, forces our family to continue to have to live this nightmare over and over. There are so many idiots just wanting to be Double Naut Spies. I am wondering if they have a DNS school and maybe that was where Mike Hill got his training. Would make sense!

Chapter Eighteen

Damned If You Do, Damned If You Don't

"It's time to quit all of this that you're doing. You taught me better, you
wouldn't want me doing this, so I'm not letting you."
-Austin Turner

Have you ever been in a place in life where it felt like everything you touched turned to gold? Well, I must have been
Midas' twin brother that had the total opposite reaction to whatever I
touched. A few months following Heather's death, I hit a major spiral.
I had endured hard times, but this was a different realm. Everything
I touched was turning to shit. I was missing my wife, my life, my
happiness, my identity, my peace. It seemed when I looked up all I saw
was mire and desolation as the entire world was collapsing around me.

Mende never stopped. I believe she will always be a person who loves
control. I believe she will always be willing to put the kids in harm's

way as long as she gets what she wants. Even in the situation we were in, I was having to watch my kids be harmed and in grievous ways, some so bad that I opted to not even include on these pages. I kept fighting, because my family deserved it.

I have spent over $1,300,000.00 in court and legal fees; all while being stripped of jobs. I had to file bankruptcy twice. And throughout, Mende kept winning. She benefited from a broken system. But ultimately, her time of victory came to an end. The kids are grown, they can speak to what has happened at her hands. Now, Mende pays her boys to spend time with her. I fought for the boys and while I lost in court, I still have my kids. She won on court documents, but she has lost the love and respect of her children.

Still, during this time, all I could feel was the squeeze and the hurt from court coupled with all of my grief. I turned to people, and they fled. I wrote to friends only to discover that while I thought we were friends, I was the friend, they were not. People that I had helped and had been there for had forgotten my kindness, and repaid me with stabs in the back. People who once said they loved me, now posted hatred. I had no idea who was friend or foe.

And the loneliness was crazy, I felt like I was on an island alone. I began having a steady flow of women through. I'd drop the kids off at school and meet ladies at my house, hoping that sex would fill the void. Having someone to talk to, and the physical act of sex was a release and an escape from the reality that had overwhelmed me. I had a revolving door, hoping that eventually I would alleviate the hurt and pain. Some days, I'd have three or four women staggered at different times. I am sharing this only to say, I was miserable. I was trying to take things into my own hands. I was so desperate to stop my suffering. I knew what I was doing was wrong on many levels, but I did not care if it successfully separated me from where I was at the time. I felt like a failure for not seeing that Heather was troubled, and I was hurt that she had rather die than continue her life with the kids and me. I was hurting so bad that I couldn't describe it or even understand it.

I want to pause here. I want to talk about the hurt of Moses in Exodus 32:32. Even if you aren't a Bible believer, you can apply this. If you appreciate love and compassion, this is a remarkable display of grace. Verse 32 says, "Yet now, if thou wilt forgive their sin--;"

Dash, dash, semi-colon. Do you know why that is there?

In the ancient Greek when this was written, it shows Moses crying out to God in a tearful and heartfelt plea of agony. He loved his people, and he was interceding to God for their forgiveness. When he says, "God, please forgive their sin," he broke down groaning and crying. God recorded that in the scriptures. It's considered great agony.

Have you ever been there? Have you ever lost someone you thought you couldn't live without – a parent, child, spouse, friend? Have you been diagnosed with a disease and the doctors say there's nothing they can do – start making arrangements and get your affairs in order, there's not much time? Have you lost everything, filed bankruptcy, had your family stripped and abused? Have you had your reputation destroyed? Have you learned that the life you thought you had was nothing more than a smoke screen — all lies and deceit? Have you cried in true agony and had no words to say? You're on your knees, hurting so badly, trying to cry out but all that comes out is groans. You're weeping so hard you can hardly breathe, your soul feels like it's breaking, your body feels like it's shutting down, you're on empty and at the end of your rope, feeling so alone, so devastated and so desperate. The Holy Spirit takes that to the Father, and it is not only understood, God says, "I wrote that language! I hear you! I understand you! I know! I feel your pain and know what's in your heart." You don't need to speak out loud for God to hear your agony. He came before us and wrote the language we cannot speak.

Dash, dash, semi-colon.

That's where I was. I was as low as I thought I could go. I was getting to a place where I had thoughts of giving up. Then I would think of the kids. Someone must be a champion for them. Even if I destroyed my name, I'd do it for the chance to save them. So, I never stopped that fight. How do you fight what you can't see? I had no idea who the cowards were behind the screens. I knew my children's faces and how much they needed me to hold it together and to be a strong person for them. So, fight is what I've done.

My drinking increased. It was a coping mechanism. The women I saw became more frequent. My thinking was not clear. And when I tried to climb out of the hole I had dug, cut those women out of my life, they would seek revenge by joining in the darkness of the websites who were posting against me. People gravitated to this and talked to them like they were little puppies. It was clear what they were doing, but those girls loved the attention so much they played right into it. Then I noticed women I hadn't dated going on saying I had. Why would they do this? All the comments of "support" and "love" quickly showed that ego fulfillment was their motive.

So much of this was self-inflicted. I sought to not hurt for a moment and by doing so, created more pain for myself. It's clear to look back when you're further down the road and God has picked you up and dusted you off and set your path back straight. But in that moment, I was a fish on a bank flopping for air, trying to get through the minutes, not the hours or the days. I was fighting just to breathe.

Austin- *"I never really knew my dad as a drinker but after mom died, I had to get used to it. We had a cabinet that used to house cups and bowls that turned into something that looked like an industrial warehouse for liquor, wine, and beer. I started to notice that at the beginning of the week that cabinet would be full of those fancy looking bottles and by the weekend, those bottles would be dry as a bone, scattered about the house. Bottles in every room, empty and missing caps and lids. Each week the trips to the liquor store to purchase top-shelf liquor became increasingly worse. Bottles purchased by the dozen still to be gone at the week's end.*

Dad turned into a different person, passed out each night, most of the time in his own vomit. I'd try cleaning the bottles and the puke but the frequency of the two was so high that it was almost impossible to keep up with. This wasn't the man that I had learned from my whole life but rather a placeholder of a human just cycling through this new addiction to avoid the hurt of losing a wife and best friend. I'm not saying that this probably isn't something I'd turn to if I was in the same position. He had tried to save his wife in a scene you'd probably imagine in a horror movie, but that's still not the man he taught me to be, so I took it upon myself to help him just like he helped me my entire life. One morning, I got rid of the bottles scattered around the house and I woke him from his alcohol-induced sleep. It happened to be early on a Sunday morning, so I woke up my groggy father and toted him to the shower.

'Clean up Dad, it's time for church,' I told him. 'It's time to quit all of this that you're doing. You taught me better, you wouldn't want me doing this, so I'm not letting you.'

He reluctantly obliged and we went to church, prayed at the altar, and started his road to a new normal. It was time to be the man he had taught me to be."

I was struggling. I had never been a drinker, not even in college. I had prayed and I didn't see God. After all, he didn't save my wife. I was lonely, and the horde of women that I had circulated through had not filled the void that I was so desperately trying to fill. I had lost my confidence, my companion, and life was now filled with accusers and people trying to destroy me. For what? Because my wife decided to give up? I was doing things that were out of my norm. I was just trying to be okay. I wanted to stop hurting. I was drinking a lot of liquor. I raised my kids in church. I had taught them better than what I was doing.

I felt nothing when I prayed, so I had stopped that some time back. There I was drunk in my kitchen, asleep. I stunk and looked exactly how you are picturing it. Austin snatched me up. All the kids were on the couch ready to go. I got in the shower, and I thought, how can I change this? I'll see if they want to go eat and get ice cream. I'll divert. But when I tried it, I was stonewalled by my own children. Every one of them said, "Dad, we want to go to church, and we want you to go." I admit that I felt some tug at that moment.

I had already tried going to church a few months back, it was posted online and created some drama. I never wanted to do anything to hurt a church or pastor. I stayed away to keep it down. But even when I went to church, I didn't speak to anyone. I knew people at the church were talking bad about me already.

That day, we visited a different church, one the kids wanted to visit, one where they had sung several times. I walked in and went straight to the altar. I didn't speak to anyone. I wasn't there for them anyway. I felt hands on my shoulders and back. I didn't think anything of it. There I was, just like Moses — I was groaning by that point. I had been through so much. I had tried everything. I just wanted to stop hurting but couldn't. I had lost faith in everyone. I had lost faith in the Church. When I finished praying, I stood up and looked and those hands that were touching me, were my four children.

Proverbs 22:6 "Raise a child in the way they should go, and they will not depart from it."

There wasn't a pastor who could have gotten to me. No one in that congregation could have gotten to me. I was so guarded, I didn't trust anyone. But there were my children, the only people who could touch my heart and move me. What if I hadn't taught them that when they were young?

On the car ride home, I made a promise to them.

"I make no excuses, Dad was wrong. I made bad choices, because I was hurting. I dishonored my name, and I failed you. I apologize, and I assure you, that changed today."

And it did, I didn't drink anymore. Haven't been drunk since.

Austin- *"I always wanted to go to New York. I love music and New York is the home of Broadway. Luckily, my dad had a work trip to New York, so he invited me to tag along. Of course, I accepted, especially in the times we were experiencing. We had an awesome time. He would work during the day, and at night we'd experience the nightlife of New York. We got to see Wicked, Phantom of the Opera, and Hadestown. Each show was amazing. I loved them all and they're each my favorite on different days. The trip was awesome, until it wasn't. The night we saw Phantom, dad wasn't feeling well. He was restless and that night in the hotel, he couldn't sleep because he was in pain. He told me not to worry about it. That's such a dad thing to say. We made it through the night and the next morning it was time to head to the airport, our trip was over. I could tell he still wasn't feeling well even though he didn't tell me. He's normally pretty stubborn when it comes to situations surrounding his health or the doctors, but I knew it was bad when he started asking for help. He began to lose so much strength that he couldn't even hold his own bags going through security and he asked me to grab them. He was dragging his feet instead of picking them up and he looked sickly. We made it through security, and he opted to sit down at a tiny café near our gate because he was extremely thirsty and felt like he had run a* marathon. He drank two glasses of orange juice and two glasses of water before exiting and going to the bathroom. He was gone for a long time, but I couldn't exit the table because we hadn't paid and the waitress would have chased me down the terminal. Dad finally reemerged and looked very worried, almost as if he had seen a ghost. He struggled to get the words out, so he showed me a picture on his phone.

At first, I thought he was showing me a trap gone wrong from one of the Saw movies. There was chunky blood on the walls, toilet, floor, and I swear on the handle of the flusher. He began to explain that he had thrown up that blood, to which I was obviously alarmed. He tried to tell me he was fine and just needed more water, reverting to the originally stated stubbornness regarding his health. I tried telling him that was obviously not normal, but he insisted on getting on our flight and trying to make it home. After numerous trips to the airport terminal bathroom to vomit blood and other chunks of what he didn't know was his esophagus, he still insisted on flying home. I broke through the veil of that decision when I showed him that he was as pale as someone who only goes outside during the night. Casper the Ghost had more complexion than he did in that moment.

We hobbled over to one of the gate attendants, an older man in a red coat that worked for Delta. I frantically explained the situation and showed him the pictures, adding that it had been happening for over an hour now. He shared the same situational awareness that I had, which my father obviously hadn't, and immediately called for an ambulance. Delta opened the gangway doors and plopped down a set of stairs that closely resembled a ladder it was so steep. It was difficult to carry my father down the ladder with each bag that we had, but I managed. We made it to the taxiway and the ambulance workers were asking questions that were going in one ear and out the other, because I was focused on Dad not being able to hold himself up. About that time, I felt him convulse and knew he was about to throw up again, and what do you know, it sure was windy that day. He threw up blood once again, and it hit the wind and went all over me and all over him. It ruined both of our outfits and shoes but that obviously wasn't my first concern.

To put into perspective how bad it was, when he threw up on the taxiway, the main guy in charge of the ambulance crew sprinted in the opposite direction from us and called on the radio, 'He is throwing up copious amounts of blood.' Those words still ring in my ears today as that was the only thing I could comprehend from the entire exchange between the ambulance operators.

I threw my dad's body weight on my shoulders and continued to tote him to the open doors of the ambulance. It seemed miles away and each step I took felt like I was going backwards. My brain was telling me to move faster but my feet felt like they were in quicksand. Up and in and onto the gurney that was strapped to the floor, the female operator started an IV. I sat, distraught because I began to realize how much blood he'd truly lost. Was I about to lose my dad too? I thought to myself all the worst possible things and couldn't find a piece of positivity. It felt like the world around us was still moving but I was suspended in time thinking about life without my dad. A police escort rushed us out of the airport and to a hospital in Newark, New Jersey. The emergency room was busy because the part of Jersey we were in wasn't the nicest of places, if you catch my drift. Sketchy folks were roaming outside the hospital doors and all over the streets surrounding the hospital. You might be tempted to say that I was just being a skeptic but one of the nurses handed me my dad's watch and said, 'Don't go outside with that on, or you'll probably get jumped.' I just looked at her with a deer in the headlight's kind of stare.

I'm trying to answer the questions of a thousand people quick enough, so I don't have to leave my dad's side and I start to notice that other nurses and now doctors are leaving emergency bays and popping in from other *parts of the hospital, venturing to the room my dad is in. They began taking out Ambu bags, which is something to help a patient breathe if they're out and can't breathe for themselves. So many voices were yelling, but I couldn't hear them, the silence rung, and I noticed my dad tearing up and whispering to the doctor. I was able to make out a few words by reading his mouth, 'I'm getting kind of scared, Doc.' If that wasn't unsettling, I'm not sure what would be.*

Moments later, that same doctor approached me and told me that they may have to intubate him. That was against my dad's wishes, and he didn't want it done unless it was absolutely necessary. I told her to do what she needed, just make sure they saved my dad. I heard a piercing scream and looked up. It was my dad, his head slammed against the back of the bed and his vitals were dropping on the monitor rapidly. He was dead for a second, but they brought him back. I watched all the doctors and nurses scrambling. Is he gone? Am I alone? What do I do? Is my best friend, my dad, dead...? He came back after the hard work of the staff and I was relieved for a few seconds.

'Let's not do dat no mo,' was the exact verbiage my dad proclaimed when he woke up. Even in those times he found a way to slip in a dad joke. He threw up blood again, all over everything and lost consciousness once more. His vitals didn't stop but were very, very low. This time a head doctor started the heavy drugs to keep him sedated and began the intubation. A long tube that looked like something you'd find hooked to an enormous industrial machine was forcefully shoved down Dad's throat and, even sedated, he was trying to fight the doctors. It took multiple people to roll him to his side and keep him there. The doctor found a hole where he was bleeding internally and went in with a tool to burn it closed. After what felt like a forever struggle, he got it. There was my dad — blood-stained shirt, pants and even shoes, with a giant tube hanging out of his mouth and his vitals still all over the place. He

kept trying to yank the tube out of his mouth, even while heavily sedated, so I laid over him and forced his arms down. They eventually resorted to handcuffing him to the bed so he wouldn't try to yank out the only thing that was breathing for him.

Someone from the hospital staff asked me if I was alone. I told her I was with my dad. Apparently, when your parent isn't alert and you aren't an adult, you are placed with a guardian. I had 24 hours to get another adult there to stay with me. My grandad was able to make the flight to save me from being in a children's home in Newark. Five days went by, and Dad was still out cold. So many drugs kept him asleep, and the intubation kept him breathing. Eventually, he started to miraculously improve, and the doctor allowed for the drugs to be pulled back so the tube could be taken out.

When he woke up and realized where he was, he was upset there was a tube down his throat. He gave me an angry point and squint to which I responded, "They had to dad, to save you." He laid there and waited as patiently as he could. Finally, the team of doctors arrived to remove the tube and the first words he was able to mutter were, 'Can I have my phone to play Clash of Clans. I need to do my attacks.' Dad was back and it seemed he was back to his old self."

That day was terrifying. I remember sitting in the airport. I could feel my body getting weaker and weaker. I saw the concern on my son's face. I called a GI Doctor and sent the photos I had taken to show the amount of blood I was losing. He told me if I got onto a plane that day, I would likely die in flight.

As I got to the ER, I was getting a lot of attention, which told me they were alarmed. I asked the doctor to take care of Austin. She said she would. I watched as they rolled in what I knew to be lifesaving equipment. They were giving me blood and put bilateral 14-gauge needles in each hand. The doctor advised later that he had a hard time finding the tear and he was concerned he would not find it at all or not in time. He did, and the part he fixed was later diagnosed as Barrette's Esophagus with cancer that led me to radiation and chemo treatments. Both were hard on my body.

As I lay there unable to move, I had moments of consciousness but couldn't open my eyes. I could hear but was confused at what was happening. I'd try to take a deep breath because I felt like I was drowning and couldn't get the air satisfied in my lungs. It was miserable. I remember being in a panic and I felt tears rolling down my cheeks. Austin wiped them away.

The day I woke up, they removed the vent. I had visits from nurses and the doctors that day. The ER doctor came to see me and, holding back tears, told me she had been so worried.

"I knocked on death's door, but no one was home," I replied.

When I looked at my phone, I saw nasty messages of how I was in contempt and would be back in court. Geez, a man can't even die without crossing this bitch. Sure enough, she kept her word!

Chapter Nineteen

We Wrestle Not Against Flesh and Blood.... Umm, yes, we do!

"How far we have drifted from the eternal truths of God, humanity, and how we should behave."
-Dan Heinrich

Before the holy rollers shake the bobby pins loose from their hair, yes, I understand the Bible verse here and what it says. I understand demonic forces are always at hand. But so are assholes!

The kids and I decided that staying in the house Heather died in was just too much. We purchased a new home in the Georgian Golf and Country Club. It is not gated and does not have a guard house like our previous places, but it does have a decent golf course and the homes are moderate with good amenities. We were looking forward to a fresh start. We found a friendly neighbor wearing a Braves hat and decided to introduce ourselves. He seemed like a very nice guy, and we had a great conversation. We moved in the week before Halloween, so we were in a mad dash from the beginning. We go all out for Halloween and I mean all out!

We always decorated. The kids have movie-grade, silicon masks and gloves. They will walk the perimeter of the yard, having a good time with the neighbors. We always make a trip to Sam's Club and load up on candy, full-sized, not the crappy stuff. We make up special bags that we give out for our favorite costume or the best dressed. We play music and always have animatronics. We were told that this community had a huge gathering, police block the street, and people come from everywhere to Trick or Treat. I'm guessing I saw about 1,000 golf carts and 10,000 people came through. Being our first year and underestimating the crowd, we ran out of candy early and decided to take the golf carts out to see the costumes and just enjoy the night and neighborhood.

We got to the end of the street and Lexi's whole countenance changed. Each year, the community hosted a huge pumpkin carving event to raise money for charity. We moved in too late to submit pumpkins, which was a good thing. A dozen of the carved pumpkins had the domestic violence logo along with Heather's name. One had *A.T. Rot in Hell* carved on it. Well, welcome to the neighborhood. All the kids were looking at me waiting for a response. I tried not to have one, and the mask I was wearing helped. We headed back down the street toward home, deciding that trick or treating was now out of the question.

Heather was never hit, pushed, harmed, or bruised in any capacity. Not one photo depicting such treatment has ever come forward, nor will one ever come forward. Their smoking proof comes from the lies she told to the men she was manipulating. She used these men just as much as they thought they were using her; Heather was a liar. I would have defended her to the end and told you different until I learned she was not the woman I thought she was. That broke my heart for years. I believed in her and she took advantage of that. She was my everything, but the lies she told fostered a lot of shit we were left to face.

Those men believed what she told them, they actually thought she cared about them. One guy thought she loved him, but when talking with me, she made fun of him relentlessly. But he's still in love today. I guess I'm as big a fool as he is as well as all the others I have found out about. I no longer mourn her the way I did. I did not have the marriage I thought I had. I thought she was faithful. I thought she was loyal. But over the last six years, I have learned how very wrong I was. She was trashing me and everything I thought was sacred to us. She even told one guy that she didn't even think we were married.

So yes, I wrestle against flesh and blood, and I had no idea that my wife was warring against me. Let me tell you, it's very hard to deal with a loss, and I hurt for anyone who has had to do so, however; to deal with a loss and then learn that you were deceived and what you loved and adored was all a front, is even harder to accept. The reason is I have no way to get closure on that part. I cannot talk to her about it. I cannot go to her. It was done. She checked out. How devastating it has been to learn what I have learned over the years. And I'm still learning things now. I am learning from what is posted on social media. They educate me by talking about stuff they blame me for. Only a fool will base their "facts" on the words of a liar, and then slander and defame, knowing they are open to being sued for it. People will never change when they have that mentality. That's who they are.

You can easily identify them, just listen for the, "hold my beer and watch this," phrase.

Back at the house, I noticed the kind neighbor back outside, so I spoke and offered a greeting, trying to continue our neighborly relationship. This time he ignored me, walked into his house, and slammed the door. Weird.

The next day I got a call from the Homeowner's Association about violations. They got 150 calls over the next week. That's comical, huh? The kicker is, the kind neighbor in the Braves hat, was married to a woman who worked at the school where Mende worked, a woman who kept his balls in her purse. Bingo, that was where it was all coming from.

We tried to join the subdivision association page on social media that tells of the events, pool parties, egg hunts, food trucks, etc. We were never accepted. On the Fourth of July, the association put on a large fireworks display. We packed sandwiches and took the cart, hoping to have a nice evening with family and enjoy the festivities. We picked a spot and set up. It was nice, kids were playing frisbee, throwing footballs, music was playing. We were enjoying the time. Everyone had their Yeti coolers on their carts and their Yeti cups filled with their concoctions, and after a couple of hours, those concoctions started doing the talking. And that's when I heard it — one lousy comment from the biggest fucker in the group, wearing a tank top and flip flops. I began making my way over to him to clear matters up, and he started to look very uneasy. Still needing to impress his friends, he resolved to his unkindness.

"Excuse me," I said. "I believe I heard you making comments about me, and I don't know you, so I came to introduce myself."

"Well, umm, ah, I had heard, um, that you had, um, moved in and had lost your wife."

"No, I didn't lose her, sir, I know exactly where she is. She's dead. She died from suicide."

"Man, my bad, I shouldn't have said anything." The rest of his crew was speechless.

I continued, "You see my kids over there? Do you think I appreciate that disrespect? We live here, we're your neighbors. We have been through hell because of people like you running their mouths, who don't even know us. You were not there; we've never even met. Yet, you're expert enough to be lecturing the lawn." This instance happened every time we had any social, it was just with different people.

Finally, they started using the HOA to try and run us off. The homeowners are the board after all. I have 10k dollars in fines right now and my yard is immaculate. They will take a photo of something not in violation but say that it was left there for months and charge me per day. They are hoping this makes us want to leave. I called the association attorney, had my attorneys on and did a live zoom to show her the property. I explained the situation, and she told me it would be handled, to not worry about it. That was a year ago and they still haven't removed the charges. That's stubborn!

Through all of this, I had a bright shining star enter my life.

I had stop chasing women and was attending church with my family. I started going to a grief counseling class. There was this cute little lady that was there who had lost her husband from some sickness that I wasn't aware of at the time. She didn't talk a lot but listened. Sometimes at certain angles, she looked like Monica from her days acting on the show Friends. I would watch for her hair to be a certain way and her face to catch it. Yes, she had the resemblance.

One day we were seated beside each other and started talking. She was very kind. She was having a hard time like I was. After class we went out for coffee and talked for a long time about what it's like to lose a spouse. We spoke a language to each other that no one else could speak, a language you never really want to learn. One that quickly allowed us to bond over hurt and loss and pushed us to realize we shared a lot of common interests.

I knew it wouldn't take long for people to get wind of us and the rumor mill would take off. I had lost so many jobs, and now dating was crazy too. Most women run for the hills.

I knew I had to tell her about the drama. I also knew as soon as I did, she would probably head on down the road. I sat her down.

"Kelly, look, before either of us go too far I want tell you some things."

I tried to get as detailed as I could. She didn't seem to be all that bothered. I am not sure if she didn't believe it was as big as it was or maybe she was just waiting for the right moment to jump out the window and run. She didn't jump and run but rather thanked me for telling her. Nothing else came up about it for a few weeks. I was really starting to enjoy her company. She was attractive and funny. She also wasn't playing into all the drama. If we went out and posted a photo, here would come the Hell hounds.

I'll never forget the first call. I remember exactly who it was and how it made me feel. I was in my kitchen. I heard her answer the phone, then her voice escalated, then higher.

"You have no idea what you are talking about. He is not a murderer!"

Oh shit. I stopped what I was doing and started being nosy. She was talking to her father. The Hell sites had roped in some girl she went to high school with and convinced her that Kelly and her son, Kaedon, were in extreme danger. They sent her dad to rescue her.

When she hung up, I fully expected her to excuse herself and leave. When the trolls hit, it usually bothers people enough to push them away. Hell, I had seen this already, many times. I knew the drill; I couldn't get mad at her or the family. The lies they tell are not only scary but also convincing.

I'm not sure what made her stay through that part, but she did, and we were hitting it off and having a great time. Our chemistry was nice. It was comical to watch how hard the hate sites would try and find out our every move. We talked about it. Who has the time for this? We would be out eating and get notifications, sure enough someone spotted us, and they had a photo. How crazy is this? And how unsafe. They had no regard for the law while they yelled at law enforcement to do their job. What back-assward irony is that?

We weren't worried about what they thought. It was working for us. I was happy to be with someone who valued me, who wasn't taking me for granted. I was leery after being burned so badly, but I've paid close attention to Kelly. I know when she changes, when her norms are off, even in the slightest. Sometimes I say something but mostly I just observe. And what's different for her is that I'm not the same man. I have been damaged by how I have been treated. I am not as open and outspoken. The reason for that is when you give it all and are publicly and openly made a fool, it makes you not want to be that guy anymore. I love differently now. I am more affectionate now. And I think that is good, why would she want the same thing someone else had anyway? I am the man I am today because of the hell I have been through. I am smarter, I am more astute, I am a better leader, and I am a better partner . She benefits from my scars and the education I learned in how not to do things. We have a relationship that has been cultivated and grown the right way. I respect her as a person, as a friend. I have watched her grow and overcome demons. As CEO of a company, she is strong and independent. I like this about her. She takes care of me. She was with me through my bout with cancer, she was with me when

I landed a VP position in New York making over a million dollars a year, and she was with me when that company fell prey to the same attacks that the other companies did and cut ties.

I remember the feeling of thinking I failed Heather in missing her signs or not catching what was wrong. I beat myself up over that for years thinking I was a failure. I wasn't, I didn't miss her crying for help at all. She wasn't.

Kelly: *"I became a widow at 29 years old when my husband passed away. Our son, Hagen, was 10 years old. I had the best in-laws a girl could ask for. They were loving and supportive, and we would meet with them every Friday for dinner. It was comforting, therapeutic and made Hagen and I feel less alone as we tried to figure out what our new normal would be. I had come from a broken home, my biological mother and my dad divorced when I was very young. My childhood was hard, especially when my parents didn't get along – it was a living nightmare. My biological mother used me as a pawn in their divorce, tried to make me believe my dad hated me and left me for another woman, kept me away from my father for months and then only allowed one weekend a month, one phone call a week, and that was recorded and timed. She'd unplug the house phone from the wall and hide it or take it with her when she left me home alone, so I couldn't call my dad. Any of this sound familiar yet?*

My mother remarried and my stepfather didn't like me because I looked like my dad. He made it clear I didn't fit in with them. He knew that if he could hurt me, it would also hurt my dad. My dad knew he couldn't do anything about it because the court system almost always sides with the mother. He would appear in court with picture evidence of child abuse, including photos of my head busted open with a broom handle as I was forced to stand in the front yard with my hands on the big pine tree and take my beating. Cars passed, no one stopped. I told whoever would listen; DFCS never came to my rescue. I even ran away after a really bad beating, found my way to my church and asked the ladies to call the police. I then called my dad and both he and DFCS showed up at my house and saw bruising all over my body, fresh whelps. I still had hair falling out from where my stepfather grabbed my head and dragged me across the house, posters had been torn off the walls, there were holes in my bedroom walls and my clothes destroyed. I was forced to stay there as my stepfather and Cheryl denied having done any of it and said that I had done it myself. I watched my dad pull out of the driveway and prayed to God to just let me get in the car with him. I'd never sin again if he'd just take me away from this Hell. It is devasting as a child when you're taught the police are there to help and protect, especially children. Years later, my dad borrowed money from my grandma for a lawyer after he received a letter I wrote saying I couldn't take it anymore and wanted to die. The letter was stained with tears. This was the breaking point. You see, my father's love and determination to protect me was immeasurable and unbreakable; I saw the same in Andy as he walked me through all he and the kids had been through thus far and how hard he was fighting.

It was a long time before I shared my childhood with Andy because it wasn't what defined me; I was an adult now after all. Those years were long gone. However, when I saw the EXACT same things going on with him and the boys, my heart broke and I told him everything I had endured as a young child and how it changed me and my relationship with my mother to this day. As I write this, it's been 14 years since I've seen her. I never thought I'd encounter another woman that could do the same things to her children that I was forced to endure. You can see the love and determination Andy has to protect his kids just like my dad had. I am thankful the boys have a dad like Andy; Lord knows you have to be tough as nails to go against everyone and be subjected to all they have been.

Andy and I had been dating a few months and my in-laws still weren't ready to meet him. It was difficult for them to see me with someone other than their son. I didn't push the issue and Andy respected their decision. We still had our Friday dinners and run-ins throughout the week. I kept them in the loop of what Hagen was up to, how he and Andy were getting along. And I was excited to be bonding with his kids. It came very naturally, especially with Lexi. She had quickly become my best bud and we spent hours in the bathroom fixing our hair, playing in makeup, having dress ups – she can wear my shoes and loves putting them on, making silly dances and singing made up songs. I cannot hold a tune and could tell she wanted to burst out laughing as it's now painfully clear I'm the only one in the house that can't sing but also the one that wants to sing all – the – time. And I do. Loudly.

Andy warned me early on that there were people harassing him and the kids, online and in public. He told me it was because they believed he killed his wife and were trying to get the police to arrest him. He said that I'd be a target when they found out we were dating and if I didn't want to move forward, he'd understand and always be my friend should I or Hagen ever need anything. I was shocked by this. It seemed like an episode of Punk'd. Where's Ashton Kutcher? I told him I didn't know who they were, but I wasn't scared of some bored housewives on a gossip blog rant. Bring it. All my social media is private and I'm a low-key person. I go to work and come home – nothing to hide. How naive I was. . . I'd learn the hard way how long their reach really was and how they'd stop at nothing to hurt anyone close to Andy.

I would be followed leaving Andy's house or wherever we met in town. My tires were slashed multiple times. I even saw Mende do it once at the school where the boys were having practice. Of course, I didn't have video so I couldn't prove it in court but did testify that I witnessed it. The judge laughed at me and dismissed it. I'll never forget the smart-ass smirk on her face when she laughed. She really does have everyone in her back pocket.

There was some type of Vaseline substance smeared all over my car twice and it has been keyed. My tag was run illegally resulting in my home address, phone number, tag number and place of employment being posted online for all to see, along with pictures of myself and my son. It was run by a female named Susan who was from Georgia, spent time in the military and was living in Indiana. I know this because she bragged about it on social media. She had no regard for breaking the law or endangering me and my son by doing this.

I was scared to sleep in my own home, was forced to install security cameras, extra lighting, upgrade all my locks, and buy a guard dog. I even thought about buying a new car. I'd check the doors and windows at least twice before going to sleep. It felt unreal. I was just dating this amazing man that loved his kids and we were happy. Why every time we went somewhere or posted something online would it be met with hate and threats? I'd constantly get calls and texts saying Andy was a murderer, that I'd be next, that he was an abusive man that beat his kids. But if you could see inside the home, all you would see is us having fun, joking, enjoying each other's company, game nights, movie nights, and cooking dinners.

One afternoon, we were outside playing wiffle ball with the kids. I had gotten dirty so when we went inside, I began digging through the laundry, looking for the smallest shirt of Andy's I could find. I found a shirt that would fit, it was Lexi's. She told me it was a family shirt, that everyone had the same one, and that I could borrow it. At one point in the night, I was being silly, and Andy snapped a picture of me and posted it online. Within hours, our phones were blowing up and there were posts everywhere online saying I was wearing Heather's shirt, trying to be her, and that Andy was making me dress up like her. The list went on and I was speechless. This would be repeated with my shoes. I have one brand of shoes that are my absolute favorite – Christian Louboutin – the famous red bottom shoes. I remember buying my first pair about a year and a half prior to meeting Andy. I wore them on our date nights, and he later posted some pictures of our time together. The posts said that not only had I worn Heather's shirt, but now I was wearing her shoes. What? Can't two women like the same brand of shoes? Not only were there multiple posts online, social media tags, phone calls, and text messages, but I received random notes in my mailbox. How crazy is that? All the notes and posts sounded the same but were equally unnerving. I'd be told that Andy was going to kill me, I'd be next, get out while I could, don't trust him, he's a murderer, manipulator, liar, a psychopathic narcissist, and will use me for my money or sex. You name it, it was said over and over. Calls to my boss were made saying the same things. I was involved with a criminal and needed to be let go. Jesus! I haven't done anything; I'm just dating Andy. I'm not sure why the firing squad had me in their scope, but Andy warned me. I could see why it ran people off. They had this down to a science and it was their goal to do all they could to disrupt his life, and anyone involved with him, all in the name of 'saving them.' Their version of saving someone was trying to wreck their lives and ask hundreds of questions to see if anyone would say something bad about Andy. All I had saw was a good man who was kind to me and my son and loved his family.

By that time, the gossip about who Andy was and allegations about what he had done were everywhere. There were posts out looking for people who might know me personally. When they found a few, they got to them, making them think I was in danger, and Hagen as well. They wanted to rally together to save me and took it a step further. People reached out to my dad and my in-laws to try and save us. Everyone I knew, plus people I'd never met, were contacting them telling lies about Andy, how Hagen and I were in danger. By that time, I had fallen in love with Andy and his family, so, of course I defended the man I loved because I knew what they were saying was wrong. My family and my friends, some of which I had known since middle school, all believed the websites and what complete strangers were telling them. My word, what I had seen, my daily accounts of how my life was going, how my relationship was, meant nothing to them. They chose to believe people without facts and whom they didn't know. So, I stopped communicating with them. Why should I try and convince someone of something they refuse to hear? I know my life, how Andy treats my son, his kids and me. I didn't care what the gossipers said. I let my in-laws go, stopped meeting for Friday dinners and the dust seemed to settle. That worked for a little while, until I started getting WellCare visits from DFCS saying they were getting anonymous calls. They were being told Hagen was in danger, malnourished, abused and neglected. They visited my home unannounced a couple of times and then closed the case.

I thought the worst was over.

My late husband passed away from Cirrhosis. He wasn't a huge drinker but had a fatty liver, ate like a college kid – grease, salt, fatty foods – and had a horrible family medical history which all contributed to his diagnosis. Neither one of us drank any alcohol, ate beef or had salt for 5 years after he was diagnosed. I went on the same strict diet he was given from his GI doctors to help him feel supported. After he died, I started drinking. First it was just on the weekends with dinner, but ultimately developed into my having a serious problem and I became a full-blown alcoholic. You think you're a functioning alcoholic until you get sober and realize you couldn't have even fooled Helen Keller. Andy stood by me the entire time I was struggling and did all in his power to help me. He was all I had at that point, and no one would have blamed him for leaving and saying it was too much for him to endure with everything else going on, but he didn't. He never let me down and stayed by my side the entire time. I knew something had to change fast or my son would watch his only surviving parent die the same way his father had. I checked myself into a 30-day rehab program. I signed notarized paperwork giving Andy authority to make decisions in my absence for my son. He was in a private Christian school at the time and Andy drove 30 minutes one way to make sure he got there on time. I wouldn't have been able to go to treatment and get sober without Andy. I'll forever be grateful to him for saving my life. I have no doubt that I'd be gone by now if it wasn't for him.

Within days of being in treatment I got news that my in-laws, my dad and my brother-in-law found out I went into treatment, leaving Hagen in Andy's care. Jumping on the opportunity while I was away, Margie, my mother-in-law, Doug, my father-in-law, my dad and Billy, my brother-in-law filed an emergency hearing for custody. Originally, my in-laws wanted grandparents' rights because I had stopped meeting them for dinners. They said it was my new boyfriend's fault, he was keeping us away from them, he was abusive, and my son was scared of him. They were told there weren't grandparent rights, so they changed the request to full custody.

Once the emergency custody hearing was requested, DFCS, the GBI, the FBI and the sheriff's department showed up at Andy's house demanding to see Hagen. Andy explained that I was in treatment, but he had the paperwork showing I, the only living parent, gave permission for Andy to watch over, care for and make any necessary decisions for him. It didn't matter. They were on a mission. Hagen was brought outside, crying, clinging to Andy's leg, and begging to stay with him. To no avail, Hagen was placed in the back of a cop car and taken to Margie and

Doug's house. I received a phone call from Andy moments after everyone left the house and was heartbroken. I felt helpless and as a parent it's the worst feeling in the world knowing you can't do anything to protect your child when that's your most important and precious job – protect, love, and keep them safe. Not only was my son missing me, but he had just been literally ripped from the closest thing he had to a father and taken to a place he hadn't been to in months, to people he hadn't spoken to, and he knew they didn't like Andy because they'd voiced it in front of him many times. We were all devastated and tried to find a way to stop the madness.

Three weeks later I had court. After three hours of sitting through a hearing, we hadn't spoken about Hagen or myself, but instead had spent time talking about Andy, Heather, his relationship with the kids, Mende – I'm thinking, I'm on the wrong Zoom call. A witness was called, Shawn Hitt. He was asked if he knew who I was, and he said no. He'd never seen me before but knows Andy and he threatened him at a traffic light years ago and "knows Andy is dangerous." The second witness was Lani Skipper; she also didn't know me but was called as an expert to testify. This whole fiasco was all about the hatred of one man, ANDY TURNER, and it was displayed through Lani, Shawn and everyone one on that side of the court. It had nothing to do with me and was completely unfounded. My head was spinning. Hagen's guardian ad litem testified that there was no reason for Hagen to be taken from his mother. I had completed treatment, had scheduled AA meetings and check-ins with the treatment center weekly and was not an unfit mother. You can't hold treatment against someone that voluntarily goes and succeeds. My lawyer pointed out that we'd spent hours talking about someone not named in the case nor even present in the courtroom. We won the court case, and I picked Hagen up that night. Since that day in court, I've never spoken to any of them again. I guess you do wrestle against flesh and blood. . . Family is most important to me, and I have fought for my family. My former family and so-called friends turned against me when they believed lies online and attempted to take my son away. Now Andy and I have been together for five years, married for over a year and all I have ever seen is a loving, caring family man that does not deserve what he has had to put up with.

In March of 2022, tragedy struck. I had bought a house, the first house I ever bought, and it was extremely important to me. I had made dinner, cleaned the kitchen, and was in the shower after a long day. I soon heard Hagen, who normally would have already been asleep, screaming, 'MOM! MOM!' I knew something was wrong. 'The house is on FIRE!' Everything went in slow motion and the silence took over. I couldn't feel the water hitting my body in the shower. I felt nothing except fear. I don't remember if I turned off the water or not, just that my tile floor was cold when my feet landed on it. I grabbed a towel but didn't put it on and ran to the living room. Hagen was standing by the dining room table. I saw a glow on his face, like it was light outside. That can't be right – it's after 8 p.m. – it should be dark. My brain wasn't registering what I was seeing was flames reflecting through the sliding door onto his face. I look over to where he's looking and see my back deck is on fire - the covered deck right underneath my son's room. I'm telling myself to wake up like I'm dreaming. I ran to the bathroom and grabbed my phone; my battery was at 10%. Perfect. I dialed 911. I ran back and forth from the kitchen / living room, to where the deck was, to my bedroom, which was on the other side of the first floor. I yelled to Hagen panicking because it seemed like forever before a dispatcher answered the phone. I can't recall all I said but was told that I needed to get out of the house with my son. I told the operator I had been in the shower and didn't have clothes on. Her reply was, 'I can assure you ma'am, we've seen worse.' I don't know why that's engrained in my memory but that's what she said, to go outside –

even if I was naked. Okay – let's go. I grabbed leggings and a sweatshirt off my bed, but again, didn't put them on. Everything was happening so fast, and my brain couldn't process it all fast enough. Hagen couldn't grab the dog. The dog thought we were playing a game of tag, so I tackled it as gently as possible and ran out. We stood in the driveway, and I watched as my beloved beautiful home continued to burn. The fire had reached the deck roof and continued to climb up the side of my house to my son's room. The roof caught fire. I didn't hear the fire truck sirens or see any lights as I watched pieces of my burning house land all over my car, yard, driveway. It rained black shit and debris and I was trying to process. I yelled at the lady 'Where the hell is everyone?!' I started to pray, pleading over and over. I've lost so much already, please not my home, too. Please Lord – PLEASE NO! I finally heard the sirens and hung up with dispatch. I felt a draft and looked down – I was still naked and people were starting to come out to see what the commotion was. I put on the clothes I didn't remember grabbing, feeling thankful it was dark outside. I called Andy, 'My phone is almost dead. My house is on fire, the firetrucks are almost here. No, this is not a joke.' He could hear my voice shaking and told me he was on the way. Four hours and multiple trucks later, the fire was defused, and I could see into my kitchen and living room from my driveway, my roof was gone. . . and I was in shock. The neighborhood had gathered around to ooh and ahh. In my panic, I forgot my rabbit, Larry, inside and none of the firefighters could tell me if they'd found him or if he was alive. Suddenly, here came a fireman holding Larry wearing a little oxygen mask – one made for an infant. Everyone made it out alive. Thank you, Lord.

Looking back, normally at this time of night Hagen was fast asleep. For some reason he couldn't fall asleep that night and kept tossing and turning. I truly believe God was watching over us, because if he had been asleep like he usually was, the fire would've overtaken him within minutes while he slept in his bed. I was on the bottom floor at the other end of the house, in the shower. By the time I would have realized the fire, it would have been too late for me as well. As I would have been trapped with no way of escape. The fire spread so fast and was uncontrollable. There's no doubt in my mind we're only alive because God was there protecting us.

I started a GoFundMe to help with expenses of getting the necessities while we went through the insurance process. I needed help. All we had were the clothes that were on our back; we didn't even have shoes on. The next day there were yet more posts. They were crushing to read. We were being blasted all over social media. There were rumors deemed as facts by the mindless excuses for humans that Andy burned down my house on purpose, because he had life insurance policies on both me and Hagen that he was going to cash in on, that he also had a homeowner's policy on my house, oh and the kicker, I was also IN THE SHOWER so it MUST have been Andy! Don't they know you can't have a homeowner's policy on a house you don't own? I bought that house myself. It was nothing but word vomit, and everyone was eating it up, smiling with a spoon in one hand and a pitchfork in the other. They said they hoped the investigators did their job this time and found Andy guilty of arson and attempted murder. That if they could get him in jail for something, that would be better than nothing. What the actual fuck?! I couldn't believe what I was reading. Then, I see comments under these posts and curiosity got the better of me. The most hurtful comments are the ones from none other than my late husband's family and my own father agreeing with all this rubbish. They thought Andy was behind it and seemed so worried for mine and Hagen's well-being and safety, but never reached out, wrote a letter or even donated a penny. Not that I would have taken it. Nothing. Not a 'fuck you.' Not a 'told you so.' Not a 'how can I help?' It must have slipped their mind after writing awful things about Andy online for the world to read.

The following weeks were packed with investigations by the fire marshal, fire chief, fire investigator, and a forensic expert for fires. Inspections were also done by an engineer and insurance representative from my insurance company and the solar panel company. They pulled wires from the walls to be sent off for testing in a lab, they tested the burned wood, took lots of photos. It was determined that the fire was started by a faulty wire. A FAULTY WIRE from where the solar panel company wired everything in. Not my boyfriend trying to kill me!

Word was out that the fire resulted from faulty wires, and that stirred up the hornets' nest again. Here come more posts. They said that Andy was angry that my son and I survived the fire and even more angry that now we must live with him, that he's making calls trying to find out if he can cash in on any homeowner's money – for the house he doesn't own and can't get a policy for. There's nothing those people can't spin. Nothing. I wish I had this much extra time, but I'd spend it with my family, not spreading gossip about people I don't know. Two kinds of people, I guess. I guess the saying is true: People throw rocks at things that shine. The more you shine, the bigger the rocks get. What they haven't figured out yet is the more we get knocked down, the stronger we are when we get up."

Crazy enough, Kelly's unfortunate event increased my death threats. I got a call as I was driving one day and the person on the other end of the line identified himself as a federal agent. I had no idea if it was or not. He named two people, and asked me if I had ever heard of either of them. I had not. He told me they had made comments and threats to my life, and they deemed the person to want to make good on those threats. They recommended that my family and I leave for a few days and go out of town. Talk about unnerving. I wasn't sure how to take that. We had security, what if this guy was wanting us to leave so he could rob the house? Heck, I wasn't sure what to think. I really didn't want to have a full self-defense issue at the house with the family present. We slid out for a few days, I never told anyone about the call. We were having fun, making it a long weekend. I got a call, and the same guy was on the phone. He said, 'I hope you are enjoying the mountains; you and your family are safe to return home.' When I hung up, I felt an opossum run over my grave and just sat there for a moment. I am sure that non-southerners have no idea what that phrase means. Let me help teach you. Have you ever had something happen so creepy, scary, or ominous and you get this shiver that's out of the blue? When my grandfather Pawpaw used to do this, he always said 'Shew, an opossum ran over my grave.' So now you've learned some southern, that makes you part southern. Be careful, you will start talking in shorter sentences soon.

When we got home, I was bummed and frustrated with the roller-coaster I had been on. Feel good, feel bad, feel good, get let down. Then I received more bad news. Sickness hit again, another cancer diagnosis. I hid the first one from the family so they wouldn't worry and went to treatments and came home sick and pushed through and still did all the things needed. This time I wasn't able to hide it, I had someone too close, who cared enough to ask questions and be nosy. As I write this, we had been married for over a year. She was my partner, my best friend. Over the past five years of getting to know each other, things had been refreshing. I was so sick of the silence. It was good to hear conversation and a heartbeat again.

Chapter Twenty

Kidnapping

"...here is how I felt about that. You may have slept with my mother, but that didn't or wouldn't make you my dad. My dad raised me, loved me, cared for me, protected me, taught me. He is and will forever be my Superman."
-Lexi Turner

I think the greatest fear of any parent must be hearing that your child is missing. I could not imagine what it would feel like for a parent to have no idea where their child is, who has them, and what is happening to them. I remember growing up hearing stories about the Lindbergh baby, and Adam. Those drove fear in not only my parents' heart, but mine as well, even as a kid. I recall walking from my house to Paw-Paws house and picking up a garbage can lid; it was metal and had the flop handle on it. I yelled, "If any bad guys are out there, I am Captain America and I have my shield with me." In my mind, this struck fear in the heart of a would-be kidnapper. In our family people tried to do it legally!

One evening, the kids and I were in the front yard in a hexagon pattern throwing a frisbee to each other. I looked up to the familiar sight of the PCSO pulling up. A couple of officers stepped out and one said loudly, "Well, this is it. They have finally got you. You're about to lose your daughter."

The kids heard what he was saying. Confused, Lexi asked, "What did he say?"

He kept going, "She's going to be living with someone else."

Lexi fell to the grass and started crying. Here they were again, doing all they could to trigger me to get a reaction. And they got one. I'll not repeat the colorful language that was chosen to tell him to get off my property in a prompt way. I was more than upset. Who does that to a child? I was left with a stack of papers about four inches thick and the kids asking questions. We walked inside so I could figure it all out.

The pages were littered with a name that would become a nightmare for my family.

Cindy.

Cindy was Heather's aunt, although she wasn't related by blood. They weren't close at all as, according to Heather, Cindy was a heavy drinker, and she didn't like to be around her. For this reason, Heather was adamant about her not being around Lexi.

As I read, I discovered what was happening. Cindy, who was not even liked by Heather, had petitioned the court for full custody of my daughter. She believed I was an unfit parent, making allegations of abuse, molestation, showing her porn, not feeding her, and claimed I was never even married to Heather, and was potentially not even the father to Alexis.

That was a lot to take in, especially coming from someone who I had seen maybe three times in all my years with Heather. Lexi had seen her maybe twice. It was absurd, but hey, if you give lawyers money, they will take it, and file a case just to see what happens.

I knew where she had gotten her misinformation about Heather and me not being married. It had been shared on one of the Andy-hater sites and mentioned on one of the TV stations. I never knew the details, but learned throughout the trial. Some of Heather's boyfriends had planted the seed of a story in all the right places.

My long-time friend Gary, whom Heather got to sign our marriage certificate, was subpoenaed. It was believed that his signature was a forgery. One thing I knew about Gary, he was a good man. He was a godly man. He would tell the truth. I called him, apologized that he was caught up in this mess, and asked him if he had signed the certificate. He said he had not. I thanked him for letting me know.

The next day when he entered court, I hugged Gary. I absolutely hurt in my soul that he even had to be there. I was embarrassed. The lawyer asked him if I had called him, and he said I did. She asked him what I had said, he told her I asked if he had signed the certificate.*

Heather had not only told me that she had taken the paper to be signed by Gary, she was also excited that he had done it for us. They were properly filed, only she knew what she had done, and she was telling other men this like it was her escape plan. The court ruled that it did not matter that he didn't sign it, we lived as married from the date of filing, we filed tax returns, we lived together, we wore rings, and we both claimed to be married. This meant we were considered married to the court.

Cindy's claims were outlandish. She believed I was molesting my daughter based on a Christmas photo Heather took some four years earlier when she was little and going to sleep. I was snuggled up with her in our bed, it's a beautiful and loving picture that her mother took. This was the evidence she submitted for that horrendous claim. Cindy absolutely knew she was lying and on the stand even admitted she got "carried away" and overtold things to get this filed. Her allegations were total bullshit that slandered and defamed.

Lexi- *"This was hard for me. I lost my mom. I was forced to leave my friends and go to a new school. I had to not play soccer, tennis, and basketball, because people asked my dad not to come or because they wanted to make problems around me and the boys that Dad felt was unsafe. Now they were trying to take my dad and brothers from me. This person I don't even know!*

We got to court and Cindy showed photos of a bedroom and teddy bears and said that was my new room. What kind of evil person would ever want to do this to a little girl? She even went so far as to say my father did despicable things. What kind of person does this? What kind of person tries to ruin someone's life just to hurt another person? Then having other people say they are or could be my dad? This had me worried and scared they would take me from my dad and brothers.

Well, here is how I felt about that. You may have slept with my mother, but that didn't or wouldn't make you my dad. My dad raised me, loved me, cared for me, protected me, taught me. He is and will forever be my Superman. I am glad that nightmare is over, or at least that part. I hope one day the world hears and knows how they stopped the sound of playing, cheering, and laughter and filled it with dullness. A silent numbness that we despise."

All the factors of this particular hearing were heavy. They were heartbreaking, unnecessary, and unfounded. Cindy had people wearing matching shirts parading around outside, causing a scene. In the meantime, we're worried if a court that had been one-sided against me would allow my daughter, who had known nothing else since birth, to be stripped away because someone hired a lawyer and started telling lies. I looked back to see many of Mende's cronies in attendance. They paraded some photos through the court making allegations that Lexi could have been fathered by any one of the guys in the photographs. The court took a recess and ordered me to take Lexi for a DNA test and return at 9 a.m. the next day.

Let me explain what was happening. I was terrified. They had created doubt. At this point, I knew Heather had been unfaithful, but I initially thought it had been recent. Now I was learning that it has been throughout our entire marriage. Lexi was being dragged through the consequences of her mother's actions yet again. If we took the DNA test and I wasn't her father, she would be ripped away from all she knew, all she loved, and from the people who loved her. That was a miserable thought to me.

I picked up Lexi as an awful thunderstorm rolled in. As I drove, the wipers could not keep up with the rain coming down. This was how my heart felt, my car being flooded with harm. As I looked over to Lexi, I saw she was crying about as hard as it was raining.

"What's wrong, baby girl," I asked, already knowing the answer.

"Dad, what if tomorrow I have to go and live somewhere else?"

We both cried as we drove. I called Pastor Martin and he answered quickly.

"Pastor, I need you to pray for something. If you've ever gotten a prayer through, I need this to definitely be one."

He asked what we were going through and listened, obviously troubled by what he was hearing. I've always respected Pastor Martin. Anytime that I went to him, I appreciated the advice and counsel that he gave me. That time I appreciated his friendship and his prayer. He didn't wait until I hung up to pray, he prayed right then. I took comfort in hearing his voice praying because I wasn't able to. I was bitter and angry. You know that one verse in the Bible that says if you can't forgive others, God won't forgive you and He won't hear your prayers? I was truly having a hard time forgiving the people who were attacking me. It had always made me angry when they attacked my family and they hurt my children, but now, I was furious. And I was fearful. I had no idea if the next day my daughter was going to be mine or not.

I had been there since the day she was born. I had picked out all the pink a baby girl could own. I had been the one to comfort her and love her. I was there when she took her first step. I was there when she first rolled over. I had watched her grow into the most beautiful young lady there ever was. Now, due to the decisions that my wife made she could be plucked out of my arms and sent home with a complete stranger. I would have no way of knowing if this new person had good intentions or if Lexi would be placed directly in harm's way.

When we arrived at the office, we were both crying as we approached the counter. The lady behind the desk looked concerned. I explained to her what the court had ordered and that we had to have the results back to the court by the next day. She swabbed us and we walked out, both still crying.

I did not sleep at all that night. I sat up all night, worried to the point of being physically sick. The next morning, we made our way to the Paulding County Courthouse, a place I truly despise. I entered the courtroom and sat down beside my lawyer. The room quickly filled with noise and giggling as a parade of little matching shirts made their way in.

It was almost time for court to begin when my phone started buzzing. I had the ringer off as they tend to get upset about ringing phones when court is in session. I answered it and heard a kind voice on the other end.

"I'm not supposed to be calling you, but you and your daughter touched my heart so much," said the lady from the DNA office. "I have the couriers on the way up right now to take the paper to the judge, but I wanted to let you know that you are Lexi's father."

When I heard this, I was overwhelmed with emotion. I slid back in my seat and could not control the tears. My lawyer looked at me with a look that said, what the heck is wrong with you?

"I'm the dad," I said and turned around to the people seated behind me. I just gave a thumbs-up because I was not able to form a word at that moment. The judge came in and read the results. He then reprimanded Cindy for her misuse of social media and told her she was not to use any form of media to spread lies or speak badly of me or my family. What is she doing right now? She's on social media and TV talking bad and putting herself in Contempt of Court. Court should be taken seriously and handled in a professional manner. Everything should be documented and factual and presented in a logical way. I am often amazed at how people will enter a courtroom and tell lies but are so gung-ho to take someone down that they overlook details and present a sloppy case. This almost always leads to their demise. And how will she defend what's printed and recorded after a judge ordered her to stay quiet? I would expect her to deny having posted anything and play the *anyone could have logged into my account* scenario. However, actually recording herself, that she is going to have a tough time defending.

I loved watching Superman as a kid, in my mind the good guys always won and evil always lost. In real life it's not that way. But in this case, she failed in the kidnapping and exposed herself in her quest for destruction of a family. As have they all. They only succeeded in bringing sadness and causing those moments of hurt. Like Christ over three days, Superman always came back. Our family is as the phoenix. We emerge from the ashes stronger, tougher, and united in our love as a family that refused to succumb to the subjection of misery. Who are WE? Turners!

*Complete court transcripts can be found under 18-cv-002306-P3, signed Dec. 12, 2018 02:27 p.m.

II.   Defendants' Relationship to the Child

As shown by DNA evidence, Defendant is the biological father of the minor child at issue in this case. Plaintiff has submitted argument and testimony questioning the validity of the marriage between Defendant and the child's mother, Heather Turner. The Court finds that a marriage certificate for Andy and Heather Turner was filed with the probate court on February 1, 2011, and that Andy and Heather Turner held themselves out as a married couple from that date forward. Even assuming *arguendo* that a forged signature or self-officiated ceremony rendered the marriage invalid or subject to attack, the minor child at issue was born prior to any declaration that the marriage was invalid and it would make no sense to conclude and would be against public policy to conclude that Defendant was not the legal father of this legitimate child. See Hall v. Coleman, 242 Ga. App. 576 (2000).

In determining what is in the best interest of the minor child in this case, the Court first looks at each party's knowledge and familiarity of the child and her needs, along with the love, affection, bonding and emotional ties existing between each party and the child. Plaintiff, although maintaining a close relationship with the child's mother, Heather, has only seen the minor child at issue a handful of times over the past nine years. Plaintiff contends this is because Defendant has not allowed her to foster and develop a strong relationship with the child. Nevertheless, based upon the testimony received, the Court does not find familiarity, strong bonding, or emotional ties between the Plaintiff and the minor child. The Court further notes the findings of the Guardian ad Litem concerning the limited relationship between Plaintiff and the child.

Defendant, on the other hand, is the biological and legal father, and indeed the only father figure the minor child has ever known. The child has lived with Defendant since her birth and he has been her sole caregiver since the passing of the child's mother. Defendant demonstrates the expected knowledge and familiarity with the child one would expect given their relationship. In addition, there appear to be strong emotional ties, love, affection and bonding between Defendant and the child. The Guardian ad Litem reports that Defendant appears to be a good father based on his investigation to date. The child is actively involved in school, making good grades, and reported by the school to be "content, happy, and roundly accepted among staff and peers."

Neither party is to make disparaging comments concerning the other party to the child or where the child can overhear them. Neither party is to use social media to make disparaging comments about the other party.

Chapter Twenty-One

Behind The Veil

"My Mom died in April too..."
"I hate this month"
"Oh, God, I might be dying"

A veil is such a significant item. The very word has multiple meanings which are bouncing inside my head. For my free thinkers, get ahead of me, and let your mind race at what a veil is and what it's used for. I am going to break it down for you to explain what I am trying to expound in this chapter.

Veil #1

First, let's go to the Bible. The Veil was in the Temple, and it separated people from the Holy of Holies. Only the high priest could enter the area behind the veil. He would enter this place where the Ark of the Covenant was sitting and there, he would make the sacrifices for the people for the atonement of their sins. The people, anyone other than the priest, did not have access to the area to pray and get in touch with God. In fact, the high priest would tie a rope to his leg before entering and the reason for this was simple, if he had sin in his life that was not confessed and dealt with and entered into the realm where the Holy Spirit was present, he would die. Since no one else but the high priest could enter, they would have to use the rope to pull his body out.

Now fast forward.

When Jesus was on the cross and he had uttered the last and seventh saying from the cross, in his tongue, he yelled tetelestai (τετέλεσται), or "It is finished" and "Into Thine hands, I commit My Spirit." After this event the Bible teaches us of a great eclipse, the rocks rent themselves, and the earth began to quake, but something special happened here. The VEIL was rent (torn) in two, but it was torn in a unique manner, from the top to the bottom. Why is this significant? When Jesus died on the cross, God tore the veil in the Jerusalem temple from top to bottom. Only God could have done such a thing because that veil was 60 feet tall and four inches thick. What once was a symbol that said, *Keep out! Keep Out!* Now says, *Come in!* You can now come boldly before the throne of God with your supplications. "Come unto me ye that are heavy laden, and I will give you rest." I do not have an agenda to offend anyone religiously, but I will say this act did away with the priesthood. There was no longer a need for a priest to go behind the veil; we do not need to confess our sins before man because we now have direct access to an almighty GOD.

Veil #2

I also recall a veil in one of my favorite childhood movies and current Broadway musical. I would assume everyone in the world, except Karli Land, has seen The Wizard of Oz and the musical adaptation Wicked!

You have members come before the throne of the mighty, great, and powerful Wizard of Oz to make their supplications. One little pupper runs over to the veil (curtain) and pulls it aside and you see a mere man running the contraption that is the Wizard of Oz. The veil hid the true identity of the wizard. It was a covering, a cloth, that separated you from seeing what was really taking place so that you only saw the illusion that was being cast in front of you. Having learned a deep understanding of *the veil* in seminary, and having had the opportunity to go to Jerusalem and stand where Solomon's temple once stood, gave me a clearer understanding of what God meant for the purpose of the veil. I was able to witness the actual place where God rent the veil. Still, I was happy when Toto pulled the curtain back and exposed the little old man that was pretending to be the great and powerful Oz.

Veil #3

And last, my happiest moment was when a woman came walking into a room where I stood, wearing a veil over her face because tradition says it's bad luck to see your bride before you are married. This veil is in place to obscure the view until that moment after the vows are said and it is time.

I have had to pause in writing this, as I'm sitting on a Delta flight on a 757-200 at 38,003 feet in the air, going over 600 mph, and I am weeping out loud with passengers looking at me. Picture what I saw. Heather and I exchanged our own vows that we had written. The promises that we made before an almighty God to each other. Now it's time. I reach over and take that white lace veil with designs that are as clear in my mind's eye now as they were to my eyes at that moment. I pull it up to reveal a slender and beautiful neckline and observe her breathing heavily. I see her chin and her beautiful, perfect soft lips, pink with the lipstick she chose. Her white teeth smiling so big! And then those eyes. Set like wolf eyes, sometimes grey and sometimes blue. Always breathtakingly beautiful. Now I see her whole face. So beautiful and perfect. We both began to cry from overwhelming emotions as we hugged and kissed. That veil never went back over her angelic face again. I didn't want it to. I loved looking at her.

That wasn't the last veil though. You see, Heather had a veil I was oblivious of. The other three veils, when removed, made me excited and happy, and I loved what I saw and learned. But this veil had an extremely opposite effect. It was crippling, hurtful, and left a lifelong void. When this veil was removed and I could see inside, I saw a world she had been living in without me.! A world that she had created, and I wanted to forget it existed once I learned it was there. A world of men and lies. A world of stories and promises. A world of photos of her, which was sacred to me. A world that shattered our world as husband and wife.

You see in this chapter I show some of Heather's and my personal life. Our communications between a husband and a wife. Moments that are tender and raw and real. You never hear a woman saying she's leaving, you hear her say she loves, appreciates, and needs me. I left out the things of sexual nature for decency but she would openly share her desires. And she shared her hurts also. Do you know who has the entire list of these texts other than me? PCSO. They have her phone still today with the last photo she took of us on it that I was promised and never given. The GBI, the FBI, and Secret Service have access to every one of our texts. Not once does she say she was leaving. She was never harmed or upset. We were happy in our lives. Behind that veil was a woman having affairs and telling lies. Heather wrote emails to men and people have now claimed those allegations as facts, saying that the words are Heather speaking from the grave. Yet what she said to those men changed with each guy she wrote and was never anything that she spoke to me.

I tell you emphatically, she was never leaving her husband and children and the life she had, especially for someone living with his mommy. She got caught in that world as it collapsed on her, that is what my heart believes. Along with the hurts she had, she made a choice that we still feel today. That hurt me and hurt the kids in many ways. She made a choice for us.

In this screenshot, you can see a portion of a photo of me in the driver's seat. Heather had called to tell me to put on my seat belt. And, of course, I did as she asked! We talked quite a bit on this day. I was working in a new position after leaving my job in Canada to be home more, but had several weeks of training. She told me that she had a hard time with me leaving on this particular day because Pop's health was in decline.

I knew she was having a difficult time with Pop about to die, and it was near the anniversary that she found her mother dead. The entire week, I made sure to tell her often that she was loved and appreciated. I tried in small ways to plant the seeds that she was cared for. You can see I mentioned her hugs from that morning. We often had coffee together before I left on trips and we would sit and talk. On this morning she got a little emotional about me leaving and got up and just hugged me. It was one of those hugs where you just hold on and bury your head. I just held her and kissed the top of her head. You see her response: "Thank you, honey, I greatly appreciate all that you do and all of your love. I love you, too!!"

I know for years many people have heard and believed so many things that were not true. People have said that she had been planning for a year to leave me and the kids. There was not a day that she ever told me any such thing. In fact, every day she told me she loved me and appreciated me. Every day was affectionate. I chose to release these screenshots to prove the point that you cannot believe everything you're told. I thought we had a great marriage. It devastated me when I learned of not just one affair but many and how long the affairs had been going on. Heather made me believe she loved me and was a faithful, loving, and caring wife.

I asked her if she was wearing the green dress again. It was one of my favorites. She had gotten up early just to spend time with me that morning. This was a norm when I was leaving so, we could spend time together. I hated that I would miss seeing her in that dress. She always looked good in it.

Yes sir, was her regular response. I also said ma'am to her. It was part of teaching the kids and just how we did things. I remember thinking as I was driving about what all I miss out on being gone. Us men that travel do miss a lot of the family time and the little things. She offered some encouragement by reminding me it was only for a couple of days.

When I arrived at Park n Fly, I let her know I was there. She responded that she was glad I was safe. We talked when I was on the plane, like usual, and when I landed.

I'm sharing this one as it tells an important story. We had talked, and Pop was about to die. I couldn't get my commercial flight changed, so, unbeknownst to her, I chartered a private jet to bring me home. That's what I am referring to when I ask, "Do you realize how much I love you?" I was making every effort and would have done anything to get to her so she had support during that hard time. My plan was to surprise her with the early trip home later that night when we spoke.

She wrote "I'm sad" and I knew she was hurting. I was trying to be extra supportive. I lost my grandad and grandmother. It's tough. I asked her how I could help.

I have thought about this text a lot. I have wondered about it. She said, "I don't think you can help this time, babe." I always was a fixer and tried my best to make sure she and the kids had everything and didn't have any heartbreaks. Sometimes we are just powerless. I assumed when I read it that she meant I couldn't do anything about Pop dying. It likely was. But could it have also meant more? Had she already felt the walls caving in after she had the meeting to be released from her job? Was it from the fear of her private emails going public?

Again, for the people who choose to just believe what they are told.

This whole exchange is pretty self-explanatory. Her willingness to feed me cheese and nuts doesn't sound like an exit strategy. Sounds like a good wife telling me about healthy options to eat and us being playful and flirty. This happens to be the same day that people reported that she was locked in a room and held down. That's quite a talent from halfway across the country. But these people always have the "facts."

I am picking up from previous texts and calls here on this one. I'm telling her she's most important. Again, we're talking about my work trip and me coming home to which Heather responds, "I will need you when something happens." This is her saying, "Work today, but I'll need my husband to depend on when Pop dies."

I replied, "I'll be there, always."

Look at Heather's response. "I know."

Do you know how she knew? Because in all the time we had been together, I had been consistent. I had been there. I had displayed love and not just verbalized it. This is why those imbeciles, with no facts, who slander and say she was harmed and mistreated, look absolutely foolish. Sadly, when they put that out there, their people gravitate to this and go burn candles and buy purple shirts and put out purple lights and threaten our family. Heather was loved and adored always in this house. And she KNEW it. People with supposed "facts" are boldly stating what they "KNOW" as if they were in our home. If they were, they would have different statements. Never was there a complaint, a report, a bruise, or an allegation until she died of her own volition. Then, from boyfriends and family, this comes out to slander and hurt our family and for six years they have thought this is acceptable behavior. Heather did not care for them. She lied to all of them just as she did our family. She was never leaving her home, kids, security, and husband. Especially for someone who was living with his parents because he couldn't even support himself and today is living with his sister. He couldn't afford Heather's hair appointments or makeup alone. People who grew up and didn't have dates to the prom and lacked social prowess are naive enough to believe whatever they are told. I am guessing that he is the type that would go to a strip club and think the dancers are really in love with him. I believe that if they hadn't pressed her and if she hadn't feared that her private life was about to be made public, I honestly feel in my heart that she would not have chosen the path that she did.

We had been talking about my flight and she mentioned she had ordered a naughty teacher outfit with glasses. That's the beginning conversation. She had told me she was looking forward to wearing this for me when I returned home.

Then you see me asking how she is, and asking not for the masked answer but how she is really doing. I knew she was hurting over Pop like anyone losing a grandparent. She had always displayed strength and being level headed. I responded with support and love, as you can see.

She sent a photo of Pop resting. He was very sick. She tried to call me but I was in flight.

"My Mom died in April too..."

"I hate this month"

"Oh, God, I might be dying"

You can see through these texts that her mental state was really sliding. Her mom's death of an overdose, Pop dying, and dealing with the surfacing of her multiple lives was bubbling.

I didn't know how to respond to this as these texts were out of character for Heather. I asked if she needed anything and told her I was sorry. She replied, "Lol," obviously a smart-ass reply. I called her immediately. I said, "Honey. I realize you're going through a lot. I don't have the words, I don't know what to say to comfort you, I am at a loss. I didn't mean to upset you; I am here and I'm trying." You could hear frustration, hurt, and anguish in her voice. She was crying and talking about her mom, and Pop, then she wanted to know where I was. She scolded me to not text because obviously, she was on edge. I got to her and when I walked in, she ran to me, buried her head, and cried on my shoulder. I held her for what seemed like 30 minutes, not moving, just holding her as she bounced and cried and grieved. When she pulled back, she kissed my cheek softly and said, "I missed you so much."

The next day was a busy day. We talked a lot. I sent one text, as I had been scolded prior. It was simply... "Just wanna say I love you."

This is May. Heather is back at work and trying to get back into a routine. She says she loves me. Tells me to please be safe. Her apology is for the late response as she had to wait for bathroom breaks to use her phone.

I always told her she was precious cargo. She was.

This was two days before she passed away. You never see anything negative. There's never an, "I'm leaving." Never anything but love and care and normal interaction. People without the facts should hang their heads for the lies they have told. This is two-way communication, undisputed, and the other half of the conversation is on her phone, in police possession. They have the facts.

Heather was sent home from work this day. I did not know until later in the day that she had been asked to come in the following day to give a decision on whether she would leave voluntarily or be fired. She made the plan to spend this day shopping and preparing for our dinner together. In our last group of texts, Heather's last text to me was simply, "Love u." For the remainder of that day, nothing seemed out of the ordinary. We have photos of that night that our daughter took. Obviously, you can see the happiness, love, and fun we shared. What you can't see is the pain, or plan she was hiding behind those eyes.

She planned our meal and this night in advance. It is not a coincidence that she lined all of these up as she did and when she did. I have no doubt that it was thought out on her part to let me know she cared but felt trapped in the situation she created. She had made mistakes, but she wanted to show she loved me.

Chapter Twenty-Two

Life's University-
Conclusion

"...each time I asked myself, 'Why is it that people do the things they do,'
I immediately answered those questions with, 'Why is it I do the things
I do?' My conclusion: Listen intently. Be kind. Love with all my might,
and give thanks daily to my God."
-Andy Limbaugh

That one single day and event brought on by the decision of one person has altered my life and my children's lives indefinitely. In looking back at all I have learned, gathered, and obtained, I think I have a solid grasp of what led to that decision by Heather, although I do not claim to know everything. No one was closer to her than this family. Those that are speaking the loudest are the ones with little knowledge and limited exposure, yet they are the ones so willing and eager to turn up the silence on those they try to destroy. I do realize much more information could be out there that Heather had hidden. But we, as a family, are not seeking to learn any more or add to our heartbreak with the wrecking ball of multiple lives she lived. It is without doubt that Heather lived a double life, and she did this very effectively and efficiently. To be able to convince so many people they were important to her, she used her wit, personality, and body to gain whatever it was she gained. She did this all while others viewed her as the perfect thing, she had created herself to be for them. We, as her family, thought she was the perfect wife and mother, all while other men were convinced that she was in love with them as well. What is sad in this story was the life she created was what also seemed to be a large part of what destroyed her.

Another bit of reasoning that I have drawn to a conclusion is that one of her God-given gifts was also her curse. God made Heather extremely beautiful, and this got her a lot of attention. I always felt she handled this attention appropriately. She would come to me and share about who had hit on her, she brought me cards that had been given to her, she told me stories and we laughed together. I told tell her that I was not a jealous man; I was secure in the love of our marriage, and I knew where she slept at night, even on the days I was gone providing for the family. That security I had in how she handled things was her cover-up. It kept me at bay, and I never felt like I had to check or doubt her. Her beauty was her curse as men could not resist hitting on her daily and she couldn't resist the attention or the thrill of sneaking around. Based on some of the notes I have read and a few I still have in my possession, I believe that many of the men were getting too attached and she could no longer control the secrets of the world she had created. This, coupled with a firing brought to light all her emails and why she was really fired. Our family believes she was afraid our family would discover what she was doing behind our backs, and I don't think she wanted to face that or endure the devastation that would cause. I will never understand how she could talk so badly about me which was obviously a ploy to gain sympathy, money, and possessions from those men, and then come home with so much love for me and the kids, cooking dinner, playing and laughing so seamlessly. I was married to a master of illusions.

I have learned a lot about myself through this in being publicly burned in effigy and seeing what I thought were friends, good people, and even family turn and stab me in the back. People I loved and respected, former pastor friends who publicly posted on those sites and would preach against gossip while doing it. We had many people tell us they loved us and supported us and then talk bad about us behind our backs. I had to endure hearing people say they hoped I went to jail and didn't care what happened to the kids. We've had to sort out things destroyed and be in constant awareness of who was going to try and harm us or vandalize us next. I struggled in many ways. You see, they do not make a handbook on how to deal with all hell breaking loose in your life. There isn't a *living through my spouse's suicide while being publicly blamed by her family, lovers, and bandwagon jumpers* for dummies book.

I struggled as a man. I wanted to give up many times. I struggled in my faith, and that's why this book was written with the words and raw emotions as it was when things happened. I wanted you to see my humanity, my failures, my hardships, my lack of knowledge to handle situations as a father and a man. I wanted to show that I made every effort to make right decisions and how I failed to do so. Also, as you see how I was affected in my spirit and mind, and it took a toll on my physical health, you can see me rise from the ashes and never give up because my love for my family is greater than the hatred of this world.

My love for my children was the sole purpose to strive and endure the shots, so they wouldn't have too, so they could have an easier walk through the fires. Through those very children I have learned some valuable lessons. Martha King, who I talked about in the first chapter, made an impact on my life. Yes, she was different, unique, but her loving way changed me forever. My children brought me back to another King I met as a six-year-old boy under a Christmas tree after a Christmas play pricked my heart and the Holy Spirit drew me in. Yes, I had a head knowledge and more than most. Yes, I knew what to do. But when that failed and that very church structure was used as a tool to destroy our family, it turned to bitterness, anger, and frustration. I am thankful that my children realized I just needed a little bit more time with The King to get myself back on track. We have been trusting Him to correct and guide us through this maze of hell ever since.

I have a renewed faith in my God and His love for me and our family. I can see his hand as I look back, leading and guiding and orchestrating. I didn't realize it then, but I can explain to you now where He was and how He intervened. I learned like Moses in the desert, Elijah in the wilderness, and Job as he endured suffering, and even Christ on the cross, alone and forsaken. But these feelings are emotions and not facts, as we were never alone. God allowed the separation from church people and churches. He used family, friends, and jobs, not to hurt and destroy me, but to separate me from toxic things that were going to anchor me down so He could lift me up and bless me in His way. I believe as much as I absolutely despised every moment of going through this, God will get honor and glory and others will be encouraged. I believe lives will be saved from suicide, families helped, court battles prevented, but mostly the feeling of hopelessness and despair will be dissipated.

Proverbs 16:9 says, "A man's heart deviseth his way: but the LORD directeth his steps."

When I was bitter and angry, when I wanted to give up, and when I was at death's door, God was leading me to this moment, for this moment, at such a time as this. Why did my family and I have to suffer? Because maybe one of you is struggling in some capacity and at the brink of giving up. Maybe you are contemplating ending it all and our story shows you that your family IS NOT better off without you. That you are special, needed, and loved. That your decisions can hurt the people you love way more than you ever imagined. I believe in my heart if Heather knew that those men, her family members, and the Jethros who in her name took cause against HER family, she wouldn't have done what she did. I do believe that the kids and I were her greatest love, but her warped sense of an exciting life took the lead.

I want to say this as well: when you see people, spread love. Everyday spread love, you may not know what that person is going through and the hell they are enduring, and your simple act can be a catalyst to encourage that person or prevent them from making a bad decision. When people hate you and seek to destroy you, love anyway. I responded to many people in many fashions — some ignorance, some anger, and some hostility — and this bred more of the same. I realized I was spreading seeds that would harvest one day and I did not want to plant that field in my life. I want to spread love and if it's met with hate and guile, that's on them but I will not let their energy hold me down. It's not worth it. Stress is a killer. When people lie, I no longer feel it is owed a response. If you let them lie long enough, they will prove you right. For years I read how they knew, KNEW, that any day would be the day they would come get me and haul me away in cuffs. They knew it! They did not know anything. I knew I had done nothing wrong as did my family, and we knew we had truth on our side.

Little Hill told me that he would never close this case unless I did exactly what he wanted, which was to sit in the same place where that very department committed child abuse and child endangerment even though their oath was to protect and serve and be "formally" interviewed. I know without doubt what this game is and how he would love to have my words that could be twisted and manipulated. So, if that means he won't close the case, so be it. He can sit on those cell phones and play those Xboxes. I view abusing power and harassment as a crime, even if you're wearing a badge.

You have created enough silent screams and silent moments in my life.

Our family decided to go back to my hometown. I always loved living there, the schools, the people. Yes, there are a few there that lack the ability to think for themselves and I determine someone's character based off of how they treat others. I don't judge others because of what someone says about them. I am capable of analysis and deciding what I choose to think. So many people want to take others' opinions of what they think about someone and adopt them as their own. Why would they do that? That other person may be motivated to that opinion by negative or evil means, and here you have jumped on board and encouraged that behavior and made it stronger for the wrong. That shows a person's total inability to think for themselves. Some people in my hometown who have known me for over 35 years, who I have never had a cross word with and only been kind to, have posted hateful things or shunned me in person. I chalk it up to the inability to think and reason on their own and believe it has more to do with them than me. A look back at how I have treated them, and a conversation should be all it takes to clear any elephant in the room.

We bought a large tract of land with the sole purpose of going back home. The plan was to build and give the kids a safe haven. We recently completed a 10,000-square-foot garage, because I had this dream garage in my mind. The boys and I have created some businesses that we plan to launch and develop. So, we have control of life and destiny. Mostly, we just want peace, to love our lives, and find a new normal and happiness.

When the garage was completed, our entire family walked out in the middle of the property and stood. There were birds chirping, geese flying overhead, the wind gently blowing through the trees and across the ponds, and the ripples were hitting the banks creating tiny splashes. Tree frogs were croaking in the distance. We had a family of deer that were grazing, which we see out here every day. There we stood, eyes closed and listened, standing in a circle with my family, hearing and feeling the happiness we share together. Hearing laughter, hearing the very voices that endured for this moment of breaking the silence.

Afterword

"In this book, you will experience the highs and lows of a family that endured tragedy. Where some would have folded; through faith, they are choosing to move forward. Suicide and depression are REAL! Let's talk! As a creative, I've seen and heard several stories. This book is part of the healing process for Andy and the kids."
-Edward Perkins | PerxWerx Music LLC

https://988lifeline.org
The 988 Lifeline provides 24/7, free and confidential support for people in distress, prevention and crisis resources for you or your loved ones, and best practices for professionals in the United States.

Acknowledgements

This book has been a very difficult book to write, however, living the stories contained within the pages has been ever more laborious. I know without a doubt I could not have completed either without the love and support of my family and co-writers.

Austin, thank you for reminding me of what I taught you at the right times. I love and appreciate the man you have become. Thanks for the hard work and always being willing to carry the load. I never realized I would raise my best friend. Thanks for all the times you woke me up, laughed, and had lunch at 2 am. The time we have spent together has been my joy in these dark days.

Kaedon, thank you for the support and well-timed laughs when I needed them. I appreciate the wisdom beyond your years that you possess and your desire to grow and always rise above all obstacles. Thank you also for our friendship, outside parental bonds, which makes life more fun when we can just spend time together.

Bronson, thank you for the support and work that you gave and have contributed in helping with this project and in life. I'm proud of your God-given abilities and natural leadership. The little things like losing to you at video games and hearing you talk trash and how we travel have helped me heal.

Baby G (Lexi), I thank you for the love and fight that you have shown. The display to never give up or be dismayed at the face of evil. You have rallied and overcome so much at a young age. May these lessons learned and forged in fire prepare you for the destiny God has for your life. Thank you for 1000s of hugs, tears we've shed, laughter even when we didn't think we could, and the awful dancing. May you always be Daddy's little girl.

You are my children, and you are loved greatly!

To Jon, my mentor, teacher, friend, and adopted father. I can never thank you enough for what you instilled in me that allowed me the knowledge and strength to endure the battles fought. You are loved and missed. RIP! Me la vedo quando Torno.

Kelly, thank you for joining the fight and helping me in areas where I couldn't help myself. Your sacrifices are appreciated from the heart.

To the people who never doubted our family and were always true, you are appreciated deeply.

Love and thankfulness to you from even the secret chambers of my heart.

Andy~